COMPUTER-AIDED QUALITATIVE
DATA ANALYSIS

COMPUTER-AIDED QUALITATIVE DATA ANALYSIS

Theory, Methods and Practice

Edited by

Udo Kelle

with Gerald Prein and Katherine Bird

SAGE Publications
London • Thousand Oaks • New Delhi

Editorial selection and matter and Introduction © Udo Kelle 1995
Chapter 1 © Udo Kelle and Heather Laurie 1995
Chapter 2 © Raymond M. Lee and Nigel G. Fielding 1995
Chapter 3 © Marrku Lonkila 1995
Chapter 4 © John Seidel and Udo Kelle 1995
Chapter 5 © Ian Dey 1995
Chapter 6 © Tom Richards and Lyn Richards 1995
Chapter 7 © Luis Araujo 1995
Chapter 8 © Ernest Sibert and Anne Shelly 1995
Chapter 9 © Sharlene Hesse-Biber and Paul Dupuis 1995
Chapter 10 © Günter L. Huber 1995
Chapter 11 © Udo Kuckartz 1995
Chapter 12 © Edeltraud Roller, Rainer Mathes and Thomas Eckert
             1995
Chapter 13 © Charles C. Ragin 1995
Chapter 14 © Gerald Prein, Udo Kelle and Katherine Bird 1995

First published 1995

SAGE Publications Ltd
6 Bonhill Street
London EC2A 4PU

SAGE Publications Inc
2455 Teller Road
Thousand Oaks, California 91320

SAGE Publications India Pvt Ltd
32, M-Block Market
Greater Kailash – I
New Delhi 110 048

British Library Cataloguing in Publication data

A catalogue record for this book is
available from the British Library

     ISBN 0 8039 7760 3
     ISBN 0-8039 7761 1 (pbk)

Library of Congress catalog card number 95-069819

Typeset by M Rules
Printed in Great Britain by Biddles Ltd, Guildford

Dedicated to the memory of
Renate Tesch

Contents

About This Book

The idea of publishing a handbook about qualitative methodology and computers arose at a conference about 'The Qualitative Research Process and Computing' in Bremen in 1992.[1] During the discussions about this project it rapidly became apparent that such a handbook could not be a mere collection of conference papers. To provide readers with a coherent overview most of the papers originally given at the conference were completely rewritten. Additional articles were commissioned by the editors to ensure that the handbook presents a truly representative overview of the most recent developments in computer-aided methods for working with textual data, and the discussion of their impact on qualitative methodology.

Fortunately, due to the availability of electronic communication, this was accompanied by an intensive discussion that itself stimulated joint papers which could have been included. While working on the introductions to the different parts we developed a system of mutual reviews between editors and authors. So we feel that the book is very much a product of a discussion process within a decisively open atmosphere. This is also true for the selection of articles. Some readers, who may be used to the strict segregation of methodological paradigms and approaches, may be surprised to find followers of an interpretivist and hermeneutic tradition together in this volume with authors who propose a strictly formalist approach to hypothesis testing during the analysis of qualitative data. But the editors – although themselves devoted to an interpretive tradition – felt strictly committed to methodological pluralism and considered it their task to provide a representative overview, rather than to further extend age-old schisms.

Comparing this volume with earlier publications in the field (for example, Lee and Fielding, 1991; Tesch, 1990) one could clearly conclude that at present this is a very rapidly developing field. So, our main concern as editors was to cover the newest developments concerning methods of theory building, qualitative hypothesis examination and strategies for combining qualitative and quantitative methods, which are discussed in Parts II, III and IV respectively. Key issues in the debate about general methodological questions are addressed in Part I, with the clear purpose of advancing the present discussion. The introductions to the different parts give an overview of the different chapters by showing how they relate to each other, to previous discussions and to discussions in qualitative methodology. A closing chapter about software should help the reader who wants to employ one of the analysis strategies discussed in the book in his or her own research project. Readers who are not acquainted with the whole field are recommended to first read the introduction to the whole book, which gives an overview of the history of the field and introduces the basics of computer-aided data handling in qualitative research.

We gratefully acknowledge the help of the German Volkswagen Foundation, which made it possible to organize the conference and without which this book would have never been written. We would also like to thank all those who participated in the electronic and face-to-face debates before, during and after the original conference and during the development of this volume. In particular we are grateful to Anne Shelly and Ernest Sibert for their great hospitality and illuminating discussions, and Ray Lee for the crucial support he provided in bringing this project to fruition. Above all, we are greatly indebted to the late Renate Tesch who was not just a pioneer in the field of computer-aided qualitative data analysis and one of the most outstanding figures in the developing community of qualitative researchers devoted to the use of computers, but also a supportive colleague and close friend to many of its members. Due to her readiness to help, discuss and challenge her friends and colleagues we owe her far more than can be described in a few sentences.

Udo Kelle
Gerald Prein
Katherine Bird

Note

1. The meeting was organized by the Special Research Centre 186 of the German Research Council ('Deutsche Forschungsgemeinschaft') and the Centre for Social Policy Research in Bremen, and funded by the German Volkswagen Foundation.

List of Contributors

Luis Araujo is a Lecturer in the Department of Marketing at the University of Lancaster. His interests lie in a network approach to organizational market structure; inter-organizational relationships; strategy-making processes; and qualitative methodologies, including the use of computer-aided qualitative data analysis software. As well as contributing to *Advances in International Marketing*, vol. 5 (ed. D. Deo Sharma, 1993, JAI Press), he has forthcoming chapters in *The Formation of Inter-organizational Networks* (ed. Mark Ebers, Oxford University Press), *Rethinking Marketing* (ed. Richard Whittington et al., Sage) and *Theory and Practice in Competence Based Competition* (ed. R. Sanchez et al., Kluwer).

Katherine Bird is a Research Assistant at the Special Research Centre 186 of the German National Research Council at Bremen University. At present, she is interested in the development and application of computer programs for the analysis of qualitative data.

Paul Dupuis is Assistant Director, Advanced Technology, Office of Information Technology at Boston College, Massachusetts.

Ian Dey is a Senior Lecturer in social policy at the University of Edinburgh. His substantive research has been mainly in the areas of employment and development. As well as developing the software package 'Hypersoft', he is author of *Qualitative Data Analysis: A User-friendly Guide for Social Scientists* (1993, Routledge).

Thomas Eckert is Assistant Professor for educational science at the Albert-Ludwig University, Freiburg. His research interests are qualitative and quantitative research methods, school-effectiveness research, teacher professionalism and adult education. His publications include *Erziehungsleitende Vorstellungen und Schulverständnis von Lehrern* (1993, Lang, Frankfurt) and a contribution to *Schule und Unterricht* (ed. Gerd E. Stolz and Bernd Schwarz, 1994, Lang, Frankfurt).

Nigel Fielding is Professor of Sociology and Deputy Dean of Human Studies at the University of Surrey. His current research interests are in software for qualitative data analysis, and criminology – particularly the relationship between unemployment and crime. His recent books include *Using Computers in Qualitative Research* (of which he was co-editor, Sage) and *Community Policing* (Oxford University Press). He is editor of the *Howard Journal of Criminal Justice* and, with Ray Lee, co-editor of the Sage Social Science Software Series.

Sharlene Hesse-Biber is Associate Professor and Chair, Department of Sociology at Boston College, Chestnut Hill, Massachusetts. She is co-developer of HyperRESEARCH, a software program for qualitative data analysis. She is currently conducting research on the impact of computer-assisted instruction in the college classroom. She recently co-authored the article 'Closing the technological gender gap' which appeared in *Teaching Sociology*, vol. 22, 1994.

Günter L. Huber is Professor for educational psychology at the University of Tübingen, Germany. His research interests are people's implicit theories, cooperative learning and interindividual differences. Forced by the demands of qualitative approaches to these fields he wrote the software package AQUAD. He also edited a book on *Qualitative Analyse: Computereinsatz in der Sozialforschung* (1992, R. Oldenbourg Verlag).

Udo Kelle is a Senior Researcher at the Special Research Centre 186 of the German National Research Council at Bremen University. His major research interests are empirical social research methodology, epistemology, theories of rational action and biographical research. He is the author of *Empirisch begründete Theoriebildung* (1994, Deutscher Studienverlag) and a contributor to *Openness in Research* (eds Maso, Atkinson, Delamont and Verhoeven, 1995, Van Gorcum).

Udo H. Kuckartz is Professor of Methodology and Evaluation at the Institute for Rehabilitational Studies, Humboldt University, Berlin. He has been a contributor to the sociological research methodology literature, particularly in the area of the application of computer software to the analysis of qualitative data. His recent publications include *Textanalysesysteme für die Sozialwissenschaften* (1992, G. Fischer-Verlag) and contributions to *Umweltbewußtsein und Massenmedien, Perspektiven ökologischer Kommunikation* (ed. G. de Haan, 1995, Akademie-Verlag). He is author of the software programs MAX and WINMAX. He is also working on environmental sociology.

Heather Laurie is a Chief Research Officer at the ESRC Research Centre on Micro-Social Change, University of Essex, where she is the

Survey Manager for the British Household Panel Study. Her research interests include the use of multiple methods in social research; survey methodology and large-scale survey data; the analysis of longitudinal panel data; women's labour market participation; and the distribution of resources within the household. Her recent publications include contributions to *The Sociological Review*, with O. Sullivan (vol. 39, no. 1, 1991), *Mixing Methods: Qualitative and Quantitative Research* (ed. J. Brannen, 1992, Avebury), and *Changing Households: The BHPS 1990-1992*, with D. Rose (ed. Buck et al., University of Essex).

Raymond M. Lee is Reader in Social Research Methods in the Department of Social Policy and Social Science, Royal Holloway University of London. His research interests are in research methodology, the sociology of labour markets and the sociology of religion. His most recent work has been concerned with the methodological problems associated with research on 'sensitive' topics, and with the impact of new technologies on research methods in the social sciences. He is author of *Doing Research on Sensitive Topics* and *Dangerous Fieldwork*, and has co-edited *Researching Sensitive Topics* (with Claire Renzetti) and *Using Computers in Qualitative Research* (with Nigel Fielding), all of which are published by Sage.

Markku Lonkila is working as a Researcher at the Department of Sociology, University of Helsinki. He became acquainted with qualitative methods when writing his master's thesis in sociology on the street musicians of Paris. He went on to complete his licentiate thesis on computer-assisted qualitative analysis (in Finnish), and is currently preparing his doctoral thesis on the social networks of teachers in St Petersburg.

Rainer Mathes is Director of Regionalpresse Frankfurt a.M., Germany. His research interests are political communication, content analysis, and market and media research. His publications include *Kommunikation in der Krise* (with H.-D. Gärtner and A. Czaplicki); 'The role of the alternative press in the agenda-building process: spill-over effects and media opinion leadership', in *European Journal of Communication* (with B. Pfetsch, vol. 6, 1991).

Gerald Prein is a Senior Researcher at the Special Research Centre 186 of the German National Research Council at Bremen University. His major research interests are longitudinal data analysis, monographic methodologies, institutional analysis and the sociology of everyday life. He has contributed to a number of publications in this area, and most recently to *Softstat '92: Advances in Statistical Software 4* (with

Udo Kelle, ed. Frank Faulbaum, 1994), and to *Bildung, Gesellschaft, soziale Ungleichheit: Internationale Beiträge zur Bildungssoziologie und Bildungstheorie* (ed. Heinz Sünker, Dieter Timmermann and Fritz-Ulrich Kolbe, Suhrkamp).

Charles Ragin is Professor of Sociology and Political Science at Northwestern University, Illinois. His main interests are comparative and historical sociology, methodology and political sociology, with a special focus on such topics as the welfare state, ethnic political mobilization, and international political economy. His recent publications include *Issues and Alternatives in Comparative Social Research* (1991), *What is a Case? Exploring the Foundations of Social Research* (with Howard S. Becker, 1992), and *Constructing Social Research: The Unity and Diversity of Method* (1994).

Lyn Richards is Reader and Associate Professor of Sociology at La Trobe University, Melbourne. Her main research interests are qualitative data analysis and family sociology. Her recent publications, all co-authored with Tom Richards, include contributions to *Artificial Intelligence and Creativity: An Interdisciplinary Approach* (ed. T. Dartnall, 1994, Kluwer), and the *Handbook of Qualitative Research* (ed. N. Denzin and Y. Lincoln, 1994, Sage).

Tom Richards is Reader and Associate Professor of Computer Science at La Trobe University, Melbourne. His main research interests are artificial intelligence and computational qualitative data analysis. As well as co-authoring the above with Lyn Richards, he is co-author, with Hoi-Kau Yuen, of 'Knowledge representation for grounded theory construction in qualitative data analysis', in the *Journal of Mathematical Sociology* (vol. 19, no. 4, 1994).

Edeltraud Roller is Senior Researcher at the Wissenschaftszentrum Berlin and Lecturer in political science at the Free University, Berlin. Her research interests are political attitudes, public policy, quantitative and qualitative methods. Her publications include *Einstellungen der Bürger zum Wohlfahrtsstaat der Bundesrepublik Deutschland* (1992, Westdeutscher Verlag), and, with R. Mathes, a contribution to *Kölner Zeitschrift für Soziologie und Sozialpsychologie* (vol. 45, 1993).

John Seidel is at Qualitative Research Associates, Amherst, Massachusetts.

Anne Shelly is Senior Research Associate in the School of Computer and Information Science at Syracuse University. Her research interests are student and teacher thinking, researcher thinking, qualitative methodology and symbolic computation techniques applied to induction-based research methods. She is co-author, with Ernest Sibert, of QUALOG (a software program for computer-assisted qualitative data analysis using logic programming), and of a chapter in *Qualitative Analyse: Computereinsatz in der Sozialforschung* (ed. G.L. Huber, 1992, R. Oldenbourg Verlag).

Ernest Sibert is Professor of Computer and Information Science at Syracuse University. Though his investigations have ranged over processor architectures and realtime data acquisition systems, he has worked primarily in the area of computational logic, especially logic programming and its applications. He is creator, with Professor J.A. Robinson, of LOGLISP – the first system to integrate logic programming with LISP in a way which allows the programmer to combine the two styles at will. Current studies include massively parallel implementations of logic/functional languages, data-parallel computing techniques generally, and various uses of LOGLISP, of which QUALOG is the most important.

Introduction: An Overview of Computer-aided Methods in Qualitative Research

Udo Kelle

The purpose of this book is to give an overview of new computer-aided techniques for the management and analysis of textual data in qualitative research and of the current debate about the methodological impact of these techniques on the research process. Apart from providing a summary of the following discussions, this introductory chapter is also intended to introduce a reader unfamiliar with computer-aided methods in qualitative research to this subject. The initial sections contain a brief historical overview of the development of computer-aided qualitative data analysis whereby some epistemological aspects of the relationship between qualitative methodology and computer-use will also be discussed. Following that it also outlines basic elements of 'computer-aided qualitative data analysis', namely the use of textual database management systems for the automatization of manual coding, indexing and sorting operations.

Computers and qualitative data – some epistemological remarks

It was not until the early 1980s that qualitative researchers discovered that the computer could assist them in working with their data. Considering the history of social science computing, this is a remarkable fact, since software for handling textual data had long been available: in 1966 *The General Inquirer*, a program for computerized quantitative content analysis (a kind of analysis based on frequency counts of words using a content-analysis lexicon) was introduced to the public (Stone et al., 1966). The program assigns words in a given document to whatever categories are specified in the lexicon and calculates the frequencies of occurrences or co-occurrences of words belonging to each category the analyst is interested in. Either a previously developed lexicon (for example, the '*Harvard Psycho-sociological Dictionary*') or a user-defined dictionary can be employed. The program helps with the construction of the latter by dissecting the text into single words which can then be grouped by the analyst on the basis of semantic similarity.

Programs similar to *The General Inquirer* began a train of development in history, linguistics and literary studies that led to the emergence of a whole scientific community concerned with computing in the humanities, who organize their own international conferences and publish their own journals (for example, *Computing in the Humanities*). For a long time a similar development did not occur in the social sciences. The use of software for computer-aided textual analysis attracted only a limited group of experts in the field of content analysis. The majority of social researchers who used texts as their main empirical data source (namely those doing qualitative studies in the tradition of interpretive and interactionist approaches) were reluctant to integrate information technology into their analytic work.

This reluctance not only reflected the distance of these scholars from the mainstream methodology of quantitative survey and experimental research where, during the 1960s and 1970s, the computer became an indispensable aid. But this caution also grew out of the epistemological roots of interpretive research that were anchored in phenomenology, the Oxford philosophy of language and continental hermeneutical philosophy (see Giddens, 1976): these philosophical approaches had shown that ambiguity and context-relatedness have to be regarded as central characteristics of everyday language use.[1] Following these approaches it is impossible to make sense of written or spoken messages in everyday contexts – an operation which is also the basis of hermeneutic *Verstehen* – without a 'tacit knowledge' that cannot be easily formalized.

One of the fundamental realizations provided by the ground-breaking works of Alan Turing about the general concept of an information processing machine has been that computers require exact and precisely stated rules which are completely context-free and contain no ambiguities. Thus, the attempt to apply the logic of a Turing machine to the domain of human understanding must be regarded as a rather dubious endeavour, as has also been argued by critical computer scientists (see Dreyfus, 1972; Dreyfus and Dreyfus 1986; Winograd and Flores, 1986). Empirical support for these considerations could be found in the fact that, despite two decades of intensive efforts in the domains of machine translation of natural languages and the recognition of the human voice, computers still have severe difficulties in understanding or translating natural languages.

It is worth noting that the early criticism launched by some social scientists against quantitative approaches to content analysis – for which the first programs for computer-aided analysis of text were developed – followed a similar line of argumentation by stating that quantitative content analysis is too atomistic and oversimplistic to really capture the semantic content of texts (Kracauer, 1952/53: 632).

Given these considerations, many qualitative researchers, particularly those working in the interpretive tradition, considered the idea that computers could be used for the analysis of text in the same way they were used for the analysis of numerical data to be inappropriate, if not wholly absurd. However, these reservations were also strongly influenced by the paradigm of computer-use prevalent in the era of the mainframe. At that time the use of computers required special training and was accompanied by high costs in terms of money, skill acquisition and human resources. The idea that electronic data processing machines could one day become an indispensable tool for the storage, retrieval and manipulation of mere text was far away. Instead, computers were mainly seen as calculators performing arithmetic operations. Following this paradigm of computer-use, electronic data processing devices were seen by many social scientists as tools for nothing more than the statistical analysis of numerical data (or the quantitative content analysis of textual data).

This situation was radically changed by the advent of the Personal Computer. Like other *hommes des lettres* qualitative researchers discovered quite quickly the enormous possibilities for text manipulation that were offered by the new technology. But given the limited user-friendliness of early operating systems and software environments many users (especially those working in a DOS environment) were also compelled to acquire a certain expertise in computer-use. After a strenuous apprenticeship, some of them experienced real enthusiasm when they discovered the numerous possibilities for working with textual data offered by the new technology. Consequently, the dominant paradigm of computer-use began to change from 'computers as number-crunchers' to computers as devices for the intelligent management of data, incorporating facilities for the storage and retrieval of information that were far more complex and convenient than any manual system of information retrieval used previously.

With this paradigm shift it became clear that, although computers cannot analyse textual data in the same way as they analyse numerical data (that is, by employing algebraic procedures), they can nevertheless be of great assistance to qualitative researchers. The central analytic task in qualitative research – understanding the meaning of texts – cannot be computerized because it is not an algorithmic process and hence cannot be considered a mechanical task. However, there are mechanical tasks involved in interpretive analysis, most of which are concerned with the management of data material. The qualitative research process often generates huge amounts of unstructured textual data, such as interview transcripts, protocols, field notes and personal documents, which if not managed properly, can result in 'data overload' (Miles and Huberman, 1994) with the researcher drowning in

the data. This problem aggravates a second problem typical of qualitative research. Since data analysis and theory construction are more
closely interlinked than in other kinds of enquiry, the researcher generates many theoretical concepts in this ongoing process which are
often recorded across numerous notebooks, manuscript pages and
index cards. Keeping track of the emerging ideas, arguments and theoretical concepts can be a mammoth organizational task. Qualitative
researchers have developed a variety of methods for coping with these
problems comprising mechanical and therefore computerizable tasks.
The next section outlines this development from manual to computerized methods of data management in qualitative analysis.

The mechanization of cut-and-paste techniques

Regrettably, techniques that have been developed to cope with the
problems of data overload and the organization of theoretical notes are
only treated marginally in the technical literature and their methodological impact on the research process is rarely discussed. Usually
these techniques consist of the construction of some sort of manual
storage-and-retrieval system, after the textual data have been *coded*
and *indexed* and after theoretical ideas have been recorded as *memos.*
  Turning first to coding, one of the earliest descriptions of coding textual data can be found in an article by Howard Becker and Blanche
Geer:

> We have tentatively identified, through sequential analysis during the field
> work, the major perspectives we want to present and the areas . . . to which
> these perspectives apply. We now go through the summarized incidents,
> marking each incident with a number or numbers that stand for the various
> areas to which it appears to be relevant. This is essentially a coding opera-
> tion, . . . its object is to make sure that all relevant data can be brought to
> bear on a point. (Becker and Geer, 1960: 280–281)

In Glaser and Strauss' famous monograph *The Discovery of Grounded
Theory* (1967) coding is the central prerequisite for constant comparison (which in this book was regarded by both authors as the basis of
qualitative theory building). Here coding means relating chunks of
data to *categories* which the researcher has either previously developed
or which he or she develops *ad hoc.* 'The analyst starts by coding each
incident in his data into as many categories of analysis as possible, as
categories emerge or as data emerge that fit in an existing category'
(Glaser and Strauss, 1967: 105). In practical terms this means 'noting
categories on margins, but can be done more elaborately (for example,
on cards). It should keep track of the comparison group in which the
incident occurs' (Glaser and Strauss, 1967: 106).
  The same applies to the notes the researcher records during data

analysis and which form the basis for the emerging theory. Glaser and Strauss termed these notes '*memos*' (Glaser and Strauss, 1967: 107) and recommended that the analyst write them, as well as codes, on a copy of the field notes (Glaser and Strauss, 1967: 108). A similar piece of advice was given by Miles and Huberman concerning what they called 'marginal remarks' (Miles and Huberman, 1994: 67). Other researchers, of course, prefer to write their theoretical ideas on separate slips of paper or index cards.

An important task of data management is to draw together all the text passages and memos which have something in common. For this a storage-and-retrieval system has to be established that permits the retrieval of text passages and notes when they are needed during analysis. As far as the text segments are concerned, this means that the researcher has 'to get the material out of the chronological narrative form of [the] field notes or interview write-ups and into a storage system where [s/he] can easily order and retrieve it' (Lofland and Lofland, 1984: 132).

Before the advent of computers, 'cut-and-paste' techniques were the most widely used methods of organizing the data material in this way – the researcher had to 'cut up field notes, transcripts and other materials and place data relating to each coding category in a separate file folder or manila envelope' (Taylor and Bogdan, 1984: 136; see also Lofland and Lofland, 1984: 134). Some authors recommended the use of index cards, for example Miles and Huberman in an earlier version of their monograph, *Qualitative Data Analysis* (published in 1984 before computer programs for qualitative analysis became widely available): 'Coded field notes can be photocopied, cut into chunks and each chunk attached to a 5 × 8 card' (Miles and Huberman, 1984a: 66).

However, a serious methodological problem arose with this technique: the researcher was forced to remove the cut-out text passage from its original context and it could easily happen that, when reading the different text segments relating to one topic, he or she found most of them meaningless. One strategy for coping with this problem was to include with the text passage information about its original site, so that the researcher could trace the path back to its context (Miles and Huberman, 1984a: 106).

However: 'Cards and file folders are reasonably workable if the number of sites is small and the data collection not extended. But they are increasingly difficult and very time-consuming as the database gets larger' (Miles and Huberman, 1984a: 67). Hence, data overload remained a serious problem even when manual methods of storage and retrieval were used. As early as 1984 Miles and Huberman advised researchers to use a computer if large amounts of data had to be analysed, but they made only cursory remarks about how electronic

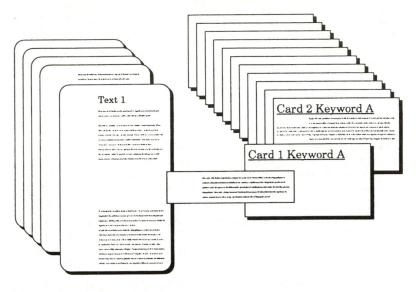

Figure I.1   *Cutting and pasting*

data processing could be applied to qualitative data management. In the same year a special issue of *Qualitative Sociology* was published that exclusively focused on qualitative computing (Conrad and Reinarz, 1984) and which marked the arrival of computer technology in a broader community of qualitative researchers.

The first attempts to computerize manual storage-and-retrieval procedures were made using standard software: either the operation of cutting and pasting was simply transferred to a computer environment using an ordinary word processing program to copy text segments from one file to another; or a standard database management system, for example dBase, was used to store every text segment as a single record in a database especially constructed for this purpose.

Whereas using a word processing program for cutting and pasting has hardly any advantage over manual methods, the use of database systems offered some extended possibilities for data organization, for example, making it possible to sort text segments according to many different criteria simultaneously. Nevertheless, the retrieval facilities remained rather limited, and certain restrictions were imposed on the research process. For example, using a standard database management system like dBase required the researcher to define the record structure for the storage of the text segments before entering the data. This made it very difficult to change the coding scheme during the ongoing process of analysis. Thus the process of data management did not fit well with the methodological requirements of a research tradition whose main principle was that the categories that serve to describe or explain the phenomena under investigation emerge while analysing the data and not before.

Furthermore, these techniques did not help to solve the great methodological problem of cut-and-paste techniques mentioned above: when using word processing or standard database systems the text segments still had to be removed from their original context.

New approaches to electronic coding and retrieval helped to overcome this difficulty. One was based on a principle quite often applied for the construction of *non-formatted textual database systems*. The original textual data remained unchanged throughout the process of coding because the codes were stored separately, together with addresses of the coded text segments. Consequently, the 'decontextualization' of text segments did not occur during coding, but only during the retrieval of text segments. Metaphorically speaking, one could say that the use of a standard database system creates an *electronic index card catalogue*, whereas constructing a non-formatted textual database of this kind leads to the creation of an *electronic concordance*. The latter has two central virtues: (1) in principle it is possible to electronically restore the original context of a text segment, and (2) the coding scheme can be changed much more easily than with a standard database. The other

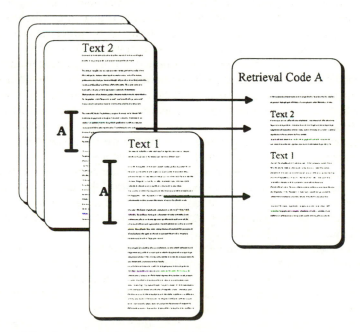

Figure I.2   *Computerized cutting and pasting*

approach was based on the Hypercard system for Macintosh computers. Although text segments have to be stored separately from the original text on 'cards', a linkage with their original context can nevertheless be established.

Since the mid-1980s a great number of software packages have been developed (mostly by qualitative researchers with advanced computer programming skills) that are mostly based either on the principle of non-formatted databases or that use the Hypercard technology (for more details see Chapter 14). In the early days most of these programs were mere code-and-retrieve facilities which only allowed for (1) the attachment of codes to text segments and (2) the retrieval of all segments from a defined set of documents to which the same code had been assigned. However, it very soon became apparent to the developers and users of such programs that a whole variety of additional features could be realized with such software that greatly exceeded simple coding and retrieval. Among the operations that, in principle, can be conducted with a non-formatted text database or using the Hypercard system are:

1. Facilities for the recording of *memos* that the researcher can electronically link to codes or text segments and then retrieve separately or together with text segments.
2. Features for defining linkages between codes so that whole *networks of codes* can be constructed together with facilities for the graphical display of these networks. Such networks could also be used for retrieval purposes, for example, permitting a researcher to retrieve all text segments that are attached to all codes within a certain sub-network.
3. *Hypertext systems* that allow for the definition of direct connections between text segments without using codes so that the analyst can spring from one text passage to a related one or retrieve all connected text segments without referring to codes.
4. The use of *variables* that can be attached to documents and can be used for *selective retrievals* where the search for text segments is restricted by certain limitations, permitting for instance the retrieval of statements about certain topics from only those interview participants who have a certain characteristic in common. For example, a qualitative researcher investigating the division of household labour among married couples could first of all retrieve all the text segments in which wives talk about housework and contrast them afterwards with text segments on the same topic from interviews with husbands.
5. Algorithms for searching for *co-occurring codes* can retrieve, for example, all text segments to which two or more codes were

attached, the overlap of all text segments to which certain codes were attached, or passages that contain a specified sequence of coded text segments, or where coded segments are separated by a certain specified distance. Such operations could be employed by a researcher interested in the relationship between certain events. A biographical researcher interested in the relationship between the categories 'critical life event' and 'emotional distress' could, for example, examine all text passages that were coded by these two categories.

6. Operations can also be designed for the retrieval of *quantitative attributes of the database*. For example, frequency counts of the occurrence of certain codes in a given document can be used to help identify the kind of 'core categories' mentioned by Glaser (1978: 71). Similarly, statistical procedures could be used to test the robustness of the coding categories, for instance in computing intercoder reliability.

These various new options have been included in different ways in the software packages that were developed to assist qualitative researchers, leading to rapid developments in the emerging field of computer-aided qualitative data analysis. Looking at the scene now, one will even find that these developments have culminated in a race between developers to include as many of these features as possible in the newest versions of their programs.

General methodological aspects of computer-use in qualitative research

Discussions about the methodological impacts of these new techniques and about their potential costs or benefits have accompanied this development from its conception, with discussants expressing both strong optimism as well as great concern. The optimists focused on the aspect of *rigour,* claiming that the use of computers would make qualitative analysis more systematic and transparent, thus enhancing its trustworthiness (for example, Conrad and Reinarz, 1984; Richards and Richards, 1991d; 1994; Araujo, 1992; Mangabeira, 1992) and also on its potential to enhance the creativity of the researcher (see Richards and Richards, 1991d; 1994). Those who were concerned concentrated on the danger that the researcher could become *alienated* from the data by a machine which had shifted from being an aid in doing qualitative analysis to its definition (Agar, 1991: 182), thus stimulating different kinds of *analytic madness* (Seidel, 1991: 107).

The first two chapters of Part I relate to this discussion. Drawing on their experience as qualitative researchers and research consultants Udo Kelle and Heather Laurie try to answer the question of whether computers really can enhance the validity of qualitative research results. The authors argue that the concept of validity which is employed has to be appropriate to the requirements of qualitative research and they warn against simply borrowing validity concepts from quantitative methodology. Using examples from research practice they show that computer-aided methods can be very useful for adding validity and trustworthiness if the researcher pays attention to the different meaning of validity concepts in different research paradigms.

The question whether the computer can alienate qualitative researchers from their data is addressed in Raymond Lee and Nigel Fielding's contribution. Starting from empirical investigations among qualitative researchers who use software for working with textual data, they come to the conclusion that the fear of computers 'taking over analysis' is quite often overemphasized: in practice researchers tend to cease using a certain package rather than submit themselves to the logic of a software program totally different from the logic of enquiry these researchers want to employ.

The question of whether a machine can transform the logic of the research process in an undesirable way quite easily translates into the question of the relationship between the logic of data analysis incorporated in a certain software package and the logic of data analysis proposed by a certain methodology. Given the heterogeneity of qualitative approaches it is essential to examine the relationship between different approaches in qualitative research and the use of computer-aided techniques. Apart from the works of Tesch, who very roughly distinguished between 'descriptive/interpretive' and 'theory building' analysis (Tesch, 1990), until now there have been no serious and intensive investigations of the relationship between single methodological approaches and computer-aided methods. In Chapter 3, Markku Lonkila discusses the role of grounded theory methodology in the context of computer-aided qualitative data analysis. In fact there are many domains where computer-aided methods are particularly useful for a research strategy in this tradition. But grounded theory and computer-aided qualitative analysis also share some very problematic aspects, as Lonkila points out: both overemphasize coding and in doing so neglect other forms of textual analysis, especially the kind of fine-grained analysis employed in discourse analysis. And in both cases the researcher runs the risk of losing contact with the data by concentrating too much on his or her concepts as opposed to interpretively analysing the data.

It becomes clear from both Lee and Fielding's article as well as Lonkila's contribution that the problem of the researcher becoming alienated from the data does not primarily lie with the computer but with a researcher who prefers a certain analytic style. John Seidel and Udo Kelle address this problem of alienation from the perspective of coding. In Chapter 4 these authors argue that the distinction between two different modes of coding is crucial to avoid serious confusion: codes can either represent signposts to certain text passages or they can denote certain facts. The first type of coding is characteristic for an open and inductive style of enquiry employed by an interpretive analysis of textual data in the tradition of hermeneutic and interactionist approaches. The second type relates to a deductive style of textual analysis in the tradition of classical content analysis. Although the authors emphasize that it may be very fruitful to combine these two approaches, they also point out some serious methodological dangers that arise when they are simply merged without taking certain precautions.

New methods of computer-aided qualitative analysis

In Part I the discussion focuses mainly on the topic of whether computer-aided methods are appropriate for the kind of work usually done by qualitative analysts. This discussion rests to a great extent on experiences with 'code-and-retrieve' software, developed in the mid-1980s, that primarily focused on the computerization of cut-and-paste techniques. Since then the tools mentioned above (such as facilities for constructing hyperlinks, for network building or for searching for co-occurring codes), which in principle could be incorporated in a textual database management system, have inspired many developers and users to propose new methods for analysing qualitative data. Most of these methods and the software for implementing them have only been available for a short time and so there is not yet a great body of experience among qualitative researchers comparable to that with code-and-retrieve software. For this reason, most of the chapters in Parts II, III and IV which discuss these new methods are written by the researchers who proposed these methods, many of whom have also developed software for their implementation.

The central goal of Parts II, III and IV is to present and discuss these methods and to clarify their underlying principles and 'models of the qualitative research process'. Practical aspects of software use are not covered; the reader who wishes to learn more about the software most appropriate for the analysis strategies outlined in these parts may refer to Chapter 14 about software.

Computer-aided methods that apply to three different areas of qualitative analysis will be discussed: (1) procedures for linking elements of the qualitative database and building networks that assist qualitative theory building, (2) methods of qualitative hypothesis examination and (3) strategies for integrating quantitative analyses into the qualitative research process.

Using linkages and networks for qualitative theory building

As mentioned above, the earliest coding and retrieval programs were based on the mechanization of cut-and-paste techniques and enabled the analyst to define linkages between codes and text segments so that all text segments attached to the same code could later be retrieved. But the data structure by which this is realized – in most cases the attachment of pointers to codes that contain addresses of text segments – could, in principle, also be used for a great variety of other linkages: linkages between memos and text segments, between memos and codes, between codes themselves, etc. By applying such a technology whole networks of codes, memos and text segments could be constructed. Additionally, by using pointers, *hypertext systems* could be implemented that allowed text segments to be linked to each other without having to attach codes to them.

The computer-aided development of networks has provided a powerful tool for *qualitative theory building*. For instance, an option to link codes to each other can be extremely helpful, since for most analysts codes represent the theoretical concepts they develop while generating a theory about the phenomena under investigation. Consequently, a network of codes can be regarded as a representation of the emerging theory. With some of the more advanced software packages currently available it is also possible to graphically display such networks, for example ATLAS/ti, Hypersoft, NUD.IST or WINMAX (for more details see Chapter 14).

Advanced retrieval facilities that can be implemented while using such a network approach could offer additional features that assist with theory building. If codes are linked to form a network it would, in principle, be possible to implement routines that retrieve text segments attached to all codes that are linked to a certain 'core category'. And, if the network of codes forms a hierarchical tree structure that represents, for example, theoretical categories at different levels of abstraction, it would be possible to retrieve all segments that are attached to all subcodes of a given code.

In Part II of this book the application of different kinds of linkages and networks to qualitative theory building is discussed. In Chapter 5 Ian Dey demonstrates how this approach can be used to avoid the dangers of fragmentation always inherent in a methodology based on coding and retrieval. The possibility that the 'decontextualization' of text segments will seduce researchers into an almost systematic neglect of the context of text segments has been discussed in the methodological literature for quite some time. A good example of this is Agar's report of a research project where coding and retrieval resulted in a mere 'report on shared topics of concerns together with samples of how those topics were represented in an interview' while 'detailed theories of actions, states and results that were embedded, utterance by utterance, in those segments' (Agar, 1991: 181) were totally disregarded. Dey points out that a methodology of computer-aided analysis that employs linkages can help the researcher to avoid these dangers in two ways. First, defining linkages between text segments and their original context allows this original context to be rapidly restored. And, second, establishing direct linkages between text segments ('*hyperlinks*') allows patterns and relationships between different elements of the text to be taken into consideration during the coding process.

In Chapter 6 Lyn Richards and Tom Richards discuss various methodological aspects of the construction of hierarchical networks of code categories. Hierarchical relations between categories play a significant role in qualitative theory building. Computer programs can be used to represent these hierarchical structures by connecting codes to each other. Given these technical facilities the lack of methodological discussion in the previous literature, with respect to the necessary preconditions for the construction of hierarchical categories and the dangers and pitfalls of this process, becomes painfully apparent. Richards and Richards try to close this gap by addressing some of the crucial prerequisites for hierarchical tree construction; the distinction between *factual* and *referential categories*, the consistency of the hierarchical structures and precautionary measures for avoiding the proliferation of code categories. Finally, the authors present some retrieval strategies which are useful if hierarchical categories have been applied or constructed during the coding process.

In Chapter 7 Luis Araujo presents concrete examples of theory building with the help of hierarchical categories. The author outlines some practical implications for the construction of code schemes and shows how a roughly predefined coding scheme can be iteratively refined.

Complex retrieval procedures and qualitative hypothesis examination

At their earliest stage of development most of the software programs for computer-aided qualitative analysis could only be used for *ordinary retrieval*, that is, retrieving all text segments to which a certain code has been attached. Nowadays, almost all such software packages offer some complex retrieval facilities, based on the search for *co-occurrences of codes* in a given document. These features can be used to explore possible theoretical relations between code categories and thus to generate hypotheses. Several authors have also proposed using these facilities for strategies of *qualitative hypothesis examination*.

In Chapter 8 Ernest Sibert and Anne Shelly give a comprehensive introduction to the logical and computational foundations of this process. Although the analysis of qualitative data has to be regarded as a creative endeavour that relies heavily on the researcher's interpretive and conceptual abilities, it also always comprises deductive inferences that can partly be automatized. The authors outline how these mechanical parts of the researcher's reasoning process can be computerized by constructing a knowledge base containing the location of codes in a document and by employing techniques of logic programming.

When using the co-occurrences of codes as a basis for qualitative hypothesis examination one can, in principle, proceed in two different ways:

1. Either the search for co-occurring codes is used to retrieve all text segments to which the codes investigated are attached, and the analyst then examines the original text to identify evidence or counter-evidence for his or her hypotheses. With these results the hypotheses can not only be rejected or accepted, but also modified or specified on the basis of the empirical material. Thus the automatic deduction system serves as a heuristic device for hypothesis examination and refinement, and not as a hypothesis tester in the strict sense. This is the strategy proposed by Sibert and Shelly.
2. Or the mere fact of a co-occurrence is itself regarded as evidence or counter-evidence for a certain hypothesis. Here a deduction system of the kind described by Sibert and Shelly could really function as a *hypothesis tester* making the process of qualitative hypothesis examination similar to that in statistical analysis. This method is described by Sharlene Hesse-Biber and Paul Dupuis in Chapter 9.

Nevertheless, the idea of qualitative hypothesis examination may provoke controversial discussions since it contains many as yet unsolved methodological problems. Particularly those researchers working in the tradition of an interpretivist and interactionist approach will feel uncomfortable with the idea of employing automatic procedures of hypothesis examination during the process of data analysis. The introduction to Part III addresses some of these issues and discusses the meaning of notions like 'hypothesis' and 'hypothesis examination' in the context of qualitative research as opposed to the methodology of statistical hypothesis testing.

In Chapter 10 Günter Huber relates techniques of logic programming (that form the basis of qualitative hypothesis examination) and co-occurring code searching to qualitative theory building. By presenting examples from research practice the author shows how computer-aided techniques for qualitative hypothesis generation and examination can be employed. Additionally he demonstrates how the method of logical minimization (also described in Chapter 13) relates to qualitative hypothesis examination and how it can be integrated into qualitative theory building.

Between quality and quantity

With the introduction of computers to the analysis of qualitative data some authors hoped that this development would lead to the long-standing dichotomy between qualitative and quantitative data analysis being overcome. Such approaches try to combine hermeneutic methods of *Verstehen* with the statistical analysis of standardized, numerical information derived from unstructured textual data. In this way, it is hoped, the strengths of both approaches could mutually reinforce each other: the intersubjectivity and reliability provided by standardized information derived from large samples on the one hand, and the intimate knowledge of the single case or text passage achieved by interpretive analysis on the other.

In performing this kind of analysis one of the essential questions would be how to transform the meaning of the analysed textual 'raw data' into a quantitative data matrix in a scholarly and systematic way. In Chapters 11 and 12 two proposals are made as to how this can be done.

In *hermeneutic-classificatory content analysis*, presented by Edeltraud Roller, Rainer Mathes and Thomas Eckert, the textual data are first divided into units of analysis according to certain formal characteristics. Thereafter, a detailed and elaborated coding scheme is developed. Unlike classical computer-aided content analysis, coding is not performed automatically but regarded as an interpretive task in which several codes are attached to each unit of analysis thereby generating a data matrix. The quantitative analysis of this data matrix is followed by a thorough and fine-grained in-depth interpretation of texts segments retrieved from frequent ('typical') or highly untypical, marginal, cases.

In contrast, the method of *case-oriented quantification* presented by Udo Kuckartz in Chapter 11 does not require the application of a theory-driven code scheme developed beforehand. Furthermore, this kind of analysis, whose theoretical background the author traces back to the concepts of *typification* outlined by Max Weber and Alfred Schütz, starts with a thorough hermeneutic analysis of the whole case. During this analysis, those variables that can serve as a basis for constructing a typology are identified. After assigning values to these variables, all cases are grouped according to their similarities or differences, employing statistical techniques of exploratory data analysis such as cluster analysis, or correspondence analysis. Like Roller and her colleagues Kuckartz returns to the original textual data after performing the statistical analysis in order to conduct further fine-grained hermeneutic analyses.

However, the quantitative analysis of numerical data derived from qualitative textual material poses some serious methodological difficulties. The application of widely used statistical methods will be difficult if – as is often the case with qualitative data – their mathematical prerequisites, such as the requirement for random sampling, cannot be easily met.

Roller and her colleagues attach great importance to meeting these requirements, whereas Kuckartz proposes the application of statistical procedures with few prerequisites, such as cluster analysis. A quite different approach to solving this problem is presented by Charles Ragin in Chapter 13. He chooses not to use statistical procedures, but to apply principles of Boolean algebra to formalize the process of multiple comparisons of cases intuitively employed by many qualitative researchers. Like Kuckartz and Roller and her colleagues, Ragin also starts by generating variables from qualitative material. The next step of the analysis is to identify certain variables as possible causes and others as possible outcomes. The goal of the method of 'logical minimization' presented by Ragin is the identification of all possible configurations that produce a certain outcome.

If one looks back to earlier debates on methodological issues, especially those concerning the advantages and disadvantages of qualitative vs. quantitative methods, it seems fair to assume that the merits of the approaches presented here, which are intended to bridge the gap between quality and quantity, will be controversial. As with concepts of qualitative hypothesis examination, researchers who are devoted to hermeneutic and interpretivist traditions may object to these approaches, while arguing that quantification strictly goes against the intentions of interpretive methodology.

However, it will be difficult to settle these disputes (if it is possible to settle them at all) exclusively on the basis of abstract methodological and epistemological considerations. When a reasonable number of empirical investigations have been conducted using these methods it may be easier to judge their value. After the first decade of computer-use within qualitative research much experience has been gathered with coding and retrieval facilities, which has led to a more informed discussion about these facilities. The new methods for computer-aided qualitative data analysis – using networks for qualitative theory building, methods for qualitative hypothesis examination and for the integration of interpretive analysis with statistical methods – are still in their infancy and there are only a few researchers who have gained extensive experience with them. Given this background many of the chapters in this volume may be regarded as opening shots in this debate.

Note

1. Take as an example Wittgenstein's concept of a language game which is governed by rules that cannot, in contrast to 'algorithms', be fully explicated and formalized.

PART I

GENERAL METHODOLOGICAL ISSUES

1

Computer Use in Qualitative Research and Issues of Validity

Udo Kelle and Heather Laurie

Will computers make the research process more transparent and will they improve the validity and reliability of its results? Soon after the first attempts were made in the early 1980s to use computers for the mechanization of manual tasks in qualitative analysis, these questions were raised and some qualitative researchers were really thrilled by the prospect that computers could add trustworthiness to a methodology which had always suffered from the reputation of seducing the researcher into employing an unsystematic, subjective or journalistic style of enquiry.

It was such hopes that inspired optimistic forecasts like that of the editors of a special issue of *Qualitative Sociology* about computers (Conrad and Reinarz, 1984). The authors expressed their expectation that computers would make the qualitative research process more transparent and rigorous while systematizing procedures that previously had been unsystematic (Conrad and Reinarz, 1984: 4) and enabling researchers to codify exactly how they analyse their data (p. 6). At the time these words were written there were only a very few software programs for qualitative data analysis on the market and this software was used by only a handful of researchers. Other researchers who did not know these programs and who wanted to use computers for their work had to draw on standard software and to undertake the tedious task of adapting it to their requirements (for example, by using database programming languages) or to write their own programs.

A decade later the situation has changed completely. A great variety of programs developed by qualitative researchers for the special demands of qualitative data analysis are available (see Chapter 14), and many researchers have gained experience with this software. As a consequence, there is an increasing body of literature about practical and methodological issues (for example, LeCompte and Preissle, 1993: 279–314; Lee and Fielding, 1991; Richards and Richards, 1994; Tesch, 1990, 1991; Weitzman and Miles, 1995).

Given this situation, the issues raised by Conrad and Reinarz and their optimistic forecasts deserve reconsideration. For this purpose we will present some methodological reflections that arose from our own research practice and from the experiences of colleagues who used computer-aided methods for analysing their data and whom we assisted as methodological consultants.

But because the notion of validity itself has given rise to some controversies among qualitative researchers we feel obliged to refer at least briefly to the current debate about validity issues in qualitative research. We can of course not give a detailed account of the numerous discussions on the issue that have taken place during the past two decades and would recommend that the interested reader refer to current writings about the topic (for example, Altheide and Johnson, 1994; Eisenhart and Howe, 1992; Hammersley, 1992; Kvale, 1989). This section only serves the purpose of clarifying our standpoint in this rather controversial discussion in order to enable the reader to relate our further arguments about validity and computer use to some of the recently stated opinions in the validity debate.

The validity debate in qualitative research

In contrast to scholars in the classical domains of quantitative research, such as psychometrics or survey research, the qualitative community has not yet agreed about the meaning and the proper use of the terms 'validity' and 'reliability' in the context of qualitative enquiry. The adherents of an extreme position would fully deny the appropriateness of these terms for qualitative research. 'We don't do validity and reliability' Smith (1984: 380) notes, thereby expressing the opinion that the epistemological foundations of the qualitative paradigm would under no circumstances allow the application of these standards. The underlying assumption (nowadays often linked to a constructivist position) is that qualitative methods have their roots in a paradigm which is distinct from other approaches of scientific enquiry and makes its own 'knowledge claims'. A supporter of such a position would refer to the fact that reality can be interpreted in different ways by individual and collective actors and from that would draw the conclusion that multiple realities exist and are valid in their own terms and therefore cannot be judged from outside. Of course, the emphasis on the importance of members' perspectives and interpretations, implicit in this approach, is one of the hallmarks of the qualitative paradigm. However, a radical relativism does not automatically follow from this. Furthermore, as Hammersley points out, such a position is always in danger of becoming self-refuting:

> However it is a view that can carry radical implications if we apply it to researchers themselves, as we surely must if we are to be consistent. Once we do this, we are led to ask whether research reports are not simply constructions that reflect the nature of the researcher and the research process, rather than representations of realities. (Hammersley, 1992: 196)

But in practice only very few researchers who advocate such relativist positions are prepared to accept such consequences and to regard their research reports as mere constructions. Instead it will be at least implicitly claimed that they represent a correct account or a 'thick description'[1] of the interpretations and the world-views of the people in the empirical field under study. We would like to call this the 'implicit realism'[2] which is embodied in almost every presentation of findings from qualitative investigations.

The other extreme in the debate is represented by those social scientists who repudiate any validity claim regarding qualitative findings since the usual standards of experimental research would not apply (see Kerlinger, 1979: 270), thereby not paying attention to the fact that numerous social phenomena could never be uncovered if methods of 'naturalistic enquiry' were not used, that is if people were not observed and interviewed in their natural surroundings. Countless phenomena investigated by gathering data in naturally occurring settings could never be obtained in experimental settings where conditions could be controlled by the researcher. Therefore, the attempt to validate qualitative research findings with experimental research's replication model presents a fundamental contradiction to the methodology itself.

The middle ground position between these extremes would maintain that every result of an act of scientific enquiry does, to a certain extent, represent an 'image' or a 'model' of a real-world process (even if this real-world process is itself an act of interpretation). From this perspective the process of scientific enquiry itself must be open to an assessment in order to examine the validity of its results. Nevertheless, the criteria used must be applicable to the specific kind of enquiry. Adherents of this middle ground position (for example, Hammersley, 1992; LeCompte and Preissle, 1993) have sometimes been criticized because this position 'has often led to the development of criteria that are in agreement with the postpositivist criteria; they are merely fitted to naturalistic research settings' (Denzin and Lincoln, 1994: 480). As mentioned earlier, the application of criteria developed in the context of experimental research, such as replicability, would clearly go against the intentions of qualitative enquiry. Nevertheless, the *epistemological core* of traditional validity concepts deserves a closer look. As Tschudi (1989) has pointed out, it is the *ubiquitousness of human error* which served as the starting point for the development of these concepts. The aim of the validation process is not to prove the perfect agreement between research results and 'reality' (an endeavour that would necessarily lead to an infinite regress), but to identify possible sources of error. In this perspective a result can be regarded as provisionally valid if every possible precautionary measure is taken to avoid mistakes: 'At best, one can know what has not yet been ruled out as false' (Cook and Campbell, 1979: 37). In our discussion of the relation between computer use and validity we will refer to this 'fallibilistic' approach and examine two of the many problem areas qualitative researchers deal with: first, sampling issues and, second, problems of the consistent and 'reliable' application of coding schemes. In both problem areas computers may be a useful tool for identifying and coping with sources of error.

Sampling issues

In comparison with large-scale survey research, qualitative researchers have always worked with rather small samples. Even in the early days of qualitative research this practice provoked methodological criticism of their findings, since they were regarded by critics as mere anecdotal accounts from individuals who may or may not be representative of the population under study (see Bain, 1929: 155; Lundberg, 1942: 169).

Managing complex textual data with computers offers the potential for increasing sample sizes, an idea which sounds attractive to many researchers on both methodological and policy grounds. Increasing sample sizes may be seen not only as a means of countering colleagues' criticisms, but also of convincing policy-makers (who are frequently also the funders of research) that the findings produced validly represent the views of the population under study. From this perspective the computer is sometimes seen as a tangible aid for the defence of research findings.

However we should keep in mind that the logic of sampling in qualitative research is quite different from that employed within quantitative surveys. In quantitative research cases have to be selected at random as a prerequisite for the application of statistical methods which serve to *examine the generalizability* of findings. Since sampling error will be smaller with large samples, the probability that measurements made on the sample reflect the true values in the population will improve with increasing sample size. For this reason quantitative researchers are interested in collecting large samples.

In contrast, qualitative researchers are generally not concerned with statistical generalizability, but with *discovering new phenomena* through a careful in-depth analysis. Even a single case study, for example a field study in a certain institution, can provide new and fruitful insights into the distribution of organizational power. But it is unclear to which other organizations or types of organizations these findings can be generalized. Of course, a second study may be conducted in a different organization to see whether these findings also apply here. But, as Lincoln and Guba (1985: 297) have pointed out, it would be in a certain sense misleading to say that the researcher conducts the second study in order to generalize the previous findings. Furthermore, he or she is interested in finding out whether the findings can be transferred to an organization which is in many respects different to the first one. But a central prerequisite for this kind of comparison is that the two organizations are not chosen at random but selected purposefully according to theoretically relevant criteria. Qualitative methodologists have developed several kinds of purposeful sampling (Patton, 1990: 169ff.), with 'theoretical sampling' (Glaser and Strauss, 1967: 45ff.) being the most prominent technique. The main purpose of these sampling procedures is to allow for systematic comparisons between cases that are similar or different in certain respects defined in line with the research interest.

Consequently, qualitative researchers usually do not regard a large sample as a value in itself like their quantitative colleagues, since qualitative research methodology does not entail concepts like statistical generalizability or statistical sampling error. However, increasing sample sizes may have a positive benefit in a qualitative setting for different reasons. Multiple comparisons between purposefully selected cases are crucial for a qualitative study to identify patterns and to develop theoretical categories. But due to limited resources the case number is often too small to allow for all desired comparisons. An increase in sample size allied to the use of electronic storage and retrieval facilities may therefore add greater breadth to the scope of the analysis while maintaining the depth of interpretation which can be regarded as the hallmark of qualitative analysis techniques.

However, it is crucial to be aware that a simple increase in sample size alone does not necessarily imply that the research findings will be more valid. Nor does a larger sample automatically imply that the findings can be generalized to the population under study in statistical terms. The central issue here is how the sample is drawn (is it a random sample or a purposefully selected sample?) and the main purpose of the research being carried out.

An important issue regarding the economy of the research process has to be mentioned here. In our own research experience, as well as that of colleagues, we have observed an interesting paradox concerning computer-use in qualitative analysis. Although the technology facilitates the clerical handling of voluminous textual material this does not necessarily translate into a quicker or easier analysis. Instead, there is a real danger of being overwhelmed by the sheer volume of information that becomes available when using computer technology. The amount of time and effort required to prepare the data and enter it into the program is not inconsiderable and increases in tandem with sample size. One should therefore be aware that the potential benefits of a larger sample size may be outweighed by the extra costs in time and effort required for data preparation and data entry.

Coding schemes and reliability

Almost all computer-aided methods of qualitative analysis require some coding or indexing of the data. The origins of coding and retrieval methods were 'cut-and-paste' techniques which represented 'folklore techniques' widely applied in qualitative research (for more details see the Introduction and Chapter 4). However, there are several other strategies for analysing textual data, such as fine-grained hermeneutic analysis or paraphrasing techniques (see Mayring, 1990). Many qualitative researchers exclusively use such strategies with limited amounts of data and therefore are less motivated to apply coding methods or cut-and-paste techniques. Some recent investigations have demonstrated that the implementation of computer-aided methods by a research team that had previously not used coding methods can cause serious difficulties (see Chapter 2), because its members may find it extremely difficult to develop a common coding scheme or to apply such a scheme consistently.

In the context of quantitative research one would address this as a problem of 'reliability', since a coding frame would only be regarded as reliable if in any subsequent re-coding exercise the same codes could be applied to the same incidents, which means that the coding could be repeated by a different coder within an acceptable margin of error.[3] To attain this goal one would be careful to construct coding categories which are mutually exclusive and unambiguous.

But again one must be careful not to confuse the requirements that arise in a hypothetico-deductive (H-D) research design with the demands of qualitative researchers employing an exploratory research design in order to develop theories on the basis of the data. Since the aim of an exploratory research design is usually not the testing of ready-made hypotheses but the development of categories and hypotheses grounded in the data and their further refinement, codes will be used in a quite different way than in hypothetico-deductive, quantitative research. In an H-D approach to the analysis of texts (for example, quantitative content analysis), codes would serve to condense the relevant information contained in the data, so that this information can be accurately represented by a matrix of numerical data. This can be referred to as a '*factual mode*' of coding (see Chapter 4 and Chapter 6), while in open research a '*referential mode*' is most widely (by some researchers exclusively) employed. In referential coding codes serve as 'signposts to' and not as 'models for' the information contained in the data. Hence, codes used for *referential coding* do in many cases not represent specific, precisely defined facts or incidents, but general, vaguely defined topics. While helping the researcher to retrieve relevant information from the raw data these 'topic-related codes' can be regarded as heuristic devices, but not as (reliable) representations of certain entities. Of course it could be argued that it is nevertheless of crucial importance to apply these codes consistently to ensure that the same text segments are assigned the same codes, since otherwise different members of the research group would draw upon different information when referring to the same topics. But since during an exploratory study the coding scheme is constructed in the ongoing process of data analysis, a more sophisticated investigation of the reliability problem is needed here. It would be helpful for this discussion to distinguish between two stages of exploratory research or data-based theory building, each requiring a different approach towards reliability: first, a stage where the analytical framework, the categories and their properties, are developed and hypotheses are generated and, second, a stage where these hypotheses are further refined.

Coding for hypothesis generation
The stage of hypothesis generation is that where 'open coding' (Strauss and Corbin, 1990) takes place and the coding scheme is developed. Since data collection takes place in unstructured settings, and in most cases with the close involvement of the researcher, the codes are often based on an intimate knowledge of the field, and almost inevitably carry subjective interpretations. Furthermore, they are related to the theoretical perspectives and interests of the researcher, so that different analysts will notice, and therefore code, different things in their data. For instance, a researcher who is interested in gender conflicts could code an interview with a black single mother in quite a different way to a researcher who is mainly interested in class relations. But this does

not necessarily pose 'threats for validity'. One must keep in mind that it is possible to produce an endless number of equally valid, but not contradictory, descriptions and explanations of the same phenomenon (Hammersley, 1992: 199), depending on which aspects one focuses on. Given that the main goal at the stage of hypothesis generation is to discover new phenomena and to develop new insights, a diversity of codes can be rather fruitful, while the search for a consistent and stable code scheme at this point of the investigation carries with it the danger of blocking the path of discovery.

Coding for hypothesis refinement

The coding scheme will become more and more concrete, solid and structured in the ongoing process of analysis, serving as a basis for the developing theory: certain codes will be dropped and links will be established between the remaining ones, and the analysis focuses on one or two codes to which subcodes are attached. If this process is conducted within a research team it may be accompanied by lengthy negotiations. Projects whose members have divergent theoretical perspectives and research interests can now undergo a phase of serious instability.

The completion of the process of analysis varies according to the methodological standpoints of the researchers involved. Many qualitative researchers will regard the construction of a solid conceptual structure that can serve as a theory about the domain under study as sufficient, and will put an end to data analysis at this point. But others may still want to employ procedures to prove or check on their already developed hypotheses, not for the purpose of 'hypothesis testing' in the classical sense, but to develop and refine their hypotheses further (see Introduction to Part III for the difference between hypothesis examination in quantitative and qualitative research). If codes and their allocations to text segments have been stored electronically, computer-aided methods of information retrieval provide a powerful tool for enhancing validity at the stage of hypothesis refinement. An example of this was apparent in one of the authors' own research projects (Laurie, 1992): one of the research questions in this project was whether married women earning a wage tend towards pooling their wages with their partners' and sharing in the management of household finances. As expected a relationship between women's earnings and the sharing of household money could be found. But closer analysis using multiple retrieval procedures revealed the importance of distinguishing the source of income entering the household from the type of access women had to money defined as 'household money'. Many women expressed guilt over expenditures which they could not define as legitimate household expenditure, whereby the type of access they had to bank accounts served in many cases as a gatekeeping mechanism. While exploring how the legitimation of expenditure was negotiated by individuals in differing circumstances, we were able to refine our crude initial proposition that women's paid employment leads to equal access to household money: we found that employed women tended to have complex financial arrangements with their partners. In particular, those in full-time paid employment combined elements of shared control with independent access to their own money.

In this project two main advantages were gained by the use of computer-aided methods. First, easy and quick retrievals helped to explore the data more fully than would have been possible by manual means given a sample size of just under one hundred households. Second, the facility to have easy access to all of the collected data increased our confidence that interpretations were not based on one or two highly untypical cases.

If some sort of hypothesis examination is conducted, the reliability of the code scheme is indeed of crucial importance. If the codes have been applied with a different meaning at different points this can produce contradictions which are artefacts of the coding process and which at worst lead to spurious conclusions. But if codes are assigned to text passages consistently, a stable coding scheme will provide a more systematic analysis and therefore greater confidence in the findings, since the same criteria are applied to all the data. This means that an analysis which is highly selective or which neglects critical information in the data is less probable.

Conclusion

In this chapter we have suggested that computer-aided methods can enhance the validity of research findings from qualitative studies in two ways: first, they can assist the management of larger samples and, second, given that a reliable and stable code is applied they offer facilities to retrieve all relevant information about a certain topic. This increases the trustworthiness of qualitative findings considerably because these facilities can ensure that the hypotheses developed are really grounded in the data and not based on single and highly untypical incidents.

Nonetheless, one must be careful not simply to borrow validity concepts and validation strategies from different research traditions, since their application to qualitative data analysis may lead to spurious conclusions. In particular, a large sample does not represent a value in itself in a qualitative context. Instead of being concerned with sample size one has to apply theoretically informed, purposeful sampling strategies in order to ensure that the investigated cases display theoretically relevant aspects of the empirical domain under study. A large sample size in qualitative research does not serve the purpose of generalizing findings to a population but of broadening the scope of the study. Since a scholarly qualitative analysis of large samples is tedious and time-consuming, even with the help of electronic data processing devices, one should ensure that the sample size really does meet the analytic requirements. Finally, implementing a consistent and stable coding scheme at too early a stage of data analysis may really have a hazardous influence on hypothesis generation. Therefore, it may not be desirable to strive for the reliability of a coding scheme at all stages of the research process, although it is of course a crucial prerequisite for hypothesis refinement.

Notes

1. A notion that carries a lot of realist implications!

2. One will find this implicit realism even in the works of the most ambitious critics of 'postpositivist' and 'realist' positions. For example, Norman Denzin begins his monograph on *Interpretive Interactionism* with the words 'Interpretive Interactionists attempt to make the world directly accessible [sic!] to the reader' (Denzin, 1989: 10).

3. A method has been proposed by Blackman to determine intercoder reliability, using tables of agreement, 'confusion' matrices and Scott's π. The information from all these calculations can be used to improve the code definitions and procedures. The purpose of this operation is to help the researcher to improve the clarity and precision of coding and, hence, the quality of results (Blackman, personal communication). This technique has been integrated into the software package QUALPRO (see Chapter 14 about software).

2

Users' Experiences of Qualitative Data Analysis Software

Raymond M. Lee and Nigel G. Fielding

Choosing the right package for qualitative data analysis is always a problem, even for those with experience of other kinds of software. Unbiased information at the right level can be hard to come by. Nor is technical information about program specifications all that is relevant. Ever since the advent of Computer-Assisted Qualitative Data Analysis Software (CAQDAS) programs, researchers have been concerned with the epistemological consequences of their use. In an earlier paper we likened this to the fear of Frankenstein's monster, and commented (Lee and Fielding, 1991: 8):

> The anxiety comes from the fear that the machine will 'take over' the analy-sis. Researchers, and their audiences, will be seduced by the convenience and credibility of the program's rendering of sense. As we celebrate the pro-gram's output, and especially its form, we will no longer have an awareness of the process by which this product was brought about. Qualitative research, especially ethnography, will be commodified, without the knowl-edge of process that formerly made the final analysis a product we could believe in.

Such concerns reflect the traditional preoccupation of qualitative researchers with epistemological matters, a historical recognition of the way in which computers transformed quantitative research, and, perhaps, even a measure of technological conservatism. Whatever its origins, discussion about the transformation of qualitative research by computers has so far been mostly speculative. Empirical assessments of how qualitative researchers actually use computers have been lacking. To remedy this situation we decided to embark on a small-scale research project that would look at users' experiences of CAQDAS programs.

In this chapter, we draw on preliminary findings from qualitative fieldwork which we have conducted on user experiences with CAQDAS.[1] The research study we carried out is based on focus group methodol-ogy rather than interviews with individual users. This is because we have sometimes, although not always, found individual users surpris-ingly unclear about precisely how they use a program. Fortunately, however, the sharing of experiences in a group context promotes fruitful discussion of the kinds of issues we are to be concerned with in this paper. Focus groups with past or present CAQDAS users took place during 1992 and 1993. The groups were convened at various sites throughout Great Britain and included users of a wide range of currently available programs, such as The ETHNOGRAPH, NUD.IST, HyperRESEARCH and Hypersoft (for more details of these programs see Chapter 14). The group discussions covered a range of topics including: how users heard about the program and from whom, what use had been made of it, the nature of their research, the character of their research team, how they had analysed their data using the program and their reactions, both positive and negative, to the software, its availability, documentation and support. Groups lasted between 90 and 150 minutes and were tape-recorded and transcribed verbatim, with transcripts fed back to participants on request.

We begin by looking at the *program acquisition process*, including how people first encountered the software, their motivations for using it and problems relating to the distribution and supply of particular packages. From this we move on to consider issues relating to *program documentation*, ease of use and institutional support for non-quantitative computer use in the social sciences. A major concern of this chapter is with the *process of coding and categorizing qualitative data*. Concerns include: the merits of 'on-screen coding', the way in which programs interact with the user, the use of analytic memos, the problems of coding in teams and the circumstances under which users reverted to manual methods. However, our central thesis throughout is that, far from being solely technical matters, user experiences and problems relate in a fundamental way to the *social environment* in which research is carried out. Here we have in mind considerations such as the place of qualitative research in the social science division of labour, hierarchical relations in small working teams and issues posed by resource constraints and sponsor expectations.

Program acquisition

How do people hear about programs?
Our focus groups began by asking people about how they had first heard about the program. As one might expect, informal networks were one source of knowledge about the software. One person, for example, heard about The ETHNOGRAPH while standing over the departmental photocopier talking with a colleague about the problems of handling large amounts of qualitative data. There are signs, too, that information about CAQDAS programs is being introduced into postgraduate training programmes. A number of the focus group

members had initially used the software for their dissertation research.

Second, and related to this, a number of users traced their initial acquaintance with the software either directly or indirectly to events such as a particular conference, workshop or seminar on the topic. The significance of this from our point of view is that a number of such events have been funded by external funding bodies. In most cases, the funding outlay has been modest. One message from our study seems to be that investment of this kind does seem to be effective in encouraging the diffusion of new methods and technologies.

The other issue we would like to mention briefly is that of piracy as a source of program acquisition. Obviously we were dealing with people who were non-pirates by definition; they had registered their software. We asked, however, if they knew of pirated software and about their own reasons for not pirating. There seemed to be general agreement on three points. First, the generally low cost of CAQDAS programs discourages piracy. Second, in the UK, recent legislative changes have shifted the culture in universities to one that is anti-piracy. Third, the temptation to pirate software is related to availability. Software sometimes takes a long time to arrive from abroad; one researcher had therefore resorted to using a pirated copy of a package while waiting for a legal copy to be delivered.

Why do researchers decide to acquire a program?
To preserve the anonymity of the researchers we will not describe in detail the actual projects on which they were working. In scope they ranged, however, from small-scale Master's dissertation projects, through a PhD thesis to a number of rather large multi-person, and in some cases multi-method, projects. When we asked our focus group participants why they had decided to acquire a software package several familiar themes emerged. At the planning stage, or soon after data collection had begun, researchers began to realize that they would have *data management problems* arising from the size and/or complexity of the data to be analysed. In fact we suspect that, whatever the size of their project, it is common for qualitative researchers to feel that the volume of their material is too large relative to the resources they have available. Some had learned from previous experience that data analysis by manual means could be complex and time-consuming. They also feared what we have come to call the detritus problem, in other words the inevitable and sometimes frightening accumulation of the many, varied and sometimes fugitive items of data and analytically reflective material which qualitative data analysis generates. For some researchers ease of retrieval was also a factor. In one project, for instance, it was important to be able to home in on the experiences of particular sub-

groups in what is by qualitative standards a relatively large sample. Finally, we occasionally found instances of researchers being encouraged to use a package by research managers who perceive in it efficiency or productivity gains. At present, we think this is quite rare but we suspect this kind of situation is likely to become more common.

Program infrastructure

A number of background issues affect the user's experience of any software. Among these are how readily available the program is, the quality of the documentation accompanying the software, and the ease of data entry. Although CAQDAS programs are available commercially, it is hardly 'big business', and *availability problems* were cited by several users. A complicating factor is that qualitative research is not associated with computers and, as we have noted, graduate students seem particularly likely to initiate use of CAQDAS programs in their working environment. Our respondents noted that social science departments may have less call on institutional resources for hardware and software. Further, graduate students are located further down the pecking order in decisions relating to the acquisition of new technology. Difficulties were cited in persuading computing service managers that data could be textual as well as numerical and that the volume of data to be manipulated could exceed the capacity of PCs, thus requiring mainframe access and realistic allocations of memory.

One user reported:

> chasing our computer people in college for months, saying 'What's available, what kind of text-based systems are there, why can't we have text readers, how do we do this?' Trying to get them to recognize that qualitative data is the kind of data that requires analysis, requires software, I am finding that resistance is there in terms of actually educating and persuading the people who have the money and the computer networks within the college.

A further problem was that qualitative research had 'taken off' in that department's particular social science discipline and 'people are desperate to find more rigorous ways of dealing with data, they are fed up with being accused of being soft and woolly, and they are looking for ways to demonstrate to their colleagues that they have gone through a rational process'.

Mention was also made of the more straightforward problem of a *delay in shipping* software once ordered. Considerable delays were cited, and the view that 'if they could just send off and take a week . . . [to] get a copy', then piracy would be reduced. There were some criticisms of *documentation*. Some users spoke of the need for more information on the time they should expect to take on different parts of the operation. Printing sorted output was a case in point. If one was searching, it could take 30 to 45 minutes per sheet to print and 'I would really like more information along those lines, what it does.'

Of course, unclear documentation is a feature of many programs, including, it must be said, many commercial packages. It is not difficult to see how such relatively straightforward problems may deter the inexperienced user.

Data entry issues related to the perceived advantages of using CAQDAS. An initial attraction was simply as a means of textual database management so that 'you could actually go in and pull out what you needed without saying "I know what I need but I can't find it."' All but one user subsequently became persuaded that, provided they could implement and master it, CAQDAS offered a 'much more systematic approach than conventional methods' which 'does actually make you look at performance, you can't ignore the data'. But users with long experience using computers in qualitative research found that data entry revived old anxieties and frustrations. 'I've always had a love/hate relationship with computers and I think that's partly my feeling towards The ETHNOGRAPH. Because I can remember as an undergraduate in the days when we used to have cards, going across to the Computer Centre with all my questionnaires with 1,000 cards, which was two boxes, and you had to stack them all in manually and the turn-round time was about a week and a half.' An error on 'one tiny comma or full stop' could throw everything out. Although 'when it works it's wonderful', users needed to bear in mind the tedious background work.

However, the principal concern relating to data entry was that of the *size of the data set*. Apart from a lot of transcription, often bulk affects the analysis. One user who was working on a large number of in-depth interviews reported: 'I thought "I wonder what they are thinking about something", press the button, out comes about 8,000 sheets, I have to really home in on exactly what I want.' Another had seen colleagues doing the 'cut-and-paste' procedure and 'chucking out bits and piles of comments there and I thought there must be an easier way of doing this'. Even though her sample was small, the data were sufficiently extensive – one interview alone exceeded 100 pages – that she had progressively repeated the coding operation until she had a fine-grained set of codes and a selected data sub-set.

> I have been through the data and I coded everything. I ended up with about fifty codes, every single comment on that data was coded, and then I started to look at what my codes were and what they meant, then I did counts to see what sort of things were repeatedly happening and from that I then had to select a very small amount of data and I managed to come out with three interesting phenomena from the data.

The longest of her transcripts took seven hours to code. Clearly, the iterative coding process described here would considerably increase time spent on data entry.

An alternative to the daunting task of transcribing and then repeat-coding all the data was to transcribe selectively from the outset, but users were conscious that this ran against a strongly established view in qualitative research concerning 'immersion' in the data.

However, all but one of the users were doubtful, whatever their experience, that they would return to 'manual' methods. The decision did not relate to size of data set – at any rate, those who had cut their teeth on a large data set would not be inclined to use manual methods for small data sets. The pay-off when they came to search was suffi-cient incentive. One who was analysing fifty-five semi-structured interviews by manual methods (because the research group had not acquired any software) noted that 'every single issue that I want to write about I've got to get all fifty-five out, divide them into mothers and non-mothers and then get the issue I want and then get the bit, it's a nightmare'. However, the breadth of codes was an issue: broad codes and large data sets meant that a search could be 'a giant thing taking up three days'.

Coding

The coding process loomed large in the accounts that users gave of using a package. Their comments generally reflected a feeling that the mechanical aspects of coding were laborious and tedious. Those who seemed to fare best with the computer were individual researchers who had small- to medium-sized data sets which they approached with a fairly delimited theoretical interest. Those with large data sets, pro-jects involving a division of labour and colleagues with differing theoretical pre-suppositions had more difficulty.

One issue raised by users was the tension between two-step and one-step (on-screen) coding. As far as we can judge, users had some worries about on-screen coding, feeling that it distanced them from their data. On purely pragmatic grounds, however, they tended to prefer one-step coding. It was faster. In other words, whatever the relative merits on theoretical grounds of adopting one procedure rather than the other, the pressures felt by researchers forced them to resolve the issue in one particular way.

Some users, who felt that coding was laborious, nevertheless argued that the ability to search and retrieve once the data were coded was a major compensation for the time spent doing the coding. One researcher, who for various reasons had to analyse data on her current project manually, lamented, for example, her inability to rapidly extract the segments she needed for her analysis.

One issue which is likely to emerge as program use becomes more common is how far it will be possible to transfer coded files as opposed to data files in raw text files. Either program developers will have to find ways of standardizing the internal representation of coded files or they will need to make program information available to third parties who might be prepared to develop conversion programs.

In the view of some users, the coding process itself had not become any easier as a consequence of using a CAQDAS program; indeed, some felt it was now more demanding. This may well be because it has become easier to change codes, encouraging more care over category refinement and more work on false leads. There may also be an effect from coding now being a wholly separate procedure to transcription and data entry. In these respects, there is at least a case that program use subtly leads away from the process Glaser and Strauss (1967) described as 'open coding'. For example, a package such as The ETHNO-GRAPH permits up to twelve codes to be assigned per line of text, with seven levels of 'nesting'. Clearly, those who expect the use of a program automatically to make the coding process easier could readily become frustrated.

What happened when users became frustrated by their experiences in using a CAQDAS program? Broadly speaking, they either adapted their methods of working to the exigencies which faced them, or they ceased to use the program altogether. One researcher, for example, developed a strategy which involved outputting all coded segments relating to a particular theme into individual files which were then analysed in detail separately. The efficacy of such a procedure depends, of course, on the degree to which the initial selection of topics may channel future analysis. Another researcher, who had coded her transcripts in a relatively fine-grained way, felt herself flagging towards the end of her analysis. At that point she began to use a kind of skeleton coding scheme for the last few interviews in her sample which allowed her to extract a limited range of relevant material. Although in her words this was 'miles faster', she nevertheless worried because:

> I'm not sure what that does to those interviews, because I think I hadn't coded those in the same way as I coded the other ones, where there was a lot more overlap, a lot more script and you tended to code what was in front of you.

In some cases, difficulties of this kind led to the temporary or permanent *cessation of program use*. We explored in some detail the circumstances in which our focus group participants ceased to use the program. One research group which had struggled with the intellectual task of developing codes found the mechanical process of coding a barrier.

> I think it [the use of a computer program] has affected us detrimentally, and
> I think it is partly because of our inexperience, but the psychological block
> that we have developed as a team in terms of having to go through this rou-
> tine of getting the codes, getting them on the machine, put us back a lot and
> it killed a lot of the enthusiasm and interest that we had intrinsically in the
> project, the whole thing became coloured by our hatred and resentment of
> the bloody program and what we had to do to put the data in, and in the end
> we all became extremely bitter and twisted and what happens except another
> day, another week had gone because none of us could actually face sitting
> there for another three or five hours getting blasted codes and typing [indis-
> tinct word] so the mechanics of it in many ways killed quite important
> chunks of time it would take up to do other things, and we also, in a way it
> became a block to us writing.

In other cases ceasing to use the program had an epistemological basis.
As one researcher commented:

> I've moved away from the commercial cut-and-paste type of analysis any-
> way, this desire that you have to find usual data, to find out broad areas of
> consensus – although you are doing qualitative research – in a way that
> quantitative researchers do, consensus of opinion on one thing.

In a number of cases there was what might be called expedient cessation. Users under pressure from deadlines went back to using manual
methods. In doing so they hoped to avoid the labour of having to go
back to the program to re-code all of their data, and instead worked
from the original transcripts or from previously extracted segments.
There is a positive aspect to this. In the past we may have overstated the
Frankenstein's monster problem. Despite the comments quoted earlier,
in the long run the social context in which program development takes
place is inherently pluralistic. It is not, by and large, driven by commercial pressures but by continuing contact between developers and
users. To be sure, particular programs have particular strengths and
weaknesses, but continued contact with users in fact encourages the
adaptation of the programs over time to multiple styles of use.
Moreover developers have recurrently demonstrated their own epistemological awareness of the problems potentially involved in program
use (Seidel, 1991; Richards and Richards, 1991d). Now it is also clear
that users will cease to use a program rather than persist with unsuit-
able use. The negative aspect is that we do not know the effect on the
analysis of the shift late in the day from computer-aided to manual
methods.

Programs in the research environment

Social scientists have grown increasingly conscious that the context in
which research takes place has an effect on the production of research
knowledge. The public face of a project, expressed in publications and

presentations, can be very different to the situation behind the scenes. When programs enter the research environment there are a number of elements which contribute to the social context of their use. These are neither matters purely to do with software nor purely features of the dynamics of small occupational groups, but of the interaction between the two.

Social research is usually conducted in small groups. Group size affects the working out of consensus on matters such as coding conventions and analytic procedure. One user reported 'very difficult problems of negotiation because there is [*sic*] three of us working in the group [and] we also have the collective information that goes on between ourselves', a comment suggesting that team members have to keep in mind not only their particular 'angle' but that of the other team members singly, plus the collective meaning worked out in some process of consensus formation. Where transcription is delegated to someone not involved in the analysis process several days would be needed to work out common meanings for codes, whereas for the solo researcher 'a lot of that is done when you do the transcripts yourself, if you aren't doing the transcripts yourself then you are not in touch with the data before you start'.

Indeed, working in a group can 'multiply' discouragement and inhibit individuals who may want to persevere in using CAQDAS by provoking fear of being seen as a 'wise guy' or rate-buster. A team whose leader felt that a failed attempt to use The ETHNOGRAPH 'has affected us detrimentally' had arrived at a 'psychological block that we have developed as a team'. The experience had called into doubt an effective working relationship which had evolved in previous collaborations.

> When we have worked up to now we have done a lot of creative work and writing, we write group reports, we write papers, we write memos to each other. And what it did was to stall that because it became the whole [obstacle] that we had to get over before we could start on anything else.

Although one should not discount the experience of those who are unsupported and abandon the software in a mood of quiet desperation, things seem simpler for the lone researcher. 'I usually just have the transcript by me and just as I went along, read it up, OK, line so-and-so I want that and that, and you do it straight on, which saves all the writing it down by the side.' It seems obvious that consistency is more easily achieved by solo analysts, even if this can lead to a narrow analysis. The implication is that, rather than a linear function, the matter of team size is essentially a contrast between one researcher and one plus '*N*' researchers.

When research teams combine individuals from several disciplines the problem of reconciling perspectives is aggravated. While some software developers have foreseen the potential in the software to advance multi-method research and triangulation of analysis, those users with experience of working on projects combining methods, including computer-based qualitative data analysis, did not report substantial convergence. The fact that team research and disciplinary differences as well as interpersonal differences had their negative side suggests the need for great care in the division of labour for working with the software. In one project each member took responsibility for coding all the segments of the interview transcripts which were related to their particular, distinctive analytic interest. After an initial and lengthy 'negotiation' to identify these interests, 'we made a big mistake' in that each took 'our own responsibilities'. Because the project leader had some training in the use of CAQDAS she undertook to reconcile the coded transcripts.

> So I was confronted with three sets of transcripts. . . . Some of those codes [had] actually changed in terms of their main direction. [A colleague] put them all together into one set, which was bloody awful. . . . One of the things I kept running up against, having eventually got a second code which we agreed, kept running into the maximum set of levels because all that had to be put in three sets of codes. . . . We were regularly coding 8, 10, 12 codes per line, it was just so complex.

It emerged that none of those who had used CAQDAS on a team project had analysed the data collectively. In the case just cited it was tried but the project leader took on the role alone in light of the coding problems. In the others, the CAQDAS user in the team was assigned the role of analysing all the qualitative data.

In our previous commentaries on the subject we have suggested that it is unrealistic to expect CAQDAS to speed up the analytic process. By making the process more thorough and enabling more complex relationships to be examined it is as likely to add to analysis time. The reluctance of funders to support lengthy analysis stages, and the exigencies of qualitative data collection, mean that analysis and writing time is usually squeezed. This appears to have happened in the project which encountered problems with differently minded coders. Time had not been spent working out the practicalities of coding; the team was 'trying to jump ahead of ourselves . . . because of the time constraint', and 'it would be much more sensible for us to have a couple of days talking together on what coding is about'. Other users spoke of becoming 'totally absorbed' in the analysis process once the tedium of data entry was over. 'You'd be driving along to work thinking "I wonder if there is a tie-up between that and that" and you'd go back home and have another look. If you were cutting and pasting you wouldn't do it.' Another remarked, 'it is the excitement of suddenly you can play with all these different categories and I found myself going on and on and I thought "stop, you are getting carried away here"'.

Qualitative research can weld teams together as well as divide them. A key element of procedure which contributes to the social organization of team research is that of writing analytic memos; it enjoys a premier role in Glaser and Strauss' (1967: 108ff.) grounded theory approach, for instance. Such memos not only rehearse analysis but inform coding. As we have seen, establishing a group meaning of a code is important and time-consuming. Researchers are used to checking conventions by independent re-coding and comparison of concurrence, but no respondent had performed such checks in their CAQDAS projects. However, they recognized that the coding process was different to manual methods and missed the chance to write marginal comments.

> The way we worked before this [project] contract is to write in interpretations on the transcripts themselves, things about concepts, in the process of writing, as one does. . . . So to see The ETHNOGRAPH as a mechanical process primarily rather than being an intellectually interpretive process, that was the difficulty.

The memo problem can be partly addressed by screen-switching to a word processor file containing duplicate transcripts on which coding notes can be entered, but it is a cumbersome process.

When the codes were applied to the data and code searching began, the fact that each code would be extracted with all its associated data could well lead to a change in conceptualization.

> You have got your own ideas of what might come out [but] what can happen is [that] the content codes sometimes make you shift the theoretical balance, because you begin to see data emerging [in a] . . . different balance from what you expected, and then your more complex codes come from that.

The software was then a genuine tool for analysis: 'you've got your sheet [of data assigned to a code] and then you do the thinking, and then you start again'. However, another user felt that the software led towards an essentially quantitative model of analysis, citing that the program 'encouraged you to . . . look for similarities between your codes . . . and it cuts things up into little blocks so that you can count perhaps the sections that you had on one particular topic and compare the sections that somebody else has on that topic, and I think that is quite dangerous'. This user had reacted by conducting the major part of the analysis by manual methods.

Qualitative researchers may face special problems here. Qualitative research has no tradition of using computers, so researchers are quite likely to be naive users or have no experience beyond the basics of word processing. Indeed, we suspect that many of those with an affinity for qualitative methods use them partly because of an aversion for computers based on the link they make between numeracy and computer literacy. Confronted by difficulty in operating the program, such users seem especially likely to conclude that computing is not for them. The program is a kind of magic, and it is the user's fault if s/he cannot work it. 'One of the problems I find with students [is] that psychological barrier that you can work with machines and it's not going to bite you, you won't get it all wrong. Once you get them over that hurdle then you can put up with the [faults].' Experienced software users may be more willing to problem-solve, to find another way round the obstacle, and may be better linked into user networks which can offer advice on the basis of pooled experience. Experienced users will also know that, far from magic, programs themselves contain the products of human error.

In closing, we should emphasize that the findings discussed here represent a 'snapshot' from a particular stage in the development both of the software and of user experiences with it. It hardly needs to be said that technological developments are proceeding rapidly, and our strong impression is that use of CAQDAS packages is spreading rapidly. As our fieldwork has continued, we find some issues which are consistent with the findings reported above and some where the technical refinement of packages or the knowledge of users has changed the picture. We would only add that while we believe use is spreading, what seems to be moving even more rapidly is a feeling among researchers and sponsors who are not acquainted with qualitative analysis software at a practical level that these developments are important and that they should know more about them.

In this chapter we have explored a number of specific problems users have had in what were relatively early encounters with the first generation of qualitative data analysis packages. In so doing we have alerted potential users to some of the technical considerations which they will need to bear in mind in choosing a package. We have, however, gone beyond simply providing consumer advice. While this is a necessary task, we have highlighted a range of issues concerning the social context of computer use in qualitative research which, in our view, are likely to prove more enduring.

Note

1. Support for the pilot phase of this research came from the Department of Social Policy and Social Science at Royal Holloway University of London. The main part of the study is being funded by the Economic and Social Research Council, Grant No. R000234586.

3

Grounded Theory as an Emerging Paradigm for Computer-assisted Qualitative Data Analysis

Markku Lonkila

I call it the law of the instrument, and it may be formulated as follows: Give a small boy a hammer, and he will find that everything he encounters needs pounding. (Kaplan 1964: 28)[1]

In this chapter the relationships between grounded theory and computer-assisted qualitative data analysis are examined[2]. Grounded theory has influenced the development of several programs that support qualitative data analysis and has taken on an almost paradigmatic role in the specific methodological-technical discussion surrounding computer-assisted qualitative data analysis.

The central role of grounded theory was evident at the second and third international conferences on computer-assisted qualitative data analysis held in Breckenridge in 1990 and Bremen in 1992. Grounded theory was the qualitative method most often mentioned during the Breckenridge conference. In Bremen a special methodological session was organized for grounded theory but not for, say, discourse analysis. The leading role of grounded theory in the field of computer-assisted qualitative data analysis can also be seen when examining manuals of software developed for qualitative data analysis and articles by software developers.[3] These observations lead to the question, whether and in which ways the introduction of computers to qualitative research might be connected to the popularity of grounded theory.

The first section of this chapter will present the basics of grounded theory, followed by some critical remarks in the second section. Since it is not possible to give a thorough overview of all important aspects of grounded theory in a relatively short chapter, the emphasis will be on coding – which is the element of grounded theory that is most relevant to and has had the greatest influence on computer-assisted qualitative data analysis. In the remaining sections of the chapter I will examine the nature of the connections between grounded theory method and computer-assisted qualitative data analysis. I will present examples of the analytic operations relevant to both and introduce some advanced software packages (particularly ATLAS/ti and NUD.IST) designed in accordance with the grounded theory model.

Grounded theory in a nutshell

Grounded theory is a method for the inductive generation (and provisional verification) of sociological hypotheses and theories from empirical data.[4] Its principles have been laid out in numerous books and articles by Barney Glaser and Anselm Strauss (Glaser and Strauss, 1967; Glaser, 1978; Strauss, 1987; see also Strauss and Corbin, 1990).[5] The application of grounded theory has flourished particularly in the sociology of health, but has become increasingly popular in other disciplines as well. Here I will concentrate on the method as it is presented by Strauss (1987) and Strauss and Corbin (1990).[6]

The process of research in the paradigm of grounded theory

If the principles of grounded theory are applied, the research process can, in very coarse terms, be described as follows: the researcher starts by reading and carefully analysing a small amount of data. He or she 'codes' (read: analyses) the data (most often text) by following very detailed and complex procedures and 'rules of thumb'. During the analysis the researcher is continually asking questions about the data and checking them by constantly comparing different instances of data. When necessary, the researcher collects new data based on 'theoretical sampling': a sampling procedure directed by the categories of the emerging theory. During the whole research process the researcher writes 'memos' on, for example, his or her ideas about codes, their interrelations, new directions for the research, etc., and draws diagrams visualizing his or her thinking about the data. Continuous interaction between the collecting and coding of data and the writing of memos is essential. As the research advances, the researcher develops an increasingly abstract and complex conceptual structure, specifying the connections between the concepts of the emerging theory and regularly returning to the data to check whether this theoretical structure is in fact supported by the data.

The centrality of coding

At the heart of grounded theory is a very detailed and explicit coding of texts. In computer-assisted qualitative data analysis coding has a more formal meaning: it is conceived of as attaching keywords to text segments. In grounded theory the terms 'coding' and 'code' are somewhat vaguely defined, but it is clear that coding refers to a different operation than the formal act of attaching words to text segments.

At the most general level, Strauss and Corbin define coding as 'the process of analyzing data' (1990: 61). In *Qualitative Analysis for Social Scientists* (Strauss, 1987: 21) a code is defined as 'the term for any product of this analysis [coding] (whether category or a relation among two or more categories)',[7] but in *Basics of Qualitative Research* (Strauss and Corbin, 1990) the authors do not explicitly define a code. They use the term, however, in a context (p. 203) that indicates that a code seems to refer to a conceptual label of a category (1990: 98, 108). According to them, coding consists of three 'modes' which are called 'open', 'axial' and 'selective' coding.

Open coding   Grounded theory research commences with open coding which is basically meant to get the research going. Strauss and Corbin describe open coding as

> the analytic process by which concepts are identified and developed in terms of their properties and dimensions. The basic analytic procedures by which this is accomplished are: the asking of questions about data; and the making of comparisons for similarities and differences between each incident, event, and other instances of phenomena. Similar events and incidents are labeled and grouped to form categories. (1990: 74)

In open coding the categories are developed by focusing on their properties (attributes of a category) and examining their nature, relationships and dimensions. Each of these properties corresponds to a different continuum. For example, the property 'shade' of the category 'color' varies along the continuum 'light–dark'. 'The process of breaking a property down into its dimensions' (Strauss and Corbin, 1990: 61) is called *dimensionalization*.

Axial coding   Whereas in open coding the main aim is to freely generate new categories and specify their properties and dimensions, axial coding means working intensively with one category: 'Open coding . . . fractures the data and allows one to identify some categories, their properties, and dimensional locations. Axial coding puts those data back together in new ways by making connections between a category and its subcategories' (1990: 97). Open and axial coding do not necessarily follow each other in a linear order. They are rather two 'modes' of coding between which the researcher is continually switching.

In axial coding one tries to specify the relations of the category in question to the other categories. This is done within the framework of a 'coding paradigm' – a metatheoretical concept derived from a general theory of action (see Strauss and Corbin, 1990: 99ff.; Kelle, 1994: 330ff.) – which the researcher has to bear in mind when specifying the categories. The coding paradigm comprises the following elements:

- the phenomenon under study,
- its causal conditions,
- its context,
- intervening conditions,

- the action and interaction strategies of the actors involved,
- the consequences of the actors' actions.

For example, a researcher interested in 'pain management' might try to specify the relation between the categories 'pain' and 'pain management': 'If we saw that people with arthritis used certain strategies to relieve their pain, we might pose the question: Under conditions of Pain, what strategies do they use for Pain Management?, thereby relating the two categories' (Strauss and Corbin, 1990: 108). Similarly the researcher could examine the consequences of the actors' strategies and so forth (Strauss and Corbin, 1990: 106).

Selective coding   Selective coding takes place later on during the research process, when the researcher has already developed the categories and specified their connections. In selective coding, the researcher adopts the most important category (a 'core category') and tries to orient the study around this core category by specifying and validating the relationships between it and the other categories.

The current methodological debate on grounded theory

There is an intense ongoing debate about the feasibility of grounded theory in qualitative analysis. This debate has partly taken place elsewhere,[8] partly it is yet to come. In spite of this, analysis techniques similar to those used in grounded theory research are frequently employed in qualitative research. At the level of analysis techniques, grounded theory indeed provides a well-written and detailed explication (and for many researchers, an example to follow) of the operations carried out in qualitative research.[9] However, Strauss and Corbin fail to define clearly the relations between some of the basic concepts of grounded theory (for instance between categories, properties and dimensions: see, for example, Strauss, 1987: 14–15, 20–21; Strauss and Corbin, 1990: 70–71, and 127 showing that a category can also be a property).

The rhetoric of grounded theory can also be misleading. In grounded theory the vocabulary of hypothetico-deductive research is used, and sometimes different meanings are given to its terms (see, for example, the discussion on the 'generalizability' of research in Strauss and Corbin, 1990: 250–251), which shows how problematic it can be to simply adopt terms from the positivistic tradition. This point is illustrated by Norman Denzin in his well-argued (and basically positive) review of *Qualitative Analysis for Social Scientists* (Strauss, 1987):

> Still, this book marks the end of an era. It signals a turning point in the history of qualitative research in American sociology. At the very moment that this work finds its place in the libraries of scholars and students, it is being

challenged by a new body of work coming from the neighboring fields of anthropology and cultural studies. Post-Geertzian anthropologists (Marcus, Tyler, Clifford, Bruner, Turner, Pratt, Asad, Rosaldo, Crapanzano, Fischer, Rabinow) are now writing on the politics and poetics of ethnography. They are taking seriously the question 'How do we write culture?' They are proposing that postmodern ethnography can no longer follow the guidelines of positivist social science. Gone are words like theory, hypothesis, concept, indicator, coding scheme, sampling, validity, and reliability. In their place comes a new language; readerly texts, modes of discourse, cultural poetics, deconstruction, interpretation, domination, the authority of the text, the author's voice, feminism, genre, grammatology, hermeneutics, inscription, master narrative, narrative structures, otherness, postmodernism, redemptive ethnography, semiotics, subversion, textuality, tropes. (Denzin, 1988: 432)

A further criticism relates to lack of clear, technical explication. Grounded theory procedures and 'rules of thumb' are designed to structure the often impressionistic process of qualitative data analysis, and even though Strauss (1987) and Strauss and Corbin (1990) are among the most concrete and detailed guides to the jungle of qualitative data analysis, they are not, however, concrete enough. Sometimes painfully numerous case examples (Strauss, 1987) do not, in the end, illustrate much of the 'dirty work' of qualitative data analysis techniques. One does find passages about the underlining of keywords in the data and writing comments in brackets (1987: 60), writing the names of categories in the text margins (1987: 27), sorting memos (Strauss and Corbin, 1990: 199–200) or heading the code items for sorting (Strauss, 1987: 68), but not much about the technical and methodological problems associated with the practical implementation of these operations; for example managing and sorting the possibly large systems of codes and their inter-relations. Did Strauss use index cards to store the codes? Did he use Boolean searches (see Chapter 14)? How could he technically manage the huge amount of cross-references between different instances of the data, between data and concepts, and between concepts themselves? How could he ever be sure he did not miss anything because of the sheer quantity of these connections? One is almost tempted to claim that it is next to impossible to conduct grounded theory research without computers. However, references to computer-assisted techniques are rare in both Strauss (1987) and Strauss and Corbin (1990), although Strauss has obviously been following the discussion on computer-assisted methods (for example, 1987: 75; 1990: 200–202).

Connections between grounded theory and qualitative data analysis software

The utilization of both grounded theory and computers in qualitative analysis can be viewed as an attempt to enhance an often vague analysis process by making it more structured and rigorous. However, both could also be misused as purely rhetorical weapons to convince the readers or academic community of the scientific nature of one's research.[10] This problem was summarized by Norman Denzin, who views grounded theory as expressing the dilemma present in both pragmatism and the sociology of the Chicago school, namely how to 'be subjective, interpretative and scientific at the same time'. According to Denzin it is not clear 'that this is either possible or desirable' (Denzin, 1988: 432).

Grounded theory has exerted a particularly strong influence on the qualitative analysis programs ATLAS/ti and NUD.IST which can be seen in the structure of the programs, the developers' publications (see Muhr, 1991; Richards and Richards, 1991a–c and forthcoming), and which is perhaps partially accounted for by the contacts the developers have had with Anselm Strauss (Strauss, personal communication, 1994). The influence of grounded theory can also be found in other programs, for example Kwalitan (see Peters and Wester, 1990: 3–17) and HyperRESEARCH (see Hesse-Biber et al., 1990, 1991, and Chapter 14 for more details of these programs). In the special issue of *Qualitative Sociology* (Tesch, 1991: 4) on computer-assisted qualitative data analysis, five out of the nine writers refer explicitly to grounded theory.

In the following sections I will analyse the connections between grounded theory and computer-assisted qualitative data analysis by presenting examples of the analytical operations central to both. I will also examine the differences in how these operations are conceived of, how useful computers are for conducting grounded theory research, and the consequences of the interaction between grounded theory and computer-assisted qualitative data analysis.

Coding of data

The more or less structured 'coding' of data (or 'indexing' in NUD.IST, 'tagging' in HyperQual) is central both to grounded theory and to most of the programs developed specifically for qualitative data analysis (see also Tesch, 1990; Weitzman and Miles, 1995). In grounded theory the notion of coding is, however, understood differently than in computer-assisted qualitative data analysis. Lyn Richards and Tom Richards (1991a: 6–8) argue that by 'coding' Glaser and Strauss mean a much more complex operation than just attaching labels to text segments. Bearing in mind the above discussion of coding procedures in grounded theory, this seems justified. Coding in grounded theory is not just about isolating and naming the categories, 'but also how to dimensionalize them and discover their conditions, consequences, and associated interactions and strategies' (Strauss, 1987: 154). The distinctive feature of coding in grounded theory is striving towards theory development (Strauss, personal communication, 1994).

Constant comparisons
Asking questions and continually making comparisons – the two basic procedures of coding in line with grounded theory methodology – can be enhanced by using qualitative data analysis software. Constant comparison is made easier by the possibilities for coding and retrieval found in almost every program for computer-aided qualitative data analysis (see Chapter 14). All text segments that were coded in the same way can be drawn out of the text corpus by straightforward retrieval procedures and then compared. Retrieving and comparing coded text segments allows researchers to be more systematic in their concept development and allows a comparison of their coding results – thereby changing a traditional monologue of the qualitative researcher to a dialogue both with colleagues or with the possible judges of the research.

Linkages
Computer-assisted qualitative data analysis can also aid a grounded theorist in developing, specifying and managing multiple linkages between text segments, between text segments and codes, and between codes themselves (see the Introduction to Part II). Thus, certain functions of these programs which draw on grounded theory can be extremely helpful in axial coding, where the researcher develops the relations between a category and its subcategories within the framework of the coding paradigm, or in selective coding where the categories are related to the core category.

Memoing
In addition to coding, memo-writing is an operation central both to several software packages and to grounded theory (although here, as with coding, the contents of the notion may differ). It is hard to imagine that qualitative analysis could be conducted without the need arising to write theoretical notes or comments about the original text. In several programs the theoretical questions and notes emerging through the research can be stored in memos and sorted and retrieved when necessary.

Use of diagrams
The production of not only memos but also diagrams that serve as integrative devices is an important part of grounded theory. Is there a researcher who has not tried to sketch some kind of diagram in order to clarify and visualize his or her thinking? A quick glance at a (preferably coloured) weather map shows how a huge mass of information – impossible to grasp in the form of a table – can be transmitted in a visual form. The computer's abilities to support qualitative analysis by producing diagrams, graphs and networks integrated into the analysis of textual data have been largely neglected in computer-assisted qualitative data analysis – one of the notable exceptions being the graphical network editor of ATLAS/ti (on the importance of data displays see Miles and Huberman, 1994. On the visual features of programs for qualitative data analysis see Weitzman and Miles, 1995).

Verification
Grounded theory is not only about generating a theory but also about testing it. Every so often the researcher wants to check his or her (possibly rudimentary) 'guesses' about what is happening in the data. And testing such ideas in an orderly and logical manner is something that a computer is good at: special features have also been integrated into qualitative data analysis programs (for example, in HyperRESEARCH and AQUAD) to assist in the process of hypothesis verification (see Part III; Chapter 14; Huber and Marcelo, 1991: 333).

Theory building
The clearest impact of grounded theory can be found in programs supporting theory building, particularly ATLAS/ti and NUD.IST. On a general level, both programs claim to support the researcher in generating a theory from empirical data. In ATLAS/ti the influence of grounded theory is particularly obvious in the coding terminology used (open coding, axial coding): 'There is a variety of coding techniques available, some of which we have given names reflecting the impact of ideas and terminology of grounded theory on the design of the ATLAS/ti system . . .' (Muhr, 1993: 38–39). In the NUD.IST manual the authors write: 'Central to its [NUD.IST's] design are the premises of "grounded theory" research (Strauss, 1987), a method that has little to do with coding and retrieval of text extracts, a lot to do with catching and interrogating meanings emerging from data' (Richards and Richards, 1990: 8).

It seems clear that the development of the two programs mentioned has been strongly influenced by grounded theory.[11] But it does not follow from this that they can only be (or actually are) used in an analysis in line with grounded theory methodology. However, nearly all of the programs developed specifically for qualitative data analysis tell us: if you want to do qualitative research with the computer, you have to code your data. How you do it, is basically up to you (even if some of the programs and many of the articles written on computer-assisted qualitative data analysis suggest that the researcher get acquainted with grounded theory). It may be that at least some kind of coding is needed in most qualitative research, but it is also possible that coding is overemphasized, given the fact that a large part of the qualitative researcher's work consists of interpretation and a fine-grained hermeneutic analysis (see Chapter 4).

From technique to method

In his review of *Qualitative Analysis for the Social Scientist* (Strauss, 1987) Norman Denzin (1988: 430–432) criticizes some of the principles of grounded theory and his arguments are also relevant to programs based on this method. First, he criticizes grounded theory's conceptual-indicator model which may lead 'to an overemphasis on discovering categories and indicators, with a corresponding slighting of the actual recording of lived experience in interactional situations'. He also worries that searching for a theory 'may displace the goal of actually writing the theory of interpretation that exists in the social worlds being studied'. According to Denzin it is not always clear whether the conceptual-indicator model of grounded theory really enables the researcher to grasp the theories of the people in the field under investigation. He comes to the conclusion that 'Strauss' approach, although it attempts to articulate everyday concepts and their meanings, may move too quickly to theory, which becomes disconnected from the very worlds of problematic experience' (Denzin, 1988: 432).

Denzin's criticism can also be regarded as a relevant warning for researchers using computer software for qualitative data analysis. If the software prevents an interactive and easy movement between emerging conceptual structures and the data, the development of the theory (the construction of coding structures) may take place at the expense of extracting the essence of the original texts, that is, the interpretations and definitions of situations made by the people in the field under study (see Chapter 4).

When using grounded theory-based programs like ATLAS/ti or NUD.IST the researcher is not forced (although more than a little suggested) to conduct an analysis in line with grounded theory methodology. These programs can be – and I would estimate are – mostly used for other purposes. The researcher does not have to commit herself or himself to a specific theoretical tradition, for example interactionism. He or she can tag the data with different codes, build code structures, search for different expressions in the text or do whatever the programs allow. But, at least for a novice researcher or a student, there is a danger that the choice of techniques available (computer programs like ATLAS/ti and NUD.IST) may also suggest the choice of method (grounded theory). Consequently, there is a danger that 'computer-assisted dominance' of one method – even a sophisticated one – could do great harm to qualitative research.

Notes

1. I would like to thank Dale Berg for finding the exact formulation and reference of this quotation for me. Thomas Muhr in turn reminded me that computers differ from hammers in that they offer a wider variety of options for supporting different tasks.

2. I wish to thank all the people – too numerous to mention here – who have commented on the earlier draft of this article by e-mail. Particularly I want to name Udo Kelle and Anselm Strauss. I am naturally responsible for the views expressed in the article.

3. Exceptions exist: for example the computer program AQUAD (Huber and Marcelo, 1991) is partly influenced by Ragin's (1987) comparative method (for more details see Chapter 13). The dominance of grounded theory might partly be due to the relatively small circles of researchers and developers knowledgeable in computer-assisted qualitative data analysis.

4. In a recent e-mail exchange Strauss writes that he currently thinks of grounded theory 'really as a methodology, a way of working with the data' (Strauss, personal communication, 1994).

5. Isabelle Baszanger (1992: 52) adds the book by Schatzman and Strauss (1973) to her list of the important works in the development of grounded theory.

6. It should not be forgotten that one of the co-originators, Barney Glaser, has launched heavy criticism against these publications (Glaser, 1992). Nevertheless, this debate will not be presented here (for a detailed discussion of the differences between Glaser's and Strauss' views of grounded theory see Kelle, 1994).

7. Here a code seems to be identical to a category or a relationship between categories. Strauss also writes: 'The categories are of two types, sociological constructs and in vivo-codes.' The latter 'are taken from or derived directly from the language of the substantive field: essentially the terms used by actors in that field themselves' (1987: 33).

8. See particularly Kelle (1994), but also the book reviews and articles by Bertaux (1988); Corsaro (1992); Denzin (1988); Ekerwald and Johansson (1989); Ellis (1992); Harper (1988); Hopf (1988); Soeffner (1991) – the list is not comprehensive.

9. Grounded theory explicates detailed procedures for coding, memo-writing and drawing diagrams which in some form, I would estimate, are present in most qualitative research. However, it does not follow from this that most researchers actually produce grounded theory. Anselm Strauss answered a question posed to him by Lyn Richards, about how far people can stray from his ideas of grounded theory and still be doing it:

> The general answer is that they have to aim toward developing theory, which means theoretical coding, theoretical sampling, and constant comparisons. Many people say they are doing grounded theory and just mean, if you look at what they say they've done or actually write, they just code. Or they interpret grounded theory in terms of the 1967 *Discovery* book as justifying qualitative data or ethnography of

some kind or other; or they lay out a 'process' (à la Barney Glaser's *Theoretical Sensitivity* book), but do none of the detailed work spelling out conditions, consequences, interactions etc. (Strauss, personal communication, 1994)

10. Note the word 'purely': neither qualitative nor quantitative researchers can ever avoid rhetoric – which is basically a non-pejorative term – when writing for an audience (see e.g. Gusfield, 1990; McGill, 1990; for the use of computers as rhetorical weapons see Brownstein, 1990: 160; Lidz and Ricci, 1990: 116).

11. Matt Miles (personal communication, 1994) reminded me not to forget the influence of the hermeneutic tradition on the development of ATLAS/ti.

4

Different Functions of Coding in the Analysis of Textual Data

John Seidel and Udo Kelle

Now it was early afternoon. Gorman had met him as requested, at the Mexican Water trading post. They'd made the bone-jarring drive back into Chichinbito Canyon country. Rather quickly Officer Gorman had proved he was the sort of man who – as Leaphorn's grandmother would have said – counted the grass and didn't see the grazing.

Gorman was sitting now in Leaphorn's car, waiting (uneasily, Leaphorn hoped) for Leaphorn to finish whatever the hell Leaphorn was doing. What Leaphorn was doing was looking past the grass at the grazing . . . (from Tony Hillerman's detective novel *Skinwalkers*)

Two functions of codes

Coding is of crucial importance for computer-aided qualitative data analysis. Although codes represent the decisive link between the original 'raw data', that is, the textual material such as interview transcripts or field notes on the one hand, and the researcher's theoretical concepts on the other, most of the methodological literature does not concentrate much on coding but rather on how to work with codes and coded material.

In this chapter we will discuss two different modes of coding[1] in the analysis of textual data:

1. A code can *denote a text passage* containing specific information in order to allow its retrieval. This mode of coding is analogous to the construction of a book index: the word 'Popper' followed by a page number informs the reader that the philosopher Karl Popper is mentioned on this page. When coding an open interview the code **political affiliation** together with certain line numbers informs the analyst that in the text passage with these line numbers the respondent talks about political affiliation.

2. A code can also serve to *denote a fact*. Thus, a text segment where an interviewee expresses his predilection for the Liberal Party can be denoted by the code **Liberal Party affiliation** and the analyst can then draw on the information that the respondent is an adherent of the Liberal Party without even looking at the original text.

One can call these two forms of coding *indexing* and *summarizing*, or one can, by drawing on a distinction made by Richards and Richards (in this volume, p. 83), differentiate between the *factual* and the *referential* functions of code categories. But one must be careful not to reify this distinction: codes themselves are neither factual nor referential. Furthermore, coding always has both functions: although one can drop the reference of a code to a certain text segment, a code can never lose its referential function. There must always be some reference to some unit of analysis (an interview, a respondent or something else), otherwise any meaningful information will be lost (for example, about which member of the sample is a Liberal). On the other hand a mere index also contains factual information (for example, that the author of the book mentions certain people) even if this information is not very rich in itself. Consequently it is not the specific type of codes – 'factual' or 'referential' – but rather their use in a certain setting that determines which of the two functions plays the dominant role.

Codes as representations of phenomena

Classical content analysis (see Berelson, 1952; Krippendorf, 1980), a method for the analysis of unstructured data that has a long tradition in mass communication research, can in some respects be regarded as paradigmatic for a coding strategy whereby codes serve as representations of the investigated phenomenon. A researcher using this method who is, for example, interested in comparing the commentaries on certain political events by different newspapers will proceed by condensing the information contained in the raw data to a minimum. For this purpose the unit of analysis (for example, sentences or paragraphs) has to be determined and a precise coding scheme has to be constructed. Then, every unit of analysis can be investigated as to:

1. whether it refers to one of the defined political events, and if so
2. which attitudes towards this event the author expresses, for example affirmation, disapproval or something in between.

By applying this method a code represents a value of a certain variable, for example the value 'affirmation' of the variable 'Evaluation of political events'. The code is then attached to a unit of analysis, such as a single sentence. Each appearance of a certain code represents a certain event that is of interest to the researcher, for example an affirmative attitude expressed by a newspaper reporter towards a specific political event. In classical content analysis, coding is usually followed by information reduction: the information provided by coding is used for the construction of a new (quantitative) data corpus that can be analysed with statistical procedures, for example a matrix which contains information about how different newspapers (the rows of the matrix) comment on certain political events (the columns of the matrix). Thus, for this kind of analysis it is crucial to focus almost exclusively on the codes and not on the raw data. But this is only possible if the codes can be seen as true representations of certain facts described by the raw data. Consequently the following requirements have to be fulfilled:

1. There has to be a high degree of certainty that the codes have been applied in a systematic and consistent way; in other words, the coding must have a high degree of validity and reliability: it is essential that every text passage that is coded as **affirmation of political event A** in fact contains a positive utterance about this event.
2. The coding of the raw data must be inclusive and exhaustive; this means one must be certain that every single instance of the investigated phenomenon that occurs in the raw data is coded. This is of special importance if, by the employment of statistical procedures, the absolute or relative frequency of the occurrence of codes are used to draw inferences, for example for the support or rejection of hypotheses.

These requirements make it essential that whenever the kind of analysis is employed in which codes are used as a condensed representation of the facts described by the data, a precise coding scheme is developed before coding starts, since:

1. For pragmatic reasons alone, inclusive and exhaustive coding would not be possible if the researcher did not have a ready-made category scheme to hand right from the start. If, instead, the coding scheme was being permanently altered, it would be necessary to permanently re-code the previously coded data with the newly developed categories.
2. Objective, and therefore reliable, coding can only be conducted if all coders employ exactly the same coding scheme.

Consequently, an analysis strategy that relies mainly on the *factual function* of codes, that is where codes are used as representations of phenomena, requires a deductive approach: the relevant variables and their values (that form the codes) have to be determined before data are coded.

Codes as heuristic devices

However, this requirement for a deductive approach would cause severe difficulties in the context of a qualitative research strategy. Let us take a short look at the theoretical roots of qualitative research to clarify this point. Although there is a puzzling heterogeneity of qualitative approaches (see Tesch, 1990: 55ff.), it has often been emphasized that most of these approaches are at least implicitly based on a common underlying concept of human action, which has been referred to using notions like *The Interpretive Paradigm* (Wilson, 1970), *Interpretive Sociology* (Giddens, 1976) or *Interpretive Interactionism* (Denzin, 1989).

According to the interpretive paradigm the meaning of human action and interaction can only be adequately understood if the interpretations and the common-sense knowledge of the actors are taken into account. This theoretical postulate has far-reaching methodological consequences: the researcher must be able to gain access to the interpretations and the common-sense knowledge of the members of the social world investigated. If his or her goal is to describe their actions adequately, which is with respect to the meaning these actions have for the actors, he or she must be able to perceive the world to a certain extent in the same way as they do. Or, as Thomas and Znaniecki put it in their early study of *The Polish Peasant*: 'We must put ourselves in the position of the subject who tries to find his way in this world, and we must remember, first of all, that the environment by which he is influenced and to which he adapts is his world and not the objective world of science' (1958: 1846f.).

This demand for 'empathic understanding' of or access to the common-sense knowledge of the investigated form of social life makes it difficult, if not impossible, to employ a hypothetico-deductive (H-D) research strategy, since this would require the development of useful hypotheses before collecting empirical data. Instead, if one wants to learn something about the actor's point of view one has first to enter the empirical field. Meaningful hypotheses can be established only after gathering data, that is after establishing contact with the people in this field through interviewing or observation.

Hence, the goal of discerning the specific perspectives, world-views, 'local knowledge' (Geertz, 1973), etc. of the members of a specific yet unknown form of social world, can hardly be achieved by means of an H-D strategy: instead of constructing hypotheses before entering the field, the researcher has to go out and look at how people perceive and interpret their world themselves.

For that reason qualitative enquiry in most cases starts with observation, recording, listening, etc., which means by collecting sometimes large amounts of unstructured data, and then hypotheses and theories are developed on the basis of this material. If one wants to discuss the role of coding in this research paradigm it is helpful to distinguish between three operations in this process: (1) noticing relevant phenomena, (2) collecting instances of these phenomena, (3) analysing these phenomena in order to find commonalities, differences, patterns, structures, etc.

Noticing relevant phenomena

Noticing relevant phenomena is the central task of the researcher who enters an empirical field without ready-made hypotheses. Instead of searching for supporting or disconfirming evidence for a hypothesis, one tries to discover things that one has not previously expected. Of course this must not seduce us into thinking of the researcher's mind as a *tabula rasa*. An open mind does not mean an empty head:[2] the researcher always brings some theoretical preconceptions with him or her. But these are not 'hypotheses' in the ordinary sense of this word in H-D research, which means they do not represent explicit propositions about empirical facts. Rather, they should be referred to as (partly implicit) conceptual networks that provide us with some 'lenses' for the perception of the empirical world. We would like to address these conceptual networks as perspectives rather than as 'hypotheses' or 'theories'. These perspectives help the researcher to select relevant phenomena, and of course researchers with different perspectives will select different phenomena. But behind these differences is the simple principle in qualitative research of going out into the empirical world and noticing relevant phenomena. In the first step this translates into making observations, writing field notes, tape-recording interviews, etc., by which a general record of what one has noticed is produced.

The next step of noticing would be to identify the relevant phenomena which are contained in these general records. Identifying phenomena within one's field notes, protocols or interviews quite often (but not always!) takes the form of 'coding' (see the Introduction), which is in fact a procedure with a long tradition in the 'folklore' of qualitative research. One of the first descriptions of this process can be found in an article by Howard Becker and Blanche Geer:

> A systematic assessment of all data is necessary before we can present the content of a perspective. . . . We have tentatively identified, through sequential analysis during the field work, the major perspectives we want to present and the areas . . . to which these perspectives apply. We now go through the summarized incidents, marking each incident with a number or numbers that stand for the various areas to which it appears to be relevant. This is essentially a coding operation . . . its object is to make sure that all relevant data can be brought to bear on a point. (Becker and Geer, 1960: 280–281)

It should be noted that Becker and Geer outline a quite different process than that described earlier in this chapter. The incidents which are coded do not represent instances or examples of a general phenomenon or fact named by a code; the code only refers in a quite vague manner to one of 'the various areas to which it appears to be relevant'. The purpose is not to condense the information which is relevant for the researcher with the objective of creating a quantitative data matrix, but to 'make sure that all relevant data can be brought to bear on a point'. Here the function of codes is clearly restricted to 'signposting' – they are stored together with the 'address' of a certain text passage. Drawing on this information the researcher can then locate all the possible information provided by the data on the relevant topic. Thus coding is a necessary preparation for the two other operations that have already been mentioned: collecting instances of relevant phenomena and comparing relevant phenomena.

Collecting instances of relevant phenomena

After coding, the material can be broken into parts and then collected according to the topics which served as codes. Many texts on ethnographic or qualitative methods address this process of 'reassembling' and 'disassembling' the data, in which another widely applied folklore technique – known as 'cut-and-paste' – is often used: the text material is cut into small pieces according to the topic-oriented codes, glued onto index cards and then sorted or put into a file folder (see, for example, Freidson, 1975: 271; Lofland and Lofland, 1984: 134; Taylor and Bogdan, 1984: 136). In doing so the text segments are taken 'out of the chronological narrative form of your field notes or interview write-ups and into a storage system where you can easily order and retrieve it' (Lofland and Lofland, 1984: 132). However, this mindless and mechanical procedure that helps to collect relevant phenomena is nothing but a preliminary for the central procedure of qualitative text interpretation.

Analysing relevant phenomena

This crucial procedure is making sense of the data by analysing the relevant phenomena found in the material and collected by the mechanical operation of cutting and pasting. This is conducted by comparing the different pieces of data in order to find commonalities, differences or linkages between them. The purpose is 'the construction of meaningful patterns of facts' (Jorgenson, 1989: 107), by looking for structures in the data. To some degree this process is similar to doing a jigsaw puzzle: as with a jigsaw puzzle the analyst would start by collecting certain pieces which are similar in a certain respect. If the picture is of a landscape comprising a tree, a building and the sky, one could at first use 'Tree', 'Building' and 'Sky' as 'codes' and sort pieces according to these categories. At this point, more refined inspections of the pieces will be necessary. Shapes and colours will be meticulously examined and compared. One looks for features of the pieces that give hints as to the linkages between them. This is a similar process to that in qualitative data analysis: once the analyst has sorted the pieces that

were allocated to a certain category he or she has to study the text segments as things in themselves. He or she will analyse several parts of
them and their connections, that is the specific way they could be linked
or connected to form a meaningful picture. But unlike doing a jigsaw
puzzle, the researcher analysing qualitative data cannot refer to the
picture on the box. He or she has no model or blueprint at hand to
identify the features which would help him or her to establish linkages
between the pieces. Using a model or blueprint would be how a
researcher in the H-D model proceeds: he or she would construct a theoretical model that provides a template, to indicate which information
is relevant, before analysing data. In contrast, the qualitative researcher
employing an interpretive methodology tries to derive this information
from his or her data. In many qualitative approaches, especially in
those with strong roots in hermeneutical philosophy or phenomenology, for example discourse analysis, this would be conducted by means
of a thorough fine-grained analysis of certain text segments. Thereby,
hitherto unknown aspects of the phenomenon under study are discovered through careful and intensive inspection of the 'raw data', that is,
the original text. These are the aspects that help to combine the pieces
of information in a new way in order to gain a new image of the investigated empirical domain.

The codes employed in such an analysis strategy are imprecise and
vague, if compared with codes used for the representation of facts.
They will be attached not to precisely defined incidents in the data but
to text segments 'which seem [!] to be distinct incidents, anecdotes, or
stated opinions about discrete events' and which are 'tentatively [!]
classified into the simple [!] content categories we had decided in
advance' (Freidson, 1975: 271). But this lack of precision is a necessary
prerequisite for their use in interpretive research, which incorporates a
methodology of discovery. Here, in contrast to a methodology of
hypothesis testing, the researcher must not restrict the scope of the
investigation in advance by determining precise categories, since the
goal is not to recover certain already known phenomena in the empirical field but to discover new ones. Coding is nothing more than a
preparation for this process which is based on a careful inspection and
analysis of raw data (that is, segments of text) and on their comparison
for the sake of identifying patterns and structures.

In a qualitative analysis strategy embedded in an interpretive tradition, the *referential function of codes and not their factual function is in
the foreground*. Codes do not serve primarily as denominators of certain phenomena but as *heuristic devices* for discovery.

Confusing the different functions of codes and the resulting methodological problems

Computer-assisted methods of qualitative data analysis were initially developed to assist researchers who used codes as heuristic devices. The first software packages represented mere electronic 'cut-and-paste' tools, but at present more and more powerful facilities for the manipulation of codes are being added to many of the programs:

1. tools that enhance the construction of 'networks' or 'hierarchical trees' of code categories (see Part II),
2. knowledge-based systems that help to retrieve information about how text segments attached to certain codes are distributed throughout the whole document, whether they overlap or appear at certain distances (Part III),
3. devices for the quantitative analysis of codes and of their distribution across documents (Part IV).

These facilities offer fascinating new possibilities for analysts to 'play' with their data and thereby help to open up new perspectives and to stimulate new insights. They can also help to combine qualitative with quantitative methods or an H-D approach with interpretive research strategies. But these possibilities also contain specific dangers, because the same technical tool can be used for two totally different research strategies which employ codes differently: as indexes for text segments that are coded and retrieved by an electronic 'cut-and-paste' device on the one hand, and as representations of facts contained in the raw data on the other. Therefore analysts can – without realizing – confuse the two modes of coding: they can involuntarily switch from using the referential function of codes (that means from collecting text segments that refer in a broad and general way to a number of somewhat vaguely defined concepts) to treating codes as if they were representations of factual information.

We will call this the danger of *losing the phenomenon by reifying the codes:* the analyst starts to work exclusively on his or her codes and forgets about the raw data, although the necessary prerequisite for doing so has not yet been fulfilled: there is only a loose coupling between a code and a piece of data instead of a well-defined relation between a code and a phenomenon, since the code was not attached to denote a certain discrete event, incident or fact, but only to inform the analyst that there is interesting information contained in a certain text segment, related to a topic represented by a code.

But alongside the danger of losing the information contained in the text segment, there is also a second danger that arises when the two modes of coding are confused: *losing the context* of the information.

Like Officer Gorman in Hillerman's detective story the analyst will then start 'to count the grass and not see the grazing'.

What precautionary measures can be taken to avoid these two dangers of *losing the phenomenon* and *losing its context*? Generally speaking there are two strategies: one corresponds to the H-D model, the other is related to an interpretive research strategy.

1. If the H-D model is applied one would have to ensure that every code is suitable for representing a distinct and objectively verifiable fact whose presence could be ascertained independently from a specific context. Additionally, the analyst would have to ensure that the codes are applied consistently and in a reliable manner to the raw data. In particular one has to pay attention to ensuring that the coding is inclusive and exhaustive, that is, that every incident which is represented by a certain code category is in fact coded. Since there is already much information available about the reliability and consistency of category schemes in the technical literature on content analysis, we do not need to go into further detail. But it should be mentioned that if a researcher starts with an exploratory strategy of text analysis and then switches to an H-D mode, that means that in practice he or she starts with *referential coding* and then switches to *factual coding*, it would, in almost all cases, be necessary to (1) *reformulate the coding scheme* and (2) *re-code material*.

2. In interpretive research there are quite different strategies to cope with the problems of losing the phenomena and losing the context. Since the onset of an interpretive research tradition there has been a distinctive awareness among its adherents of the context-relatedness of the investigated social phenomena, which has inspired much criticism of the H-D model of research (see Cicourel, 1964). Consequently, there has always been concern among qualitative researchers that by applying cut-and-paste techniques 'the totality of philosophy as expressed by the interviewee – which is closely related to the goal of the study' (Wiseman, 1979: 278) can be destroyed. Usually two strategies are recommended to avoid losing the context of the text segments: (1) analysts are encouraged to acquaint themselves, by careful reading, with the entire case or document as, for example, Agar suggests: 'read the transcripts in their entirety several times. Immerse yourself in the details, trying to get a sense of the interview as a whole' before breaking it into parts (Agar, 1980: 103). (2) Several methods are proposed that help to restore or find the original context at any time: it is recommended that interviews are typed in duplicate and that one copy is always left 'intact to be read in its entirety' (Wiseman, 1979: 278). Other

practitioners advise the researcher to 'include enough of the context to understand the data fully' (Taylor and Bogdan, 1984: 137). Another proposal is to include on each data fragment the 'identification in code of the persons being interviewed, the interview number, and the page number of the typescript so that the context of the selection could be returned to and examined' (Freidson, 1975: 270).[3]

These *strategies of keeping in contact with the raw data* can not only be applied to avoid the danger of losing the context, but also to diminish the menace of reifying the codes and losing the phenomenon.

Both methodological approaches – trying to guard the reliability, consistency and inclusiveness of code use, and trying to keep contact with the raw data – address the problem of whether the researcher's theoretical concepts (which should not be confused with codes as technical devices) are really grounded in the raw data, or in other words, the *problem of validity*. But they do so in quite different ways in the context of quite different models of the research process.

The purpose of this chapter is not to argue in favour of one model as the only one that is appropriate. Nor do we want to revive old debates from the 1970s between true believers in a certain methodological credo and heretics, or to claim that there are insurmountable barriers between exploratory and H-D modes of text analysis. On the contrary, the combination of research strategies can have quite a fruitful impact on the research process if, for example, systematic exploratory procedures for empirical hypothesis generation are employed and these hypotheses are then tested by means of hypothetico-deductive methods. Nonetheless, this combination can have harmful results if it is not conducted on the basis of careful methodological considerations, in which the necessary prerequisites for the application of a certain method are taken into account. Furthermore, it must be ensured that the chosen mode of coding or textual analysis fits into the framework of the research setting and the research question.

Notes

1. I am particularly grateful to Tom Richards and Lyn Richards, whose distinction between referential categories and factual categories inspired our thinking on the different modes of coding. [Udo Kelle]

2. Thanks to Ian Dey for this nice *aperçu*.

3. Of course it is much easier to retain the original context when using computer-aided methods of coding and retrieval than with cut-and-paste techniques, since the text segments are usually not actually 'cut out', but pointers are merely attached to them. But, most interestingly, there are only a few programs that provide an easy and user-friendly facility for retrieving text segments in context.

PART II

COMPUTERS AND QUALITATIVE THEORY BUILDING

Introduction: Using Linkages and Networks for Qualitative Theory Building

Gerald Prein and Udo Kelle in discussion with
Lyn Richards and Tom Richards

The first computer programs for qualitative analysis developed around the mid-1980s were primarily code-and-retrieve facilities whose main purpose was to automate the time-consuming and tedious task of 'cut-and-paste' (see Introduction, p. 5). To facilitate this the researcher had to order the unstructured textual material by attaching codes to certain text passages, or in other words, by defining linkages between codes and text segments.

The most widely used approach to electronically storing such linkages was to connect codes to *pointers*, containing the *address* of certain text segments (which are represented, for example, in terms of line numbers) that permitted the easy retrieval of all text passages linked to a certain code.

If one examines the technical and methodological literature about qualitative analysis one will come to the conclusion that qualitative analysis often also requires other types of linkages in the ongoing process of analysis (see Dey, 1993; Miles and Huberman, 1994; Strauss and Corbin, 1990; Strauss, 1987): (1) linkages between memos and texts, and memos and codes, (2) linkages between codes and (3) linkages between different text segments.

1. *Linkages between memos and text and memos and codes.* In qualitative analysis coding usually does not mean fitting the data into a

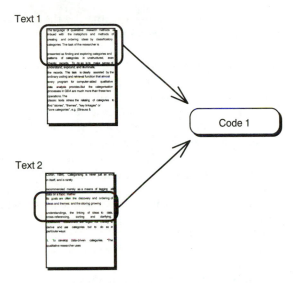

Figure II.1   *Linkages between text segments and a code*

predefined coding scheme, but the coding scheme is either developed from scratch during coding or a rough preliminary coding scheme is used and modified in line with the emerging theory. Since this process requires much 'musing over theoretical notions', Glaser and Strauss, in their first ground-breaking work on methodological issues, recommended that researchers 'stop coding and record a memo' whenever a new idea or theoretical insight occurred to them (Glaser and Strauss, 1967: 107). The notion of writing memos – a term that nowadays is sometimes used for any short text a researcher produces during the analysis process – was happily adopted by the qualitative community and has become a frequently mentioned feature in hand- and source books for qualitative research (see Miles and Huberman, 1994: 72–76; Strauss and Corbin, 1990: 197–223). Since memos are often 'the theorizing write-up of ideas about codes and their relationships as they strike the analyst while coding' (Glaser, 1978: 83) they are most useful if linked to the raw data or to certain codes. Memos can be regarded as signposts along the path between data and theory. Thus, linkages between text segments, codes and memos can help to retrace this path, enabling researchers to control the grounding of theoretical ideas.

2. *Linkages between codes.* Many of the codes will be transformed into categories of the emerging theory, others will be refined and modified for this purpose. Codes can also form the basis for the

construction of theoretical categories either by the *subsumption* of
several codes under one more general code, or by the *subdivision* of
one code into several more refined subcategories. From the perspective of theory building these operations can be directly
translated into *generalization* and *dimensionalization* respectively.
Generalization represents a bottom-up strategy: 'descriptive' codes
are combined and integrated to construct analytic categories or
'pattern codes' (see Miles and Huberman, 1994: 69–72). The oppo-
site pole of dimensionalization is a top-down strategy of theory
building in which *properties* or *dimensions* of categories are specified
(see Strauss and Corbin, 1990: 69–72). In technical terms, these
operations can be referred to as *second-order coding* (whereas *first-
order coding* describes the initial process of allocating a code to a
text segment).

3. *Linkages between different text segments.* Since in open interviews
    everyday patterns of conversation are prevalent, which means that
    respondents tend to draw on different events and ideas and jump
    back and forth between them, it is often necessary to reorder the
    transcripts of such interviews in order to collect together the dif-
    ferent parts of a specific argument or narrative. For example, when
    the chronological sequence of events is to be reconstructed from a
    biographical interview, linkages between different text segments
    will be needed. This would also be the case if one needed to com-
    pare the statements on a certain topic made by the participants in
    a 'qualitative panel' (that is, a research design in which the same
    respondents are interviewed at set time intervals). For all these pur-
    poses the use of code categories can be not only superfluous but
    even counter-productive, since the overriding aim will be to estab-
    lish direct connections between the text segments themselves.

These different types of linkages between text segments, codes and
memos have a special significance for qualitative theory building and
were employed by qualitative researchers in manual methods of indexing and building concordances before the advent of computer-assisted
methods of data administration. But only through the use of computer
technology has it become possible to construct *networks* composed of
codes, memos and text segments.

The computer-based creation of such networks can be regarded as
the expansion of the concept on which many of the first code-and-
retrieve programs were based, that is a non-formatted textual database
management system in which codes were connected with pointers to
text segments. As Muhr has pointed out, these networks can be formally described with the help of mathematical graph theory[1] (Muhr,
1991, 1992). From this perspective networks are defined as *graphs,*

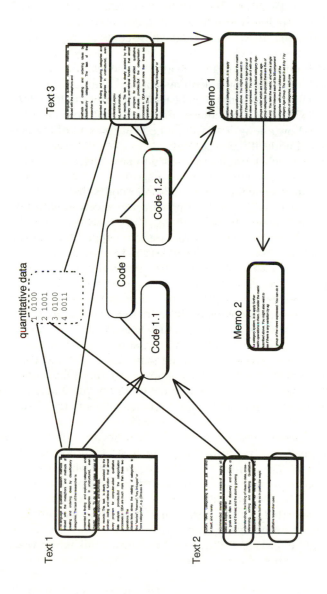

Figure II.2   *A network of linkages between text segments, codes, memos and data*

consisting of *nodes* and *edges*. 'In a subway map, the set of nodes would correspond to the stations, while the edges represent the rails between the stations' (Muhr, 1992: 1). Thus, the whole network in Figure II.2 can also be represented as a graph, whose nodes are codes, text segments, memos and quantitative data, and whose edges are the linkages between them.

If Figure II.2 is interpreted as a graph all possible relations between the nodes could be identified by describing 'paths' that follow the edges of the network. This model could then be used to construct algorithms for rather complex retrieval procedures, algorithms that would be able, for example, to follow a long path from a node at one end of the network or graph to a node at the other end.

At the same time such a graph can be used to give an account of the emerging theory by displaying its main categories (first-order codes that are linked to text segments, or second-order codes that are developed from first-order codes and have no direct connection with text segments) and the linkages between them. Thus, attention must be paid to the fact that graphs may be structured in quite different ways: either all possible linkages between the nodes can be allowed or certain restrictions can be imposed. An example for a structure with relatively few constraints would be a graph that contains *cycles* (paths may return to their origins), whereas a hierarchical *tree* represents a network that allows for fewer linkages and is therefore more tightly structured.

Each decision about how to construct such a network, consisting of codes, text segments, memos and other information, and about which constraints to impose carries far-reaching methodological and theoretical implications. In the first two chapters of this section two different strategies for using linkages and networks for qualitative theory construction will be presented and discussed and different issues and problems of theory building will be addressed.[2]

Ian Dey's main concern is to overcome the problem of data fragmentation arising from traditional cut-and-paste techniques. This problem is not only prevalent with manual techniques (where the text is literally cut apart), but also if computer-aided methods of coding and retrieval are used. Usually, retrieval entails 'decontextualization', that is isolating text segments from their original context. To cope with this problem the author proposes the use of *hyperlinks* for establishing two different types of linkages in addition to the common linkage between codes and text segments:

1. *Linkages between text segments and their context* serve to easily reconstruct the part of the text surrounding the single retrieved segment and thereby help to mitigate the possibly harmful effects of decontextualization.

2. *Linkages between text segments* help to avoid fragmentation right from the start: by employing hyperlinks the researcher can connect text segments to each other without using codes. Dey recommends this strategy as a flexible tool for the analysis of temporal or causal links between events referred to in different text segments. This strategy could, for example, be used to trace a 'conditional path' (Strauss and Corbin, 1990: 166ff.) by reconstructing from the textual data the relations between a certain incident, the conditions surrounding it, and its consequences.

Since with manual techniques that use index cards, file folders, etc., the linking of segments to each other would only have been possible with the investment of great temporal and human resources, the inclusion of hyperlinks in computer-aided qualitative data analysis can be viewed as a major innovation.

The chapter by Lyn Richards and Tom Richards relates to the application of linkages between codes and to 'second-order coding'. They focus on the construction of *hierarchical categories*, which traditionally have been widely applied in qualitative theory construction and described in the literature, for instance in grounded theory methodology, where an important issue is the development of a *conceptual structure of categories* or codes, detecting *core categories* and their *linkages*. This step has been conceptualized as 'selective coding' by Strauss and Corbin, which 'consists of *relating subsidiary categories* around the *core category* by means of the *paradigm*' (1990: 117f.). However, what has been lacking until now is a thorough methodological investigation of the nature of hierarchical categories, as well as guidelines to help researchers avoid pitfalls in theory construction. In their contribution, Richards and Richards discuss several methodological aspects of the computer-assisted application of hierarchical categories. The authors explicate certain prerequisites: the researcher constructing a network of hierarchical categories grounded in the data has to pay attention to the distinction between factual and referential categories, and to take certain precautions to ensure the consistency of the emerging hierarchical tree structure and to avoid the unnecessary proliferation of categories.

To this end *general principles* for the construction of a hierarchical system of categories are formulated. The application of these principles should ensure that categories and subcategories of a given tree relate in a consistent and clear-cut way to certain phenomena. In maintaining a logically consistent structure for hierarchical category systems, this approach may therefore help resolve a difficulty quite frequently encountered in qualitative theory building: sticking to highly detailed and fine-grained descriptions of phenomena at the cost of progressing to more abstract notions. The chapter concludes with a discussion of computer-aided *search strategies* which take account of the linkages between codes that have already been established in the process of theory building.

In Chapter 7 Luis Araujo provides an example for the application of hierarchical networks of categories in a qualitative research project. In particular, the practical example serves to clarify how coding frames must be designed and developed, if hierarchical networks of categories are to be developed. Araujo rejects naive *tabula rasa* concepts: coding is not just a process of labelling that culminates in theory building. Codes themselves are already 'theory laden': the researcher's previous theoretical knowledge and his or her specific perspective on the phenomenon under investigation is revealed in them. Araujo emphasizes that codes should always be viewed in two ways: (1) as part of the analyst's wider theoretical framework, and (2) as grounded in the data.

The process of coding data should be regarded as an important intermediary step in translating social actors' frames of meanings into the frame of theoretical discourse. Coding frames therefore mediate between the 'natural', everyday discourses of the actors and theoretical discourses in social science. The process of developing a coding frame that fits the dual criteria of being grounded in both substantive theoretical schemes and in the data consists of a number of feedback loops between theory, coding frames and data. Araujo provides examples from research practice for the construction and refinement of a hierarchical code scheme.

The chapters in this section naturally only touch on some of the features related to the potential benefits offered by the use of a network approach to theory building. Networks are indeed very flexible tools for analysing qualitative data, because the researcher can freely define nodes, how they are linked, and how these links are classified. As such the network approach does not provide a radically new approach to the analysis of textual data, but does provide new structuration tools for (1) bringing order into unorganized textual data and (2) connecting this order with the categorical structure developed from theoretical considerations.

Notes

1. The development of the software package ATLAS/ti was influenced by this approach.

2. There are a variety of software programs available that allow the researcher to build networks. For more detail see Chapter 14 about software.

5

Reducing Fragmentation in Qualitative Research

Ian Dey

This chapter addresses the problem of fragmenting data. It will be suggested that technology has been used to enhance rather than transform traditional methods. Code-and-retrieve procedures allow for comparisons to be made of similarities and differences between text segments, but they also fragment the data and discount information about context and process. This chapter explores new procedures for avoiding or overcoming such fragmentation, based on hyperlinks between text segments themselves and between text segments and the context from which they are abstracted. Three forms of linking are distinguished: links between codes and text segments; links between the text segments and the context from which they derive; and links between the text segments themselves. Some basic issues to be addressed in developing and using these procedures are discussed.

We have great difficulty in adjusting to and exploiting the potential of new technology. In the American Civil War, thousands of soldiers on both sides were killed because of outmoded tactics. The soldiers had new rapid fire rifles, but their generals still believed you had to concentrate your men in order to overwhelm the enemy during an attack. But the tactics of the mass attack were better suited to the bayonet than the rifle. In fact very few soldiers during the Civil War were killed by the bayonet, while many of them were killed needlessly by rifle fire because tactics had not kept pace with technology. This was a war of incredible heroism as soldiers marched forward in line under heavy fire, often suffering very heavy losses (Foote, 1992: 265).

Is there a parallel with qualitative data analysis? Do we continue to employ old methods, and fail to exploit the potential of the new technology which has become available? Has the computer been used mainly to enhance rather than transform existing methods? Do we carry on analysing data in ways which impose needless costs (admittedly less serious!) because we do not or cannot imagine alternative ways of proceeding?

The computer has been used to make significant improvements traditional methods of coding and retrieving data, which can now done with amazing speed and efficiency. This makes possible g thoroughness and rigour in coding, and more flexibility and sophisti-cation in forms of retrieval. We can categorize, subcategorize and recategorize data and revise or integrate our categories with ease. We can retrieve the data which meets – or does not meet – a whole range of conditions, making more and better comparisons between text seg-ments assigned to particular codes or combinations of codes.

Some of the most interesting developments in recent software have been based on developing more flexible and rigorous forms of retrieval (Richards and Richards, 1991d). These have started to realize the the-oretical potential of exploring or interrogating coded data in a much more systematic way. The construction of nodes, networks and matri-ces promises to fulfil some of the potential of computer-based analysis, as it exploits the ability of the computer to locate and collate data much more quickly and thoroughly than the human processor. However, we need to reflect critically upon the methodological biases of the technology we have introduced for coding qualitative data. There is a danger of building castles in the air – perhaps castles on quicksand might be a better analogy – unless we consider carefully the founda-tions upon which these theoretical constructions rest. The theoretical utility of retrieving text segments depends on the conceptual value of procedures for categorizing data.

Software developments do mean the ideals of qualitative analysis are easier to realize. But are we still thinking in traditional ways – as though we are using the bayonet rather than the rifle? Has the com-puter opened up new methods of analysis which we are failing to exploit? And does this failure have costs, in terms of a needless frag-mentation of the data which we can now categorize so successfully?

Data fragmentation arises from procedures which segment text. This can result in loss of narrative and an inability to analyse process and change. Text segments are isolated – conceptually and sometimes liter-ally – from the surrounding text. Whether segments are defined by line numbers or demarcated units of meaning identified by the analyst, they become 'recontextualized' in ways which abstract them from the original text (Tesch, 1990). They acquire a new conceptual significance when juxtaposed against other coded segments, but two important kinds of information are lost in the process. One is information on context, as the meaning of a segment depends on how it relates to the wider text. Another is information on how different segments of text are related in the text, for on this depends our ability to analyse a whole range of relationships within the data.

Incidentally, it may be a bit misleading to present the process of cat-egorizing data as a 'recontextualization'. This implies we have somehow made good the loss of the original context by supplying a new one – based on our own conceptualizations. But reconceptualizing the data does not mean that we can afford to ignore the original context from which it has been abstracted.

There are two ways in which the computer can reduce this information loss. One is by helping us to overcome the fragmentation introduced by categorizing data. The other involves avoiding that fragmentation in the first place. Both involve exploiting hypertext[1] to support new methods of linking data.

A stock injunction of qualitative analysis has been to analyse data in context. As meaning depends on context, interpretation requires an understanding of the contexts in which a statement is made or an event occurs. But when we categorize a text segment, we abstract it from its context in order to compare it with other segments, which we think are similar (see Figure 5.1). By making comparisons, we can acquire new insights and perspectives on what our data mean. But we cannot make such comparisons without abstracting the data from its original context. Or can we?

The computer now allows us to handle this conflict between context and comparison a bit better. We can abstract the data for the purposes of comparison, but the computer makes it easy to recover the context from which the data has been abstracted. So context need not be altogether lost when we categorize the data. Figure 5.2 represents links between text segments and their context in the data in addition to the linking through codes.

It is possible to link text segments to context through a simple hypertext procedure which takes you back to the original data and highlights the text segment in context.[2] With this approach the relevant context for each segment can be determined by the analyst. It may be the neighbouring sentences, paragraph, page, case or the whole data. Another approach would be to display comparison and context simultaneously. For example, for each text segment you are comparing

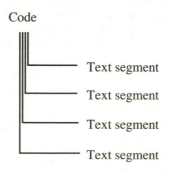

Code

Text segment

Text segment

Text segment

Text segment

Figure 5.1 *Linking text segments to codes* (each line represents a link)

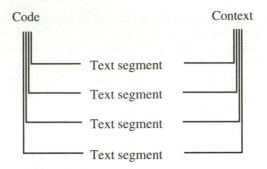

Figure 5.2   *Linking text segments to codes and context* (each line represents a link)

you might display the paragraph or page from which it has been abstracted.

Either way, the computer lets us move more easily and rapidly backwards and forwards between understanding data in context and analysing data through comparison. However, there are issues here that merit further exploration. Who defines context? Is the user free to define and redefine the contexts of a particular text segment? Or is context defined by the programmer, by the way the program has been designed? Can context be defined flexibly according to the relevant meanings of the text, or is it defined by some arbitrary standard, such as a specified number of adjacent lines?

And how does software handle the problem of thinking about as well as observing context? In many programs for qualitative data analysis (see Chapter 14), analysts can make memos capturing their thinking and attach these memos to text segments – another way of reducing fragmentation. However, the program does not automatically file these memos when you categorize text segments. You can recover memos through two simple procedures – a mouse click will take you back to the original text, and then you can display the memo you have attached to the text. But this involves work on the part of the analyst. The more work a task involves, the less likely we are to undertake it. Like water, analysis tends to follow the easiest course. If our software makes one analytic procedure easier than another, the chances are we will focus on that procedure. So software developers need to consider how to make the analysis of meaning-in-context as easy and efficient as the analysis of meaning-through-comparison.

We cannot overcome completely the tension between analysing the data in context and analysing the data through comparison. Perhaps the conflict between these two gives a creative edge to qualitative analysis. But by linking text segments and context, the computer can help us to reconcile these requirements, and in so doing help us to ensure that our comparisons are thoroughly 'grounded' in the data. Recovering context is a way of mitigating the fragmentation which results when we categorize data. Now I shall look at a way of avoiding it.

When we categorize data, we make a link between a code and a text segment. This link expresses judgements we are making, both about the data and the code we are assigning to it. One judgement is about boundaries of meaning – how we define our categories to include or exclude particular shades of meaning. Another is about similarity and difference – whether this text segment is sufficiently similar to other segments to warrant inclusion in the same category. In linking a text segment to a code, we decide that this segment is similar in some way to the other segments we have assigned to that code – and different from the segments we have not assigned to that code. These links therefore convey information about similarity and difference between text segments, based both on consistency (of our concepts) and comparison (between text segments).

Categorizing captures relations of similarity and difference, or inclusion and exclusion but, as I suggested earlier, important information is lost in the process. Take the simple example of a dog peeing on a lamppost. Here we can recognize a link between the dog's activity and the wet lamppost without implying any similarity or difference between the two. We might categorize this data – perhaps assigning the code 'animal' to the dog, 'street lighting' to the lamppost and 'expulsion of body fluids' to 'peeing'. But in doing so, we lose sight of the relationships between the different segments in the text. Information about the causal relation between events is ignored. Categorizing contributes to our analysis, but it also fragments the text and obscures our sense of narrative and process.

To capture such relationships in our data, we need to identify and record links between text segments. Linking segments was very difficult using pre-computer technology. The only practical way of linking segments was to assign them to a common category. The technological requirements for categorizing data were simple: the ability to copy and file data. It required only the technology of the card index box or the filing cabinet. There was no parallel technology for linking segments directly to each other. It could be done – by drawing arrows, writing memos and suchlike – but these pen-and-paper techniques were too awkward and cumbersome to be used systematically in qualitative analysis. Hence perhaps the traditional penchant for impression, insight, and intuition rather than systematic and rigorous analysis.

Now the computer lets us link text segments to each other easily and systematically. What could not be done physically can be done electronically. All we have to do is select the relevant segments, and make a link between them. Electronic links between bits of data are often called 'hypertext links' or 'hypermedia links' but I shall just call them 'hyperlinks'.

What does a hyperlink look like? In physical terms, it involves an electronic link between the two text segments, so that whenever we want to, we can go directly from one segment to the other. If we take two text segments X and Y, then whenever we encounter X we can go directly to Y (and vice versa). We could compare our hyperlink to a piece of string which we sellotape to two cards holding separate text segments and stored in separate locations, perhaps even separate filing cabinets. We know from the existence of the string that there is a hyperlink between the two cards, and by following the string we can go from one directly to the other (Figure 5.3).

This is a simplified view. In practice, we may attach many strings to each segment, each string being attached to other segments held on other cards or files. There is no limit (at least in theory) to the number of strings we can attach, making a set of pathways within the data, with each pathway incorporating a chain of links between different segments (Figure 5.4).

To keep track of our hyperlinks, we have to be able to identify them. In conceptual terms, the resulting complex of pathways may be more perplexing than illuminating, if we fail to distinguish between the different strings attaching different segments. Retaining the visual image, we have to colour code the strings if we are going to disentangle the different paths and not become confused by twists and turns and overlaps amongst the different strings. It is not enough just to make an electronic link: we also have to conceptualize it. Like categorizing, linking segments therefore has a conceptual as well as a mechanical aspect (for the differences between conceptual and mechanical tasks, see Chapter 8). We have to decide whether the links we identify are of chronology, causality, explanation, contradiction or whatever.

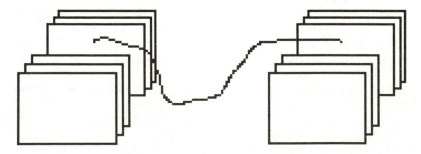

Figure 5.3   *Single hyperlink between two text segments stored separately*

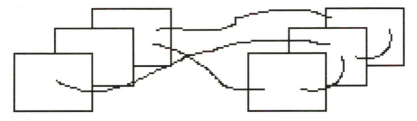

Figure 5.4   *Multiple hyperlinks between text segments stored separately*

Because we can link text segments, we can analyse data in ways not previously practicable. We can retain information about narrative and process. The difference between linking through codes and linking text segments directly is represented in Figures 5.5 and 5.6. In Figure 5.5 segments are linked through common assignment to a code (or codes), and indirectly to other segments through links between codes. In Figure 5.6, in addition to these links the segments are linked directly to each other.

Suppose we are analysing letters ostensibly written by Vincent van Gogh to his brother Theo, but actually written by Woody Allen (*If the Impressionists had been Dentists*, 1978). We want to identify causal links between the events described in Vincent's letters. We can do this by linking events and then retrieving all the causal links we have identified. The result might look like Table 5.1.

Or we might want to identify chronological links between bits of data, organizing the data into a sequence of events according to what happened when. By allowing us to identify a sequence of events, hyperlinking can be a useful tool in developing a narrative account. We are now linking the segments so that we are no longer losing information about the connections between them.

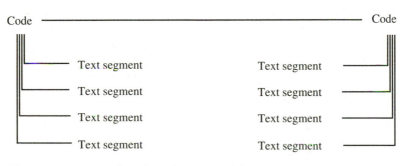

Figure 5.5   *Linking data through codes* (each line represents a link)

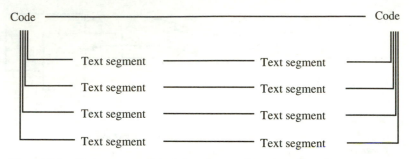

Figure 5.6   *Test segments linked directly as well as through codes* (each line represents a link)

We can combine these links between segments with the connections made by categorizing the data. For example, Table 5.2 lists examples where Vincent behaves in temperament more like an artist than a dentist and as a result the patient suffers. The computer can retrieve those causally linked text segments assigned to the codes **transposing temperament** and **patient suffering**. We can now infer relationships between categories on the basis of the links we have observed between databits. For example, we might infer that transpositions of temperament result in patient suffering, because we have recorded causal links between the text segments. We no longer have to infer causal relation-

Table 5.1   *Causal links between uncategorized data*

• Mrs Sol Schwimmer is suing me	Linked to	• because I made her bridge as I felt it and not to fit her ridiculous mouth.
• (Cézanne) is old and infirm and unable to hold the instruments and they must be tied to his wrists	Linked to	• but then he lacks accuracy and once inside a mouth, he knocks out more teeth than he saves.
• I attempted some root-canal work on Mrs Wilma Zardis, but half-way through I became despondent. I realized suddenly that root-canal work is not what I want to do! I grew flushed and dizzy. I ran from the office into the air where I could breathe! I blacked out for several days and woke up at the seashore.	Linked to	• When I returned, she was still in the chair. I completed her mouth out of obligation but I couldn't bring myself to sign it.

Table 5.2   *Causal links between categorized data*

Code: transposing temperament		Code: patient suffering
• I am in love	Linked to	• Claire Memling came in for an oral prophylaxis (I had sent her a postcard telling her it had been six months since her last cleaning even though it had only been four days).
• I was looking down into her mouth today and I was like a nervous young dental student again	Linked to	• dropping swabs and mirrors in there.
• As she sat in the chair, the draining hook in her mouth, my heart thundered. I tried to be romantic. I lowered the lights and tried to move the conversation to gay topics. We both took a little gas. When the moment seemed correct, I looked her directly in the eye and said 'Please rinse.'	Linked to	• And she laughed. Yes, Theo! She laughed at me and then grew angry! 'Do you think I could rinse for a man like you? What a joke!' I said, 'Please, you don't understand.' She said, 'I understand quite well! I could never rinse with anyone but a licensed orthodontist! Why, the thought that I could rinse here! Get away from me!' And with that she ran out weeping.

ships on the basis of some kind of quasi-statistical association between categories (Sayer, 1992).

Hyperlinking promises to be a powerful analytic tool, but it also raises some interesting problems. On what basis can we assign links between segments? Are causal links to be assigned only where they can be identified in the text, such as through the use of linking words like 'as' and 'because'? Or can they be assigned where the analyst can infer a link through interpreting the text? If links can be inferred, should any ground rules govern such inferences? For example, if we confine links only to adjacent segments of text, we adopt a far stricter rule for inference than if we allow links between widely spaced segments. Whether we adopt proximity or distance as a ground rule, we should be explicit about the procedures we adopt (see the Introduction to Part III). The procedures we adopt in categorizing data require similar scrutiny.

There is also a danger of drowning in complexity. We can have as many links as there are transitive verbs, so selectivity is crucial if we are not to become 'lost in Hyperspace'. In this respect, linking segments is unlike categorizing, where we can sustain a more open and comprehensive approach. With linking segments, we have to impose a focus upon our analysis through the conceptual perspective (or model) we adopt. For example, we might decide to focus only on causal or explanatory links within our data.

Some analysts find the imposition of a conceptual perspective on qualitative data unacceptable, refusing to bring any 'preconceived' ideas to the analysis. But an open mind is not an empty head. Take the story of the Australian who, returning from the pub, stumbles in the dark and loses his car keys. Noticing a lamppost further down the road, he goes there to look for his keys because that is where the light is. Some analysts would argue that he would be better off groping for his keys in the dark where he lost them. But he would be even better off if, like an Enid Blyton hero, he took a torch out of his pocket and used it to help find his keys. The problem is the lamppost, not the light. If the light is not fixed, we can use it to illuminate the dark and find what we are looking for. If our ideas are flexible, we can use them to develop a conceptual focus for our analysis (Dey, 1993).

There are three ways in which linking segments may aid our analysis. First, it may help us to pull out the threads of the stories we discover in our data, grounding narrative accounts in systematic observation of the way events unfold. Second, it may provide an empirical basis for inferring relationships between categories, so that our inferences are grounded in the systematic observation of links between different data-bits. Third, we can use linking as a tool to identify the configuration of factors which are linked by way of cause or consequence to particular events or episodes in our data.

It may be that linking segments provides a tool for the procedures envisaged by grounded theory – linking actions to consequences through conditions and strategies (Strauss and Corbin, 1990: 99ff.). The lack of an adequate technology may explain why the methodology of grounded theory has been so difficult to put into practice, even by its inventors and exponents. Linking segments may provide the technology needed to realize its methodological ambitions.

Perhaps also we can now explain why qualitative analysts have failed so consistently to provide an adequate account of their methods, despite the many exhortations made over the years. In the absence of tools to support systematic observation of narrative, processes and relationships within the data, analysts are obliged to fall back on the three 'i's – insight, intuition and impression. This disjunction between aims and methods may explain some of the discomfort and embarrassment which qualitative analysts experience when trying to account for their procedures.

Finally, let me anticipate a criticism of this chapter, based on the argument that there is nothing we can do through linking segments which could not be achieved through categorization. This argument might claim, for example, that we can categorize causal relationships between segments simply by assigning each event-link-event to an appropriate category. In other words, we can use categories to capture links between segments.

However, if we only categorize our data without linking it, then the inferences we make about the connections between categories depend on inferences which are not rooted in our observations. As a result, to confirm and interpret these inferences, we have to go back to the data to see if our inference is a reasonable one. We could claim an association between the categories, but to infer a relationship, such as a causal one, we would still have to return to the data to see if we can identify links between the text segments. The problem then is that we have to rely on our impressions, as without linking we have no tools for systematic observation (and recording) of the links between the databits.

My final point is that in theories of evolution, sex plays a crucial role in the development of species. This is because genetic variation and the associated flexibility in adapting to the environment are decisive factors in evolution. Perhaps the same may hold true of the evolution of qualitative analysis. By distinguishing and then linking the different elements in a narrative, which would previously have been undifferentiated, perhaps we can similarly transform the power of qualitative analysis? As my first analogy was with making war and I have now progressed to making love, this seems an appropriate speculation on which to conclude this chapter.

Notes

1. Hypertext links are electronic connections between different pieces of text. A reader can, by using a hypertext system, easily spring from one text passage to a connected one.

2. The program Hypersoft (Dey, 1992) is capable of this. For more details see Chapter 14.

6

Using Hierarchical Categories in Qualitative Data Analysis

Tom Richards and Lyn Richards

The language of qualitative research methods is imbued with the metaphors and methods of creating and ordering ideas by classificatory categories. The task of the researcher is presented as finding and exploring categories and patterns of categories in unstructured, even chaotic, records. To do so is to make sense of, understand, expound and illuminate, the records. This task is clearly assisted by the ordinary coding-and-retrieval function that almost every program for computer-aided qualitative data analysis provides.

But the categorization processes in QDA are much more than these two operations. The classic texts stress the relating of categories to find 'stories', 'themes', 'key linkages' or 'core categories' (for example, Strauss and Corbin, 1990). Categorizing is never just an end in itself, and is rarely recommended merely as a means of tagging all data on a topic. Rather its goals are often the discovery and ordering of ideas and themes; and the storing of growing understandings, the linking of ideas to data, cross-referencing, sorting and clarifying. Qualitative researchers are urged not merely to derive and use categories but to do so in particular ways:

1. To develop *data-driven* categories. 'The qualitative researcher uses inductive analysis, which means that categories, themes and patterns come from the data. Categories that emerge from field notes, documents and interviews are not imposed prior to data collection' (Janesick, 1994: 215).

2. To treat categories not as making up a formless heap but as being *linked* and *structured*. Category production and use of categories in indexing are presented as methods of *theorizing* – constructing and storing understandings, interpretations, models, ways of accessing complex data records and the relationships of categories to each other and to data. Linking categories to data is most commonly done by some process of coding for retrieval. But the more essential link is between categories. Coding bits of data as particular categories supports the processes of theory emergence and theory

construction only if the categories and their links to each other are structured and explored (Richards and Richards, 1991c).

3. To exploit the fact that categories offer not just a code-book but a conceptual structure. The category system that results from qualitative inquiry is designed not (like library indexes) as a *firm* framework for storing homogeneous contents (books) but rather as a *flexible container for complex contents*. It is a structured thesaurus of ideas, of tentative concepts and their links to data, of emerging understandings. It must have not only a structure but also ways of adapting and reviewing that structure.

4. Again unlike library indexes, the index of a qualitative project is designed to maximize references to data in as many categories as the data demands. Unlike books on library shelves, rich data records should not be in only one place. A very rich passage may be about twenty things; in accessing it through the categories we must be able to find it at each and use it to relate those categories and explore them. Researchers are enjoined both to categorize richly and to code liberally.

5. Finally, *critical examination and reporting of the indexing process is central to validation.* By reflection on and documentation of the process of category construction, the researcher accounts for and argues for interpretations. Categories need to be documented by an 'audit trail' recording not only the relationship of categories to each other, but also the origins and histories of categories.

Each of these goals of categorization has always required not just that the researcher produce categories to use 'on' the data, but that these categories (a) be rich in their contents; and (b) be given structured relationships. With the development of computer programs for QDA, the challenge of category construction became far greater as limits to the complexity and size of categorization and coding systems were removed. And more importantly, the computer provided the ability to create, rigorously use and accurately manipulate flexible yet structured category systems.

The purpose of this chapter is to set out one major (and basically ancient) theory of categories and their structural relations, and to show how to exploit that understanding of categories in computational QDA. This is the theory of *hierarchical categories*.[1]

Hierarchical categories

Genera and species, things and their parts, processes and their components, collections and their members, kinds and their instances, objects and their features, variables and their values, anything at all and examples of it: these are just some of the ways in which we organize our world and our ideas into general and specific. Think of it as a vertical direction in our 'space' of thoughts, general category above its specifics. Think of the general-to-specific as repeated through as many vertical levels as you need. For example, features of people relevant to a survey project might be the variables age, gender and religion; with religion divisible into the major groupings (Christianity, etc.), and each of those divisible into their major groupings (Orthodox, etc.), and some of those further divisible (Russian, Greek, etc.). A richer example of a hierarchy of categories might be the behaviour that people display to each other, as recorded in a field study. We might first divide this into a few major heads of behaviour, such as caring, assertive and grooming. These in turn might subdivide significantly, such as into the types of caring.

Let us call anything we are organizing in this way a *category*. It is a pleasantly neutral term, reflecting just that something goes into it, its topic, such as an idea, a religion, a country, an age-group, a process, a variable. In addition categories, particularly as a social scientist might like to employ them, can contain other things such as textual comments (memos), references to textual data (codes), a definition of the category and pointers to related categories.

When organizing categories hierarchically in this way, it is customary to call all the categories linked to a given category from immediately below its *children*; and all the children of a category are called each others' *siblings*. Hierarchies are often called *trees* because of their one-way branching nature, even if it is downwards not upwards. The single category at the top of a hierarchy is even called its *root*, and its name defines what the tree is about.

The utility of hierarchies in organizing one's thinking should be apparent from the above. Book indexes often have two or three levels of hierarchy, thesauri such as *Roget's* have several, and they're quite crucial because there is no other way of organizing the ideas in them so that you can find them. Alphabetical ordering won't do – this is not a dictionary, but a grouping of ideas. An easy-find thesaurus would begin by listing several top-level or most-general categories, such as People, Animate World, Inanimate World, Ideas, Emotions . . . . You choose the category covering what you have in mind, then look up its immediate subcategories (children), and repeat the process until you have found the group of ideas you want.

Categories in qualitative analysis

The idea of a thesaurus and its hierarchical structuring recommends itself as an organizing idea for qualitative research; so does the idea of a category. Think of a category as a container, or a computational data structure, that can hold material unified by a common definition.

Organizing categories hierarchically has powerful consequences. For one thing, the hierarchies tend to constrain the meaning of a given category. If the children of a Politics category are Democrat, Authoritarian, Aristocratic, Anarchist, this not only clarifies that Democrat is not a political party, but also that what we are looking at under Politics is views about the source or legitimation of governmental power, and not, say, position in the Left–Right spectrum or political parties.

From the point of view of coding text, this gives us a useful and clarifying way of coding people's expressed political attitudes, etc. (to continue with the political example). Bearing in mind that people belong to parties, have views about parties, have views about sources of governmental power, have views about various left-to-right ideologies; we can immediately sort coding into hierarchies that reflect these four distinctions. Under a high-level category Personal Politics we could put four subcategories: Party Affiliation, Remarks on Parties, Remarks on Government Types, and Remarks on Left–Right Spectrum. These all take appropriate subdivisions, which are the categories in which coding of text would occur.

Factual category structures
Note a significant difference between the first of these four categories and its three siblings. The first is meant to record facts: what party the person belongs to. The others are meant to index text: what the people have to say about those things. Hierarchies make recording of such facts easy. The hierarchical category Party Affiliation/Liberal (that is, the category Liberal under the category Party Affiliation) is meant to record the persons who are Liberals. How? There are two methods. One is to list their names in the memo for that category; but this doesn't easily make that fact available for analysis. The second is to index all that person's text there. Suppose, for example, that person is an interviewee; then all interviews of that person (or if they figure amongst other people in group interviews, their speech passages in the interview documents) get coded as wholes in Party Affiliation/Liberal. Suppose, alternatively, that they are people talked about, for example, in an evidence analysis project such as an historian or investigating judge might make. Then all passages *about* that person should get coded in that category.

For the sake of a title, we can call such categories *factual* (provided one doesn't try to import too much metaphysical baggage into the term) and the others *referential* (because their job is to hold coding references to the category's topic). Factual categories certainly don't hold *that* sort of coding. There may be no reference in the text at all to a person's political affiliation, and even if there were, we wouldn't be coding just those passages. The idea of a factual category is to hold *all* references to a person or thing of which a fact holds. The utility of this lies in the retrieval methods, as we shall see (for the distinction between factual and referential codes, see Chapter 4).

Factual coding has wide uses and enormous power. In an interview-based project, we could create an entire tree, perhaps with a root category called by tradition Base Data, to hold all known information about the interviewees. Major categories here would be such things as Age, Gender, Socio-economic Category, Marital Status, Religion, etc. Each of these has the appropriate subcategories, such as Age/20s, Age/30s . . .; Religion/Christian, Religion/Jewish . . . Religion/Other, Religion/Unknown (see Figure 6.1). Each interview subject would have their entire interview text coded at one category under Age, at one under Gender and so on.

Factual coding in a hierarchical system often has the structure of a variable and its values: the values of the Religion variable are Christian, Jewish, etc. This can relate closely to the content of structured interviews of the 'pick-a-box' type: What religion are you? What is your attitude to issue X – strongly in favour, mildly in favour . . .? In a hierarchical category system we can code such structured interviews quite neatly, in a way that allows for considerable interplay between qualitative analysis and the statistical analysis that the questionnaire results received. The technique is to treat an interviewee's answers as receiving factual coding

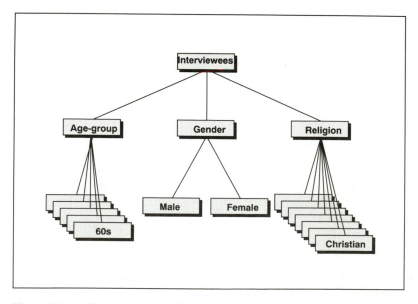

Figure 6.1   *A 'base data' tree of facts about interviewees*

not referential coding. That is, we code the entire interview under each answer the interviewee chose, for example in the category Attitude to X/Mildly in favour. (In suitable software, this process can be entirely automated so that the interviews get fully factually coded by using text search techniques without the need for the researcher ever to see the interview.)

We will return to factual categories and their structures later when we study the idea of category search, which will shed further light on the power of this sort of hierarchical categorization. For it is not just an organizational device but an analysis and theorizing tool.

Referential category structures
Referential category structures are those whose categories are intended to hold textual references to the topic of the category. This contrasts with factual category structures, whose categories refer not to the content of the text, but to attributes of the text: who said it, when, facts about the speaker, etc.

Typically the coding contents of a referential category are what the text is about. If a passage of text is discussing Napoleon, it gets coded into the Napoleon category. If it is about generalship, it goes into the generalship category. And if it is about power, or arrogance, it goes into those categories too.

In a hierarchical category system, it is critically important to see such categories as special cases of more general categories, and create them along with the Napoleon, Generalship, etc. categories. Napoleon is a case or instance of a person, so there should be a Person category as parent of the Napoleon one. This gives the hierarchical category Person/Napoleon. Depending on the researcher's interest, Generalship might be taken as a case of interpersonal relations or of military activities; leading in the first case to the hierarchical category Interpersonal Relations/Generalship. Other interpersonal relations can get added to this tree later, perhaps as examples are discovered in the text, or perhaps when the researcher thinks of them and wants to include them as a reminder to watch out for such passages, or perhaps because they want to write notes (category memo) about them. In this way the researcher might get after a while several children of Interpersonal Relations: Interpersonal Relations/Subservience, Interpersonal Relations/Consultation, Interpersonal Relations/Discussion Avoidance, etc.

It often happens that after a tree such as Person or Interpersonal Relations builds up for a while, the researcher feels that some splitting up is needed to separate different kinds of things. For example, it is usually very important to distinguish between people being discussed in the text, and the people who are doing the discussing. This is especially true if several people (unlike Napoleon) will fall into both classes. In that case we set up the hierarchical category Persons/Discussants, under which can go a Factual tree of an appropriate sort, and Persons/Subjects, under which go categories for people, each holding coding of passages talking about them. (The relation between Persons and its two children here is the housekeeping one of Ways of Occurring in the Project.) Further subdivisions may be useful too. Persons/Subjects could well have a factual tree under it, as well as the referential categories.

For many projects it can be important to include referential categories that are not so much about the subject(s) of the textual passage, as about things expressed in the passage. What emotions is the speaker expressing, what values or attitudes; is the speaker's style hesitant, definite, emphatic, casual or what; what is the speaker trying to do here? These lead to hierarchical category structures under Speaker Features/Emotions, Speaker Features/Attitudes, Speaker Features/Styles, Speaker Features/Goals. Specialists in linguistic analysis could have a field day in this tree.

Principles of hierarchical category construction

We painted a picture, above, of researchers building up hierarchical categories as they coded for rather specific categories, then thinking about the more general cases that should lie above those specifics. That is called the *bottom-up* or *data-driven* method of building trees. Equally valid can be the *top-down* or *theory-driven* method, where the researcher can formulate beforehand the range of general categories needed for the project. Either approach is legitimate, has its methodological advantages and disadvantages, and can be more or less appropriate to different types of project. In many evaluation-research projects, for example, the theoretical framework, hypotheses, topics and goals can be formulated in advance, the purpose of the project being perhaps simply to show how a particular innovation in client services provision by a company is received by different types of client. In that case the category trees (or at least the top level or two) might be formulated in advance.

In other projects, deriving for example from fieldwork, phenomenological or grounded theory (see Chapter 3) approaches, there may be little idea of what major groupings will occur, and so a strongly bottom-up development path is taken with tree construction, with a great deal of shifting around and reorganization of trees occurring throughout the project. In such cases, the development of a stable tree system with no significant additions or rearrangement of categories may signal that the analysis is completed.

But whichever way tree construction is done, some general principles apply.

> *Principle 1.* The children of a category should be cases *in the same sense* of the parent.

This is particularly important if the children might hold coding. If some children of a Religion node are particular religious denominations, we shouldn't have other children about the effects of religious belief, such as Causes Bigotry. It is better to sort these out by having Religion/ Denominations (and the denominations under that) and Religion/Effects of Belief (with the various effects under that). Now we no longer have unlike siblings. (In this scheme, the relation of Religion to its two children is not important: the two children are unlikely to hold coding. The relation is a purely housekeeping one of 'aspects that are significant in the project' and exists simply to allow the different aspects to be differentiated.)

For this reason there is usually little need to label the links between a parent and its children in a tree structure. If it is a well-designed structure all the links are of a general-to-specific kind, and in any given case of a parent, it should be clear from inspection what the exact relationship is: kind to instances, thing to parts, concept to examples, etc. If a definite specification is required, it can be kept in the parent's memo field or definition field; after all, in a well-designed tree a parent should have the same relation to all of its children, so one specification does for all the links down from the parent.

> *Principle 2.* The description of a given category should apply to all the categories in the sub-tree below it.[2] The subcategories in a tree should not switch part-way down: that is, they must remain generic with respect to the higher categories.

What does this mean? If there is a category 'Canines', then subcategories (as well as text attached to them) should be about kinds, sorts, cases or instances of canines: dogs, foxes, wolves and so on, breeds of dog, particular doggy pets. If text illustrating canine behaviour (for example, in an ethologist research project) is coded, it would cause horribly complex and illogical tree structures if this were attached to a new subcategory of the category 'Canine' called 'Behaviour'. Canine behaviour is of course not a kind, sort, instance, or case of a canine. The right way to proceed would be to create a new tree called 'Behaviour', with different types of behaviour as its subcategories. Then text passages about canine behaviour can be attached simultaneously to categories in the 'Canine' and 'Behaviour' trees, for instance by indexing them at appropriate subcategories of these trees, for example, 'Dogs' and 'Submission'. While keeping all the passages on submission together, one can then easily relate submission to dogs, cats, people, or relate dogs to any other behaviour, just by using built-in search facilities to find all passages indexed under the categories to be related and thus creating far fewer categories.

Take a more detailed sociological example: consider a tree of categories whose root is 'Attitudes', designed to capture attitudes of speakers. A researcher might give it the children: About Politics, Towards Spouse, To Divorce and so on. Under About Politics could be categories for different political positions, under Spouse the different aspects of a spouse or things a spouse does that attitudes get expressed about. And so on for the other objects of attitudes. Then *under each of these specific categories* might appear the same group: Favourable, Neutral, Unfavourable, None; or perhaps categories more descriptive of attitudes, such as Supportive, Destructive, Admiring, Disapproving, etc. (see Figure 6.2).

This would not be a good way to proceed. It greatly proliferates the number of categories beyond what is needed, it prevents the category system keeping together things that can and should be kept together, and it destroys the general-to-specific structure. Disapproving, somewhere below Attitudes/To Divorce, is not a more specific object-of-attitude than divorce. The problem with the example just given is that effectively the tree is an 'attitudes towards' tree, and the subcategories provide progressively finer classifications of the objects of the attitude. Then below all that, repeated for each finest subcategory of object-of-attitude, occurs, repeated many times, the list of attitudes of interest.

This is bad design on about three counts:

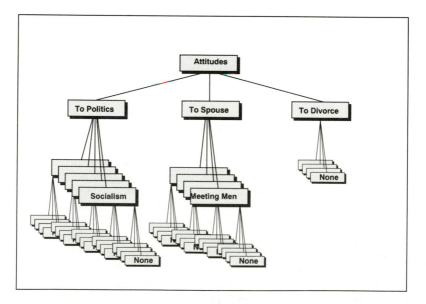

Figure 6.2   *A poorly designed 'attitudes' tree of 53 nodes*

1. the tree deserts its 'object-of-attitude' subdivision principle – trees should not change the principle of division part way down.
2. A similar or identical collection of sibling categories (the actual attitudes) is repeated many times making for an exponential increase in the number of categories and amount of coding.
3. There is no one place where all coding of the expression of, for example, destructive attitudes occurs – the coding is split up into the repeated occurrences of that category under different objects of attitude.

Now (1) might strike the reader as a little pedantic and (2) as a problem worth living with but (3) is a plain disadvantage. Because if all coding for expressions of a destructive attitude were in one place, it would be possible to analyse it: what sort of person primarily expresses it, what sort of things is it expressed toward, what other attitudes do such people express, etc.? The search for patterns is virtually destroyed, because all the system has is a few links of destructive attitudes to a few objects of attitudes, no generality which can be explored for a pattern. Realizing that serious analytical disability, and correcting for it, will also solve problems (1) and (2). In fact (1) and (2) can be treated as good indicators that something like (3) has happened and should be corrected. The alternative approach in this case is to apply the *One-place-only principle*:

> *Principle 3.* One topic or idea should occur in only one place in the index system. For example, have just one node for Destructive Attitude, not one under each node towards whose topic someone in your project has a destructive attitude.

So we can fix things by developing an attitudes tree for the attitudes themselves; which, depending on the needs of the researcher, might have as major subdivisions Personal, Social, Religious, Analytical . . ., indicating the viewpoint in which an attitude is couched; or for other purposes Positive, Neutral, Negative, under which go cases of each such as Supportive. Or these two ways of classifying attitudes might exist as two sub-trees side by side (see Figure 6.3).

And what of the objects of attitudes? We described that tree quite fully above, and all we have done since is to remove and reorganize the actual attitudes occurring below each specific object of attitudes. So we could leave the remainder as an objects-of-attitudes tree.

But, there might be a good reason to eliminate the objects-of-attitudes tree altogether, because those objects do occur elsewhere in the category system, or could do so. Some objects of attitudes, for example, might be specific people discussed by project interviewees. Then shouldn't they already occur under People/Subjects? Other objects of attitudes might be people's beliefs. Then shouldn't there be a Beliefs tree or similar, containing for example Beliefs/Political/Democracy and Beliefs/Religious/Afterlife? By having a Beliefs tree, we can code in its

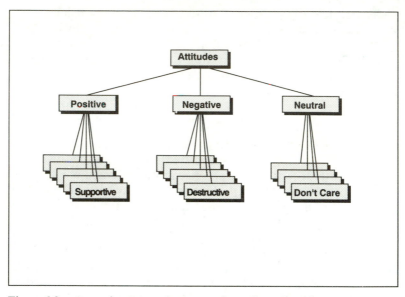

Figure 6.3   *A tree that is just about attitudes and not their objects*

categories not just text of attitudes expressed towards a belief, but who holds it, expressions of values towards it (important, morally fundamental, wicked, etc.), causes and reinforcements of the beliefs, etc. Then we have, in one place (the specific belief category) *everything* about that belief.

The careful application of the One-place-only principle will lead to organizing the project around a small number of trees with deeply different subject matters (which are the names given to their root categories). Typical examples are Persons, Places, Objects, Institutions, Ideas and Beliefs, Values, Attitudes, Needs, Activities, Events, Behaviour, Mental States. Then we never get tempted to put under Institutions categories for beliefs about them, and their activities, and the values they foster, and the people associated with them; then put many of the same categories again under Places or Behaviour. And conversely, whenever we want to find out *anything* about a particular belief: who or what institution fosters it, what behaviour it causes, what beliefs there are about it, etc. it is all found in the one place, in the category for that belief. Following the One-place-only principle like this leads not only to less coding, but to simpler decisions about coding, and a smaller, more manageable and more flexibly reorganizable category system. Perhaps most importantly it leads to far more analytical power because when all coding of all types about a subject is together in a category, that coding can be teased apart, filtered, and analysed at will. If it's not there together but spread all over the place, it can't be analysed at all.

Category analysis and search

Very often in a project, it is only the lowest categories, the ones with no children, that hold coding. Higher categories are there not to hold codes, but to provide organization and relationships between the codes; in particular to group ones that have only specific variations between them as siblings. Is it possible then to throw away all the higher categories so we are left only with the bottom ones, the ones that hold the text coding? In other words, will unorganized categories do as well as hierarchical ones? There are several reasons why not.

1. Good analysis requires easy finding and consistent using of a category. If we only have category names to go on, it can be difficult to remember the name of the category used to code complex ideas such as community service done by individuals for altruistic reasons, or even if there was one. Trees make it easy, as we argued above with the example of searching *Roget's Thesaurus*. This avoids loss and inadvertent duplication.
2. Analysis is often the search for related categories. For example, in a particular project, if you want to code a passage that describes a particular piece of anti-social behaviour, you really need to see the current array of categories for types of anti-social behaviour. Does one of them fit, or have we another type requiring a new category? In a hierarchical system, all the current types will be under the node for anti-social behaviour.
3. More significantly, unstructured categories do not present us with an organizational structure, making systematic surveying, orderly analysis and retrieval, and the presentation of one's concepts as an ordered system with meaning and coherence, impossible.
4   Adequate identification of the meaning of a category involves defining its classificatory relations: what is it a case of, what other things – cases of the same general type – must it be distinguished from? What sort of things can be examples of it?
5. Whilst most coding may occur at the lowest nodes of a tree, much can occur higher. Discussion can be about, for example, anti-social behaviour in general and not some particular aspect of it. Or, a descriptive passage about an organization may be too scanty to classify the organization, hence it can apply to a range of organization types. Particularly if dealing with physical things such as people, places or things, the text may well be about groups, classes, or kinds of people, etc. All such text needs to be coded at higher categories corresponding to the general topic in the text. Nevertheless such generic content is still relevant to the specific cases below its category – a relation that would be lost if there were no organization of the categories.

6. The systematic search for information about, or relating, categories is made far richer if categories are organized hierarchically. Here are some examples.

Example 1. There may be a lot of coding in specific categories under some more general one such as Passion. The categories with coding might even go several levels down. It can typically happen that a researcher wants to study together everything coded under any passion. Perhaps this is just to bring all the reading on it together. Perhaps it is because the researcher feels they have not handled the organization of the various passions in a useful way, and they want to collect all the text on it for re-coding in a new way. Perhaps it is because they want to take all the material on passion of whatever sort and analyse it as a whole, for example by looking for co-occurrences with other suggestive categories such as mental stability.

The obvious way to bring the coding in the entire sub-tree under such a category together, or all the memos stored there, is to have a software function which takes a given category and *collects* together all the coding, or memos, in the sub-tree below it. Note that having a Collect operation saves the researcher from having to index, for example, stream fishing passages under the more general categories that apply to it, such as Fishing and Participatory Sports. In a well-designed category hierarchy, the rule is to code a passage as low down as possible, then use Collect to fill the more generic categories as needed.

Example 2. There is a converse to Collect, that can be called *Inherit*. In this case one may be looking at a specific category and wanting to find all that is coded that applies to the category, even if it is more general and so applies to other things too. In the biological world the examples are obvious: if I want to find out all I can about cats, I should also find out about felines, carnivores, quadrupeds, mammals and vertebrates. Again, if I want to find out all that is said in tourist interviews about stream fishing, it may be desirable to look at views on fishing in general and indeed participatory sports attractions in general. The categories to examine here are the ancestors of the particular category: its parent, that category's parent, and so on up. The Inherit operation carried out on the Stream Fishing category will automatically bring together all coding in the line of ancestors above it.

Also a Collect and an Inherit together might provide exactly the pool of text or memos one wants about stream fishing: do a Collect on Fishing to bring together all types of fishing, and an Inherit on Fishing to get the generalities, then bring those results together.

This last example illustrates a desirable feature of the search of category systems, called *System Closure* (Richards and Richards, 1994). Simply, it is that the coding found as a result of any search of categories for codes, such as a Collect search, should be saved somewhere in the category system, so it is available as the subject of a later search. Here, we did a Collect on a category Sports/Participatory/ . . . /Fishing to bring together all coding on the different types of fishing: stream, rock, deep-sea . . . and kept the resulting coding somewhere as a category of its own, A. Then we did an Inherit on the same category and kept those codings somewhere as a category, B. Then we brought both lots of coding together, A and B, into one (an operation called *union*), which gave us what we wanted. Since we wanted it, we should save that bunch of coding too, for future analysis, as a third new category. And maybe now A and B can be thrown away as having served their purpose.

Example 3. Another way to make use of hierarchical coding ties up with variables and values. Suppose you want to see what differences, if any, the religion of interviewees makes on their attitudes to contraception. If you have a factual categorization of interview text by the religion of the interviewee, then it is possible, even in a non-hierarchical system, to take each religion in turn, and find all text coded by that religion and in the category for contraception. This is known as *intersection*. Each intersection operation yields the text of one particular religious group of interviewees about contraception (see Figure 6.4(a)).

In a hierarchical system, all that can be a single operation. You take the generic factual node for Religion, under which are all the categories for the different religions occurring in the project (we'll say there are seven such categories), each containing references to all the text from interviewees of that religion. You then give a single command to intersect all its children with the coding in the Contraception category. The series of results can be kept together as a *vector* of seven categories, using system closure.

The idea of vector creation can be extended to a data structure widely advocated for qualitative research (Miles and Huberman, 1994), the qualitative *matrix*. Here we might want to look at a whole range of social issues, and find out the bearing of the religion of the respondent on each. If the various social issues are kept as children of one category, Social Issues, say, we can give one command to intersect pairwise each child of Social Issues (eight of them, say) with the seven children of Religion, and keep the results in an 8-row by 7-column matrix of categories (see Figure 6.4(b)). This beats giving fifty-six separate Intersect commands and always worrying if you gave all of them, systematically, with no omissions or repetitions. And by system closure, the results are all kept, and kept together as a matrix, for future analysis.

One way of further analysing vectors or matrices in a category system is to apply further matrix operations to them. Consider the matrix described above. You might also want to see if there is any variation by age-group of the views expressed. You can do it with one command if

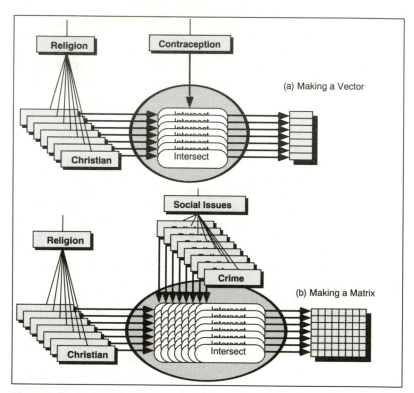

Figure 6.4   *Making (a) vectors and (b) matrices using multiple intersects*

you have a factual category Age-groups under which are the various age-group categories (suppose there are five of them). You take the matrix, and with a single command intersect each of its fifty-six component categories with the five children of the category Age-group. The result is an 8 by 7 by 5 matrix of categories, each one containing text from everyone of a particular religion and age-group about one of the social issues. This can be extended to a four-dimensional matrix by bringing in marital status, a five-dimensional one by bringing in the values of some other personal variable and so on. Each further dimension results from one single operation. This is all made possible by (a) hierarchical category structures and (b) system closure.

Conclusion

Hierarchical categories have been described as a powerful and universal technique for organizing and relating concepts, objects, thoughts and other types of topic. In QDA, such categories can contain memos (text written by the researcher about the category topic) and coding (references to passages of textual data). It was argued that hierarchical category systems provide fundamental classificatory features which weld topics into a significant totality without which there is no meaning, as well as providing useful management functions.

Ways of searching and analysing hierarchical categories have been described that do things and produce results effectively unobtainable otherwise, but which are highly important to qualitative research. In addition, the importance has been pointed out of system closure, whereby coding that results from analyses can be returned to the system in a category, to be available for further analysis. Examples were given of the use and significance of system closure in conjunction with operations that make use of hierarchies in a systematic analysis of codings.

It needs to be stressed that a hierarchical category system, and the four operations described above that make explicit use of hierarchies, are not the only features that matter in well-designed software for qualitative data analysis. For example, system closure should apply to *any* operation that results in a series of codes, such as searching text for particular words or phrases, so that the codes are kept in a category for further use. Also, there need to be many other operations on coding in categories other than the four hierarchically-based ones we mentioned. We have already mentioned intersection and union, two simple Boolean operations (see also Chapter 14, p. 194) that our examples relied on to work properly. But there are others, such as being able to restrict any operation, including the four hierarchical ones and Boolean ones, to text coded (or not coded) in a certain way, or to documents that contain somewhere (or do not contain anywhere) certain coding, or text that occurs before or after or near other text coded in a certain way. By virtue of system closure, we can use the results of any of these operations as input to further ones, or as constraints on their use, and in this way build up sophisticated and subtle analyses, and get answers to complicated questions.

Moreover, not only should there be many ways of exploring the categories and their links with data, but also in QDA the processes of recording, changing and developing ideas and results must be recorded.

Notes

1. The authors have developed the software program NUD.IST that supplies several ordinary and complex coding and retrieval functions and is especially suited to assist the researcher with the employment of hierarchical categories (but certainly not to enforce their use) (see Chapter 14 for more details).

2. In terms of the NUD.IST Index System Search functions, it should make sense to use the 'Collect' and 'Inherit' operators on any node.

7

Designing and Refining Hierarchical Coding Frames

Luis Araujo

In this chapter an example from research practice will be given for the strategy of theory building outlined in the last chapter: the development of hierarchical categories. Thus the focus will be on the interplay between the coding of textual data and the process of designing a hierarchical code scheme. In essence, it will be argued that the process of building a hierarchical coding frame involves the use of categories embedded in both theoretical frameworks as well as empirical data. Coding frames are intermediary steps in mediating social actors' and social scientists' frames of meaning. The development of coding frames is thus an iterative process, testing the representativeness of codes as categories representing a range of observations in the social world, and their relationship to wider theoretical frameworks in the social sciences.

The theory-ladenness of codes

In the methodological discussion no consensus has, as yet, been achieved as to what a code is and what role coding occupies in the process of qualitative data analysis.[1] Dey (1993), however, provides an insightful discussion of how coding is to be used in qualitative data analysis and how computers can help this process. Codes, in Dey's language, are categories and categories are relations between our cognitive models and representations of the social world, available through interview transcripts, field notes on observations, documentary sources, etc. Creating categories in qualitative data analysis thus constitutes a dual challenge: on the one hand the categories must be empirically grounded and be defined by a relation to chunks of data. On the other hand, categories must be related to a wider conceptual framework and acquire meaning only in relation to other categories. There is a parallel here with language as seen from a structuralist perspective. Language as a system of differences reveals a structure characterized by the impossibility of locating meaning in a sign, a system with neither beginning nor end, in which each term can only be defined by its negative, by what it is not.

This constitutes, in my view, a fundamental point about coding qualitative data that traditional views often underestimate: *coding is not merely a process of labelling that, with hard work and graft, will eventually evolve into a theory.* The very process of assigning categories to qualitative data is necessarily theory-informed. Our respondents inevitably use categories in their discourse and these are theory-informed too. As McCauley (1987: 304) observed: 'We are born theorizers, disposed to perceive and react to the world in certain specific ways because we must have theories (in the broad sense at least) to have any empirical knowledge at all.' This does not mean that we have to accept actors' accounts as explanations or that we have to stop the analysis at this level.

As Giddens (1976) remarks, social sciences deal with a universe that is already constituted within frames of meaning by social actors themselves and reinterprets and transcends these frames of meaning with its own language and theoretical discourse. The process of coding data in the social sciences is thus an important intermediary in translating meanings from the frames of social actors into the frame of theoretical discourse. Both languages use concepts and categories, and coding frames can be regarded as an intermediate step, mediating between 'natural' and theoretical discourses. The process of developing a coding frame that fits the dual criteria of being grounded in both substantive theoretical schemas and data consists of a number of feedback loops between theory, coding frames and data. The continuous interplay between conceptual models, categories and data allows a growing web of codes, textual segments and relationships between codes to evolve into a reasonably coherent story line that constitutes both a good 'local' theory to account for this data and a link to more general and substantive theories.

Designing a coding frame for the development of hierarchical categories

The key point that emerges from the previous discussion, and one that must be heeded particularly in relation to the development of hierarchical categories, is that coding must start with a frame that is well grounded in a theory or conceptual scheme. The mere generation of categories from labelling segments of text according to, say, actors' own use of categories in discourse, will produce a burgeoning tree of categories that is well grounded in the data but nothing more. The first resource for the construction of a hierarchical tree of concepts must be the research questions and theoretical issues one started from, and that will be reflected in the way the data are collected – for example, in the types of questions asked at interviews or from the documentary sources consulted. The analysis can then proceed with appeal to other types of resources – inferences from the data, hunch and intuition, links to substantive theories or theoretical issues, etc. (see Dey, 1993).

In order to make this discussion more concrete, I will give examples from a piece of research that has recently been completed at Lancaster.[2] The study was of a traditional British manufacturing/engineering industry and involved both machine assemblers and their suppliers and subcontractors. The focus of the study was on the content and structure of buyer–supplier relationships. More specifically, we wanted to find out how firms in this industry related to their suppliers in a number of dimensions ranging from coordination of deliveries to joint efforts in new product development. Since most machine assemblers often used more than one supplier for the parts, components and sub-assemblies they buy, suppliers compete amongst themselves to capture a further share of the buyer's business. This process of competition is mediated by the buyer's purchasing policies and by a host of other factors (for example, attitude towards information sharing, values and beliefs of managerial teams). Given that annual purchasing bills of machine assemblers amount on average to 50 per cent of their turnover, their use of suppliers and subcontractors is vital to their own competitiveness in a highly internationalized market environment.

Most of the data collected derived from tape-recordings of semi-structured, personal interviews with a range of middle and senior managers, representing a range of functional specialisms (for example, manufacturing, research and development) in both buying and supplying firms. Fifty-two managers from 35 firms were interviewed, representing a total of 78 hours of tape which were transcribed verbatim. Of the 35 firms represented, 5 were machine assemblers and 30 were suppliers and subcontractors of a range of parts, components and subassemblies. A coding frame was developed that reflected both our theoretical schema on buyer–supplier relationships and inferences from a careful reading of all the interview transcripts and other documentary sources, namely specialized press articles and company reports. The coding frame was then used to attach codes to segments of text in the interview transcripts.

The initial decisions in coding are particularly important to the extent that they have the potential to mould much of what comes later. Despite the warnings against premature closure and becoming imprisoned by powerful conceptual grids, a fundamental redirection in the theory-informed logic underlying a coding frame is distracting and time-consuming. Dey (1993: 106) presents a useful framework to weigh up the degree of initial refinement to aim for in the first attempt at coding. If the key criterion is confidence in the categories developed, then it's better to adopt an incrementalist strategy – that is, start with a few, broad categories and find ways of progressively refining them. If the volume of data is such that an incrementalist strategy would be too cumbersome and time-consuming, a more committed and decisive approach using many categories would be more efficient.

In our project the strategy followed was to start with many categories. The initial frame consisted of a hierarchical network, using a number of superordinate categories and a number of lower-level categories, most of which had been inferred from a careful reading of the data or emerged during the data collection process (see Figure 7.1 for an extract of the coding frame used in this project). In the case of what is known as face-sheet variables, coding the identity and company affiliation of respondents, we developed a detailed sub-tree prior to starting the coding of documents.

Another part of the coding frame related to substantive categories such as Competition or Relationships. These were the categories to which text segments were attached. Having derived an initial coding frame, we then proceeded to code the data always at the lowest level in the hierarchical tree. This might be thought of as a problem in the sense that it may force the researcher to zoom in on the data too early and to invest prematurely in a heavy-duty coding frame. Some software for coding and retrieval, however, allows for early commitments to be reversed if necessary. One example for this would be the operation Collect[3] which allows for data coded at lower levels in the hierarchical network to also be coded at pre-specified higher levels in the hierarchical network. It produces a burgeoning pattern of nested codes but it also preserves the option of deleting and reorganizing codes at lower

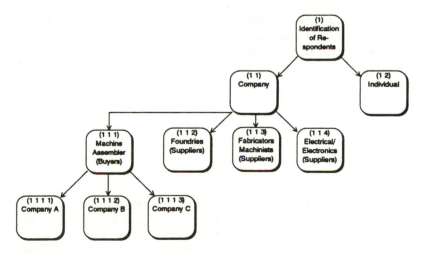

Figure 7.1   *An extract of a coding frame*

levels, if they prove to be too fine-grained for the objectives of the analysis. By retrieving and comparing data at higher as well as lower levels of categorization, the researcher has the option to re-examine and reverse early coding decisions.

Using a hierarchical code scheme to classify data

Assigning categories to data, to use Dey's (1993) expression, is a process fraught with potential ambiguities and pitfalls. First, a decision must be made on what constitutes a unit of analysis. The smallest unit of analysis is the word but unless the researcher is interested in linguistic analysis, this is not very meaningful. Lines, paragraphs and sections come next. We might want, for example, to let every answer from our respondents fit into a paragraph, which is then used as the unit of analysis. There's no hard and fast rule on how to carve up a document: we chose lines simply because this choice preserves a degree of flexibility as to how far to go in categorizing a chunk of text. We may, in principle, operate at the level of the paragraph or section but preserve the option of embedding finer-grade codes in lines or sets of lines.

The next important decision is in what sequence to code the document database. Dey (1993: 120) presents some cogent arguments as to why one should not employ a sequential approach to coding – such as code all transcripts from beginning to end and do this in, say, chronological order of interview. In our case, the decision can be made more complicated: should one start coding all transcripts following a firm-based order – that is, code all transcripts of interviews with individuals within the same firm before proceeding to tackle another firm? Or, should we code all transcripts by, say, functional specialization of the individual – for example purchasing manager – regardless of his or her company affiliation? Looking at our sub-tree on identification of respondents (see Figure 7.1), one can easily find a plethora of sequences all of which can be justified on any number of criteria.

It is tempting to argue that these issues are less important than they might otherwise be, because code-and-retrieve software can subsequently help repair some of the damage caused by an uneven first attempt at coding. Besides, to attempt a sequential and comprehensive coding of the odd megabyte of textual data is tantamount to administering oneself a general anaesthetic.

Assigning codes to data is a process of relating categories to observations. Codes are metonymic concepts in that they allow the part (category) to stand for the whole (a range of observations in the data). To say that codes are metonymic concepts is also to say that not all observations are equally good examples of a category (Lakoff, 1987).

Codes thus have radial structures with core and peripheral exemplars. Whereas most core exemplars can be derived from past knowledge and experience, observations in the data often confront the researcher with difficult categorization choices.

In forming core exemplars for lower-level codes on **learning about competitors** (code 9 2 2, see Figure 7.2), for example, we considered the typical scenarios for a firm collecting information about competitors. Customers and suppliers often pass on information about competitors inadvertently or as a gift to their exchange partners. Competitors often belong to the same trade and industry associations and their personnel may well get acquainted in these forums. Trade fairs and exhibitions provide another setting for face-to-face contacts and information exchange. Personnel exchanges may constitute another vehicle for the exchange of information.

Other exemplars may not fit this category so neatly. For example, competitors may collaborate through joint ventures, buy and sell from each other or engage in the illegal practice of industrial espionage. What started as a set of unproblematic scenarios suddenly gets confused: competitors assume a variety of roles in relation to each other and learning about competitors' activities doesn't quite fit our core scenarios. Looking more closely at respondents' language we also found that their use of the category **competitor** was not homogeneous. These inconsistencies with our initial model led us to add a new category – **criteria to define competitors** (code 9 2 3, Figure 7.2) – and to look more closely at the representativeness of our categories in confrontation with the data.

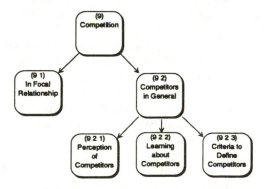

Figure 7.2   *An extract of a coding frame*

Refining and extending hierarchical coding frames

Refining and extending a hierarchical coding frame consists in a series of iterations to check the grounding of the coding frame in the data and the theoretical framework we started with. As I have argued previously, a coding frame constitutes an intermediate step mediating between 'natural' and theoretical discourses. Dey (1993: 127–128) remarks that prior to categorization, the data is organized according to the researcher's methods of data collection and transcription rather than the theoretical objectives informing his or her analysis. Once the data is categorized, it can be detached from its context and explored in our own terms. And yet this introduces a paradox in our analysis: the more the data is categorized and explored in our own terms, the more we swing the pendulum away from the frames of meaning of respondents and the context in which these meanings occur.

The use of computer software allows researchers to circumvent some of the difficulties associated with this paradox. By performing retrieval operations on coded data, data classified under the same code can be compared and contrasted. This is often referred to as the decontextualization/recontextualization approach (Tesch, 1990). The decontextualization/recontextualization method has gained an undeserved reputation for being atheoretical and for jeopardizing the holistic approach on which qualitative data analysis supposedly rests. As Richards and Richards (1994: 446–449) remark, these views are mistaken. Decisions on what constitutes a category of relevance to a study and on how to assign a category to a chunk of data are never atheoretical. The viewing, comparing and contrasting of exemplars of data classified under the same category is also a theory-informed and theory building exercise.

In our project we started refining and extending our coding frame by looking under each branch of our hierarchical network and pulling out reports on all the textual data classified under each code. If, for example, our impression from a previous reading of the data is that our classification sub-tree for competition is somewhat confused or performed at too high a level of aggregation, we want to start from there. Re-reading the decontextualized data and comparing a range of segments of text classified by that code, we found that respondents sometimes used the word 'competition' to refer to a structural property of the system in which they are embedded and sometimes as an individualized relationship, where they find themselves bidding for the same contract against an identifiable opponent. Two intermediate categories, **competition in focal relationship** and **competitors in general** (codes 9 1 and 9 2 respectively, see Figure 7.2), can thus be inserted in our coding frame to account for the different ways in which respondents use the term.

The decontextualization/recontextualization approach allows us to start exploring systematic relationships in the data and test their relevance in relation to our theoretical framework. A simple retrieval operation for a range of codes (say the family of codes related to relationships with restrictions related to face-sheet variables) can be performed, to compare and contrast how different types of individuals and organizations view specific aspects of their business relationships. For example, we grouped all the data coded under relationships (code 5, Figure 7.3) and identification of respondents/company affiliation/foundries (code 1 1 2, Figure 7.1) and compared it with data coded under relationships/commitment and identification of respondents/company affiliation/fabricators-machinists (code 1 1 3, Figure 7.1). Do foundries and machine makers conduct relationships similarly to fabricators/machinists and machinery makers? Is the product or range of products exchanged a key factor in determining the nature and evolution of a relationship? Or are company purchasing policies a key variable in discriminating between different types of relationships and should we be looking instead for customer-centred comparisons – that is, should the comparisons be centred on machine assemblers as buyers (code 1 1 1, Figure 7.1) rather than on other types of companies as suppliers?

These processes might be regarded as slicing the document database in different ways and testing the fit of different categorization schemes with both the data and a theory-based framework to explain the data. Multiplying the number of trials at slicing the document database and increasing the number of criteria for slicing, allows for the successive testing of different ways to explain the data. Cycles of decontextualization/recontextualization and exploration of relationships between categories in the hierarchical network of codes led both to splitting of categories and the pruning and consolidation of others.

Dey (1993) formulates a set of criteria to guide researchers in these decisions and highlights some of the trade-offs involved. In our project, all these decisions were guided by the objective of building on existing academic literature on the subject of business relationships and looking

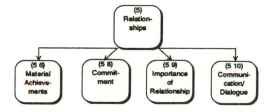

Figure 7.3　*An extract of a coding frame*

for discrepancies with existing models. Our final coding frame is thus the product of the initial objectives of our study and clearly does not represent the only way to classify the data. A researcher with a different focus would have undoubtedly built a different coding frame and produced a different account of the same data. But that shouldn't be surprising: replicability in the social sciences is problematic and the resources deployed in interpreting qualitative data are not necessarily the product of methodological recipes and codified procedures. The act of interpretation will always rely partly on the imagination, intuition, interests and background of the researcher.

Notes

1. On the different functions of coding see Chapter 4.
2. This chapter is partly based on a project financed by the Nuffield Foundation under their Small Grants for the Social Sciences scheme. Their support is gratefully acknowledged. Thanks are also due to the assistance of Miguel Henriques, a doctoral student at Lancaster, in the preparation of this chapter.
3. 'Collect' is a code-building operation used in NUD.IST, the software used to aid the process of coding and retrieval in our project. For more details see Richards and Richards p. 92, and Chapter 14 in this volume.

PART III

COMPUTERS AND QUALITATIVE HYPOTHESIS EXAMINATION

Introduction: Hypothesis Examination in Qualitative Research

Udo Kelle in discussion with Ernest Sibert, Anne Shelly, Sharlene Hesse-Biber and Günter Huber

Notwithstanding the great heterogeneity of ontological and epistemological assumptions, most qualitative approaches share a fundamental methodological claim: they are more concerned with generating new insights or developing new theoretical concepts than with testing hypotheses derived from already existing theories.

Software for the computer-aided analysis of textual data can assist this process of discovery in several ways. With its help the researcher can easily retrieve text passages relating to a certain topic within a document or across documents and identify their similarities and differences. In doing so one can, for example, contrast the utterances of different types of respondents on the same issues. Or one can compare text segments attached to different code-categories to investigate their possible relations.

Several authors have emphasized that this process of developing and refining data-grounded theoretical concepts and their relations also contains elements of *hypothesis examination* and *verification* (for example, Miles and Huberman, 1994: 262ff.; Strauss, 1987: 11ff.; Strauss and Corbin, 1990: 107ff.). From this perspective qualitative analysis is a series of alternating inductive and deductive steps: data-driven inductive hypothesis generation is followed by deductive hypothesis examination for the purpose of 'validation' or 'verification'.

On the other hand many qualitative methodologists devoted to a relativistic epistemology rooted in postmodernist and constructivist philosophy would object to the idea that qualitative research has anything to do with 'verification' or the 'testing of hypotheses' – after all, the concepts of hypothesis examination and verification form an integral part of standard social science methodologies which impose methodological models from the natural sciences onto social research (Denzin and Lincoln, 1994: 101). The notion of hypothesis testing has itself a long tradition in statistical analysis. In this tradition statistical hypothesis testing (or 'significance testing') is regarded as a strictly rule-governed process of assessing the statistical significance of empirical results, whereby empirically observed sample findings are compared with theoretical expectations. This comparison permits the computation of the probability that the observed outcome could be the result of mere chance. On the basis of these calculations a precisely formulated decision rule is applied: if the probability that a certain result is merely the effect of a random process is above the so-called α-level, the researcher has to reject the hypothesis.

Actually, one will find nothing comparable to these precise decision rules in the qualitative methodological literature. Instead, 'testing and confirming findings' (Miles and Huberman, 1994: 262) or 'verification' (Strauss and Corbin, 1990: 108) means: returning to the data (that is, re-reading one's transcripts or field notes), or returning to the field (that is, conducting new observations or interviews), in order to find some confirming or disconfirming evidence. *Precise* rules that are formulated to inform the researcher, with certainty, about when he or she has to reject or abandon a certain hypothesis are nowhere to be found.

The most explicit account of qualitative hypothesis examination so far has been given by Lindesmith and Cressey (Lindesmith, 1968; Cressey, 1950, 1971) in their attempt to apply the strategy of analytic induction outlined by Znaniecki (1934) to research practice.

In following Cressey's and Lindesmith's method the researcher starts by formulating a vague definition together with a hypothetical explanation of the investigated phenomenon. Thereafter a single case is examined in the light of the hypothetical explanation to determine whether the hypothesis can account for the investigated phenomenon in this case. If not, either the hypothesis has to be reformulated or the investigated phenomenon has to be redefined in such a way that the case can be excluded – of course the new definition has to be more precise than the preceding one in order to avoid the immunization of the hypothetical explanation; 'this procedure of examining cases, re-defining the phenomenon and re-formulating the hypothesis is continued until a universal relationship is established, each negative case calling for a re-definition or re-formulation' (Cressey, 1971: 16).

Most important for this process is the search for 'crucial cases' (Lindesmith, 1968: 15) which are cases where the chance that the researcher will find counter-evidence is expected to be high. Like crucial experiments these crucial cases are intended to permit a systematic examination of the developing theory. Thus, analytic induction in the form presented by Lindesmith and Cressey is a fallibilistic strategy in the Popperian tradition of critical realism, whereby the researcher systematically exposes his or her hypothesis to the possibility of failure.

Of course this method of qualitative hypothesis examination differs greatly from the concept of statistical hypothesis testing mentioned above, since it cannot be regarded as the application of a set of precisely defined rules. Furthermore, the empirical material not only serves as the basis for making a decision about the rejection or acceptance of a hypothesis, but also as an information source for the generation, refinement and modification of new and existing hypotheses. Consequently, it can be seen as a heuristic framework that provides researchers with general rules about how to develop a theory via the successive refinement of working hypotheses. Although Lindesmith and Cressey actually neglect the process of initial hypothesis formation and development, their strategy can be easily included among those methodologies of hypothesis generation and theory construction that are widely used in qualitative research (for example it could be used as one possible practical application of the somewhat vaguely defined concept of verification in grounded theory).

It is in this area of qualitative hypothesis examination and refinement where researchers can draw the greatest benefits from *computer-aided methods* for the coding and retrieval of textual data. If qualitative data were not organized and structured, the search for evidence or counter-evidence would be a practically insurmountable task: every time a researcher examines a certain hypothesis he or she would have to re-read several hundred, or several thousand transcript pages. This would make it very difficult to withstand the temptation to 'validate' theoretical concepts with some hastily gathered quotations, thereby neglecting negative evidence contained elsewhere in the data. On the contrary, the use of storage-and-retrieval methods can go a long way towards helping to avoid these dangers that are always prevalent in qualitative analysis due to the ever-present data overload.

In the following chapters computational and methodological aspects of the use of computerized methods of data organization for qualitative hypothesis examination will be discussed. In Chapter 8 Ernest Sibert and Anne Shelly give a detailed account of the logical and computational foundations of computer-assisted hypothesis examination. The authors emphasize that two distinctions are crucial to understanding the possible role of computational logic in the qualitative research process: the distinction between conceptual and mechanical tasks of data analysis on the one hand, and that between inductive and deductive parts of the research process on the other. As Sibert and Shelly point out, the use of computer algorithms is strictly limited to the *mechanical* tasks and to *deductive* reasoning.

Referring to Herbrand's and Skolem's works in the domain of logical fundamentals of computer science that had established the mechanizability of deductive inference, the authors give a short and informative overview of the foundations of logic programming and then go on to discuss the application of logic programming to qualitative hypothesis examination. Thus their chapter will foster the understanding of the underlying computational logic of hypothesis examination. This understanding will be extremely helpful if a programming language like PROLOG is used (either to extend the analytical functions offered by a program like AQUAD, or if the researcher wishes to construct an expert system for computer-assisted qualitative hypothesis examination from scratch).

The basis for such an expert system would be the construction of a knowledge base containing information about what codes are connected to which parts of the textual database. In examining his or her hypotheses the researcher has to break them down in such a way that a query to the knowledge base can be conducted, which means that assumptions about the phenomenon under investigation have to be transformed into a query about the (co-)occurrence of certain codes.

To illustrate this process with an example: after having read hundreds of pages of narrative interviews a biographical researcher studying the impact of critical events on the life course gains the impression that adolescents tend to speak more about the inner experiences accompanying a critical life event, whereas older people more often report the different events and incidents that took place. If the textual data are coded according to critical life events (and if, of course, the database contains some information about the respondent's age), the researcher can start to examine the hypothesis by retrieving all segments from interviews with adolescents to which the code critical life event has been attached. The same could be done with the older people's interviews and the results could then be compared.

But in the framework of a database system based on logic programming as proposed by Sibert and Shelly, far more complex retrieval facilities could be developed: retrieval facilities that inform the researcher about the co-occurrence of text segments to which certain codes have been attached and which also retrieve these segments. Using such facilities, the researcher in our example can, for example, examine the hypothesis that people who talk about critical life events also talk about emotional disturbances. By using the knowledge base system, this hypothesis would be transformed into a query about all co-occurrences of text segments coded as critical life event with segments coded as emotional disturbance.

It is of course essential for this type of analysis to determine what is regarded as a 'co-occurrence'. Using an expert system of the kind discussed, the researcher mentioned above could, for example, search for the following kinds of co-occurrences:

1. text segments coded as critical life event *overlap* with text segments coded as emotional disturbance,
2. text segments coded as emotional disturbance are *embedded* or *nested* into text segments coded as critical life event,
3. text segments coded as critical life event appear within a *specified maximum distance* of text segments coded as emotional disturbance,
4. text segments coded as critical life event are *followed* by segments coded as emotional disturbance.

The use of Boolean operators ('AND', 'OR', 'NOT' – for more details see p. 194 in Chapter 14) is of great importance for this process, since they can be employed in searching for overlapping and embedded text segments. If the operator 'AND' is used to link two codes in a search (for example, search for code critical life event AND code emotional disturbance), all text segments to which both codes are attached will be retrieved. If two codes are linked in a query through the operator 'OR', all text segments coded with at least one of these codes will be retrieved. When using the operator 'NOT', all passages to which a certain code is not attached are retrieved. In hypothesis examination the operator 'NOT' is of particular importance: to examine our hypothesis it is not only crucial to look for co-occurrences of the two codes (critical life events AND emotional disturbance), but also to investigate those cases where a critical life event is mentioned by the respondent, but there are no hints in the text of emotional disturbances (critical life event AND NOT emotional disturbance).

However, if such a strategy of hypothesis examination is applied the critical methodological question would be: in which way does the co-occurrence of codes provide the analyst with information about a certain hypothesis? Does the mere fact of co-occurrence lead to the rejection or acceptance of a hypothesis, or is it only used to retrieve the original text segments which are regarded as the basis for the decision on the hypothesis examined? In the following chapters two possible strategies are presented which answer these questions in quite different ways.

1. The search for co-occurring codes conducted with the help of a deduction system is used as a *heuristic device*: the purpose of querying the knowledge system would be to retrieve the original text to which the co-occurring codes are attached. Now the researcher attempts to answer the question about the meaning of a certain co-occurrence by a thorough analysis of the original text. Has the emotional arousal mentioned by respondent X something to do with the critical life event he describes? This is the strategy proposed by Sibert and Shelly. The acceptance of a hypothesis or its rejection (which leads to its further refinement) is not the result of the application of an algorithm (that is, of a strictly rule-governed process) but is a result of the researcher's interpretation. This corresponds to Lindesmith's and Cressey's method of analytic induction, whereby the interpretive analysis of interview texts or observations forms the basis for the researcher's decision about a certain hypothesis, and the empirical material, that is, the textual data, also serves as an information source for generating, refining and modifying hypotheses.

2. Alternatively, the mere fact of a co-occurrence is itself regarded as evidence or counter-evidence for a certain hypothesis. If the researcher proceeds in this way a deduction system of the kind described by Sibert and Shelly could really function as a *hypothesis tester* making the process of qualitative hypothesis examination similar to that in statistical analysis. This method is described by Sharlene Hesse-Biber and Paul Dupuis in Chapter 9. The researcher formulates his or her hypothesis as a 'production rule' in the form of a series of 'if-then' statements of the kind: '*If* a code A AND a code B AND a code C are present in a certain document, *then* the hypothesis can be accepted.' In executing these production rules against the knowledge base, the hypothesis tester reports on the success or failure of a given hypothesis in each document. The primary purpose of querying the knowledge base is not to provide the researcher with text segments but to use the information contained within it as a basis for decision-making. Similar to statistical significance testing, the decision-making process is strictly rule-governed and hence algorithmic. However, as Hesse-Biber and Dupuis make clear, there are certain methodological requirements and limitations to the use of such a hypothesis tester for qualitative hypothesis examination (analogous to the mathematical requirements and limitations that must be observed in applying statistical significance tests). The applicability of a mechanical hypothesis tester for the purpose of qualitative hypothesis examination depends vitally upon the type of codes employed (for more details on different types of codes see Chapter 4). Directionality of codes

(coding for the positive or negative support of a concept) is critical, since the codes must represent Boolean facts if the deduction system is to produce meaningful results. Furthermore, the reliability of the codes used is of utmost importance. In addition, the readability of the rule set as a formal specification of a hypothesis is enhanced or diminished by the choice of wording for codes. Apart from this, the authors discuss further preconditions for using an automatic hypothesis tester in qualitative research.

It is worth mentioning here, that with these two approaches two different conceptualizations of the notion 'hypothesis' come into play: for Hesse-Biber and Dupuis a hypothesis is a logically stated proposition about the presence, absence or relationship of certain facts. For Sibert and Shelly a hypothesis can also be more of a vague idea about the relations between two or more concepts, represented by codes.

In Chapter 10 Günter Huber relates techniques of automatized deduction to qualitative theory building. The author argues that it is important to differentiate between two general *'blueprints'* for theory building: a concept-driven *'blueprint for reconstruction'*, whereby the researcher defines the building blocks (that is, the empirical regularities) of the developing theory beforehand, and a data-driven *'assembly blueprint'*, whereby building blocks are discovered in the empirical material.

According to Huber these building blocks can be operationalized as linkages and configurations of code categories. In the research process, the role of a deduction system to help with the search for co-occurrences will vary according to whether the researcher uses the blueprint for reconstruction or the assembly blueprint. In the reconstruction blueprint 'backwards' deduction facilitates an examination of linkages in the text which were previously stated by the researcher. Within the framework of the assembly blueprint, the deduction system would help to find possible linkages. In this way the co-occurrences of codes can also be used as a basis for hypothesis generation, as Huber points out. Furthermore, the author shows how the method of logical minimization (also described in Chapter 13) relates to qualitative hypothesis examination and how it can be integrated into qualitative theory building. In particular this chapter will appeal to a reader interested in the practical application of deduction systems, since many informative and comprehensive examples from research practice are given.

The discussion about the potential merits and dangers of computer-aided qualitative hypothesis examination has not yet really begun. Given the great variety of epistemological standpoints in the qualitative community and the different attitudes towards the role of concepts (such as 'verification' or 'hypothesis') that originally came from mainstream social science methodology, one can expect this discussion to become highly controversial. The purpose of the following chapters is to make this an informed debate by providing explicit and detailed accounts of how the researcher proceeds when employing computer-aided methods of hypothesis examination.

8

Using Logic Programming for Hypothesis Generation and Refinement

Ernest Sibert and Anne Shelly

This chapter introduces logic programming as a potentially powerful computing environment for qualitative researchers. Logic programming, a type of symbolic computation, is characterized as formalizing natural language and human reasoning. We discuss the theoretical underpinnings of the logical programming system and its application to the mechanical tasks of the inductive-deductive cycles of qualitative data analysis. The chapter emphasizes two complements of qualitative research and logic programming: first, the use of symbols (that is, including but not restricted to numbers) and, second, the use of deductive inference.

Methodological processes of qualitative analysis

From the beginnings of qualitative research there has been a concern that the methodology is largely unexplored, undescribed and, thus, unshared. The operations of qualitative analysis tend to remain implicit; they may not be well-documented, hence they are generally not reported.

Miles and Huberman argue the need to 'make explicit the procedures and thought processes that qualitative researchers actually use in their work' (1984b: 22). The difficulties of such explicitness are one reason why *documentation* continues to be a recognized need and an unresolved problem. Documenting the analysis first of all requires the labelling and defining of the products of the analyst's procedures (for example, code categories, working hypotheses) and, secondly, describing how those products were generated (for example, what text segments were grouped together and why?). Documentation techniques, that is, those techniques which identify the set of products and describe how they were generated (and thus document the evolutionary process of analysis), must reflect the perspective and assumptions upon which the methodology rests. In the context of qualitative analysis, documentation means accounting for the cognitive evolution of the study; that is, providing a chronological account of the researcher's conceptual activities and associated mechanical tasks during the study. In addition, qualitative documentation must be consistent with the expansive, exploratory, data-grounded, inference-based characteristics of the methodology, and must have the flexibility to accommodate many types of data, many structures for entering and retrieving information about data, and many options for recording the tasks of an inference-based, evolutionary analysis process.

A documentation system for *computer-aided qualitative analysis* surely must incorporate:

1. a *database* with structure and content unique to the focus of the study and to the methodological perspective of the researcher, and
2. a researcher-developed *knowledge base*, generated inductively and containing a variety of abstract representations of the data.

By *knowledge base* we mean all of the researcher's interpretations of the data which have been entered in a systematic way so as to be accessible for computation. The coding information is a major component of the knowledge base, but we stress that other information may be included as well, sometimes a great deal of other information. All information in the knowledge base may be used in computations leading to text retrieval or for other purposes. While the ultimate aim of computations involving the knowledge base is generally text retrieval, we recognize that computations will not always lead directly to retrieval, but may simply report information deduced from the knowledge base.

Employing the above terminology, a qualitative researcher may proceed by:

1. building a database consisting of prose text (but potentially incorporating video or audio recordings, images, or some combination of these as well;[1]
2. building a knowledge base of information about the data consisting of associations (linkages) of text segments with particular codes and of information related to participants, sites, processes and ideas associated with the phenomena under study,
3. writing memoranda to record patterns, hunches, memory-joggers and working hypotheses;
4. manipulating the knowledge-base information to retrieve many varieties of text segments; and
5. using the varieties of text segments to support, reject or refine the increasingly abstract representations of the data which eventually lead to descriptions, principles, or theories.

When making analysis decisions the analyst combines *conceptual tasks* and *mechanical tasks* (Shelly, 1984). Traditionally, mechanical tasks in qualitative research are those activities by which the researcher stores, organizes and retrieves data. Conceptual tasks are those activities by which the researcher groups and labels data, then generates inferences from the data to move to a broader understanding of the phenomena under study. A researcher generates hypotheses (a conceptual task), groups and labels (that is, codes) data around topics related to his or her hypotheses (a conceptual task), then organizes and retrieves data (mechanical tasks) to generate inferences from the data (a conceptual task).

Mechanical tasks have generally been considered the mindless, routine, but necessary tasks of qualitative research. They are also those tasks which are mechanizable within computing environments. It is clear that storage and management of the database are mechanizable. Through the use of computer programs which perform more complex symbolic computations, researchers can not only retrieve text segments, but also write symbolic expressions to *build* and *manipulate a knowledge base* containing information about the data, and *use mechanized deduction* to identify text segments which represent the implicit content of the knowledge base.

In the traditional definitions of mechanical and conceptual tasks, deduction is a conceptual task because it is an activity by which the researcher generates inferences. With the advent of symbolic computing, deduction is a mechanical task because it can be mechanized. Thus, we use the following definitions of conceptual and mechanical tasks:

- *Conceptual tasks* are those tasks by which the researcher generates the products of the analysis process. Through reading, questioning, categorizing, inferring by induction and generalizing, the researcher generates coding categories, relationships, generalizations and perhaps theories. These products are generated for the purpose of conceptualizing constructs in the data at higher levels of abstraction.

- *Mechanical tasks* are those tasks by which the researcher manipulates the products of the analysis process. The researcher stores, organizes and retrieves data by using coding categories. The researcher deduces (that is, makes deductive inferences about) the validity of relationships, generalizations or theories by re-examining the data. These products are manipulated for the purpose of organizing and reorganizing the data which is the basis, the grounding, of the conceptual tasks.

Combining these processes, the researcher progresses from concrete data to abstract representations of the data. Figure 8.1 is a representation of these processes.

For example, coding data is a combination of mechanical and

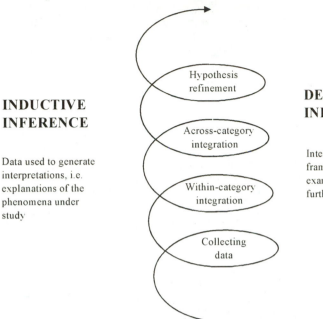

**INDUCTIVE
INFERENCE**

Data used to generate
interpretations, i.e.
explanations of the
phenomena under
study

**DEDUCTIVE
INFERENCE**

Interpretations used
frame the focus for
examining the data
further

Figure 8.1   *The induction-deduction spiral*

conceptual tasks. When the researcher codes a particular text segment
he or she ascribes some label to that piece of text. The label is a freely
chosen word or phrase, used consistently and systematically to categorize specified text segments as a pattern or focus associated with the
studied phenomenon. After this conceptual activity, the researcher
records the association of that label and that text segment for future
use. In within-category integration (Glaser and Strauss, 1967), the
researcher gathers together all text segments which are members of a
particular category and defines that category by inferring the criterial
attributes of the selected text segments. Thus, the researcher develops a
working definition (that is, a properties list) of the category through an
examination of its illustrations (that is, the text segments representing
the category).

After the definition is developed, the researcher examines new text
segments for their fit to the category by matching them against the
attributes, that is, the working definition. This activity is a deductive-
inference loop in the process of induction. The researcher uses the
code-category definition as a lens to examine additional data, which in
turn serves as the researcher's basis for refining the definition. Figure
8.2 is a representation of these processes.

Database

Knowledge Base

Data collected from:
observation,
participant(s) talk,
visual/audio media

Researcher's
representations
of the data

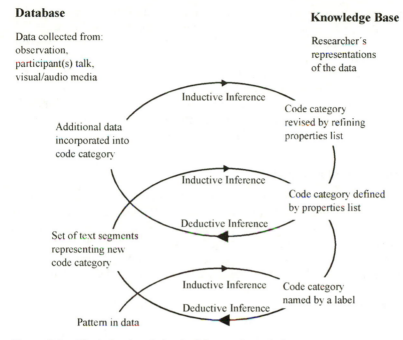

Inductive Inference

Additional data
incorporated into
code category

Code category
revised by refining
properties list

Inductive Inference

Code category defined
by properties list

Deductive Inference

Set of text segments
representing new
code category

Inductive Inference

Code category
named by a label

Deductive Inference

Pattern in data

Figure 8.2   *The induction-deduction/abstraction spiral*

The mechanical process of recording code-category membership builds a knowledge base consisting of information about the data. Such code associations are the principal part of the researcher's knowledge base. With their relevant category properties lists, they become the basis for hypothesis generation and refinement.

When the researcher develops a working hypothesis, he or she will want to explore it (or aspects of it) by examining data represented by combinations of knowledge-base information. Using some systematic method for queries which relate knowledge-base information back to the data, the researcher can identify and retrieve text segments relevant to the working-hypothesis focus.

Data retrieval is accomplished in two steps. First, by querying the knowledge base and second, by requesting the data associated with the answers to the query. It is rare that queries and resulting responses derived from the knowledge base satisfy the researcher's purpose. Text-segment frequency counts or locational information are generally insufficient. The researcher's purpose requires actual examination of those data. Without this step, the researcher has engaged in deductive inference only to the extent of identifying potentially useful data, but has failed to follow through to the point of determining how the text segments thus identified inform the refinement of the working hypothesis (that is, provide the basis for new inductive inferences).

Refining the working hypothesis by shifting one's focus on it is common during analysis; examining data from one focus inevitably leads to the need to reorganize the data, that is, to view the data through a slightly (or significantly) different lens. Thus, the cycle of inductive-deductive inferencing continues until the researcher is satisfied that the data offer no new insights and that the explanations are sufficiently generalizable across all the data.

The nature of logic programming

We suggest that logic programming offers computing facilities well-suited to the documentation needs of qualitative researchers. As a type of symbolic computation, it provides a computing environment for manipulating symbols (including but not limited to numbers), thus allowing researchers to express data and to apply computations in terms (that is, a language) that are consistent with the problem under study.

Logic programming is characterized as formalizing natural language and human reasoning (Kowalski, 1982). It has been used for some time as a language in which computer programming specifications are written. Recent work with logic programming has produced a variety of programming systems which emphasize the use of natural language and deductive reasoning (Clark and Tarnlund, 1982; Kowalski, 1979). Using logic programming, a researcher can enter data in natural language (as opposed to numbers), can build a knowledge base containing information about the data, and can request answers to queries about that information. Through logic computations, which are a type of symbolic computation, the system can make deductions which yield the explicit and implicit content of the knowledge base (Robinson and Sibert, 1984).

From the time of Aristotle, logic has been studied as an attempt to capture, in a formal way, something of the essence of rational human thought. Any system of logic requires two things: a notation or language for expressing statements, and one or more rules of inference for defining the elementary steps by which new statements are deduced from old. For example, the rule of inference traditionally known as *modus ponens* is expressed as:

From: A
and: if A then B
conclude: B

where A and B are any statements. It is characteristic of logical systems that the rules of inference depend on the forms of the statements, not on their substance. A deduction, then, consists simply of a sequence of such elementary steps beginning with a collection of initial statements assumed to be true (that is, the assertions) and leading to a conclusion. Deductions are based on form, and thus are purely symbolic operations, independent of the substance. Logic programming mechanizes these symbolic operations; it is an instance of mechanized deduction, which is a kind of symbolic computation.

The earliest suggestion that deductive reasoning could in fact be mechanized seems to have been made by G.W. Leibniz (1646–1716), co-inventor with Newton of differential and integral calculus. Although Leibniz proposed both a 'calculus of reason' and an accompanying 'universal language', he seems to have made only a fragmentary beginning on the first and had little more than a hope for the second.

It was not until the nineteenth century that mathematical logic began to be developed in its modern form, and only in the decade 1920–30 that the work of Skolem (1928) and Herbrand (1971/1930) finally established that deduction could indeed be mechanized. Subsequent study of methods for mechanizing deduction has been based largely on the work of Skolem and Herbrand, and has, in the past thirty years, grown into a substantial sub-area of computer science known as 'computational logic'. The central problem of computational logic is that of developing computer programs which can prove logical theorems. Computer scientists have worked to develop a program which, given hypotheses and a conclusion, all expressed in suitable formal notation, will establish that the conclusion follows logically from the hypotheses if the conclusion is indeed a consequence of the hypotheses.

This approach to programming actually arose from a revolutionary development in the study of mechanized deduction known as the resolution principle (Robinson, 1965). While resolution was originally developed in order to attack the general theorem-proving problem, and was an enormous improvement over previous methods, resolution-based programs still suffered from performance difficulties. Subsequent developments in resolution (Green, 1969; Colmerauer et al., 1973) led to the realization that by restricting the forms in which problems were expressed it was possible to implement much faster theorem-provers, and that these could form the basis of a programming methodology (Kowalski, 1974).

Current logic programming systems work with hypotheses expressed as statements of the form:

$$B \text{ if } A_1 \text{ and } \ldots \text{ and } A_n$$
or, in the special case $n = 0$,
$$B$$

where B, A_1 . . . A_n are primitive relational statements (that is, not complex statements constructed from logical connectives such as 'or', 'not', 'if').

We can illustrate this with an adaptation of the well-known syllogism: 'All men are mortal. Socrates is a man. Therefore Socrates is mortal.' The notation used here is that of LOGLISP (Robinson and Sibert, 1984), the logic programming system used throughout this discussion; it is a notation derived from LISP (McCarthy et al., 1965; Meehan, 1979).

```
(I– (Person Socrates))
ASSERTED
(I– (Mortal $x) <– (Person $x))
ASSERTED
(THE $x (Mortal $x))
Socrates
```

In the first line, we assert that 'Socrates is a person'. Here I– means 'it is the case that' and **(Person Socrates)** is a primitive relational expression, or predication, in which we have chosen to use **Person** as the relation, or predicate symbol with **Socrates**, which is a proper name, as the subject.

The computer responds with **ASSERTED**, indicating that the statement has been recorded. In the next entry, we assert the more complex statement that '**$x** is mortal if **$x** is a person', that is, 'all persons are mortal'. Here **$x** is a logic variable, which may be replaced by any appropriate expression. We follow the convention that symbols beginning with the character **$** are logic variables, one of a number of conventions allowed by logic programming for distinguishing variables from other symbols.

With these two assertions recorded in the computer, we enter a query requesting 'the thing **$x** such that **$x** is mortal', and the computer responds with **Socrates**, thus:

```
(THE $x (Mortal $x))
Socrates
```

The answer to a query clearly is determined by the set of assertions which have been entered at the time the query is submitted. Such a set of assertions is called a knowledge base. To illustrate, we enlarge the knowledge base with a few more assertions:

```
(I– (Born Socrates (468 BC)))
(I– (Born Herbrand (1908 AD)))
```

```
(I– (Born Turing (1912 AD)))
(I– (Mortal $x) <– (Born $x $y))
```

The first three assertions state that particular persons were born in particular years. As discussed earlier, we have chosen to use the symbol **Born** to denote the relation that the person named was born in the year stated, and have chosen to express the years as parenthesized expressions containing a numeral and a symbol indicating the year and the era (that is, AD or BC). The fourth assertion states another way of deducing that something is mortal, namely, that '$x is mortal if $x was born in some year $y'. Note that in the expression (Born $x $y) the variable $y stands for an entire expression like (468 BC).

With all this added to the knowledge base, we ask which things, $p, can be shown to be mortal:

```
(ALL $p (Mortal $p))
(Socrates Herbrand Turing)
```

ALL queries yield a list of answers, in contrast to queries formed with THE, which yield a single answer. Although the example just presented is extremely simple, it does serve to illustrate some important points:

1. The researcher may freely introduce symbols to represent the concepts of the subject of interest.
2. The expressions constructed from these symbols may be structured in any convenient way by using parentheses.
3. Assertions may be simple statements of fact about individuals, but they may also be general statements (that is, rules), conditional or unconditional, which apply to many situations.
4. The system deduces answers to queries based on the assertions present in the knowledge base.

The logic interpreter (that is, the program which carries out the deductions which yield answers to queries) actually proceeds by working backward from the original query to establish the proof or proofs by which the conditions of the query can be satisfied. Thus, when asked to find all $p such that (Mortal $p), the interpreter finds two assertions which might possibly lead to the desired conclusion:

```
(I– (Mortal $x) <– (Person $x))
(I– (Mortal $x) <– (Born $x $y))
```

If we substitute $p for $x in the first of these, we see that it suffices to show (Person $p). The only assertion which applies is (I– (Person

Socrates)), and by putting Socrates for $p we obtain one proof. Similarly, using the second assertion about Mortal we see that it suffices to show (Born $p $y). Three assertions apply. Using the first, we may substitute Socrates for $p and (468 BC) for $y, thus obtaining the answer Socrates a second time. We can also put Herbrand for $p and (1908 AD) for $y to obtain the new answer Herbrand, and similarly for Turing. In fact, the interpreter has found various ways of proving that there is something $p such that (Mortal $p), and each answer is obtained as a by-product of each such proof. The form of an answer is determined by the answer template, immediately following ALL, which in this example is just the variable $p.

Queries may include a number of conditions which answers must satisfy. An answer may be a list of expressions, not just a single word. For example, to find out for which persons birth years are known, and to find out what those years are, we construct the query:

(ALL ($p $y) (Person $p) (Born $p $y))
((Socrates (468 BC)))

using ($p $y) as the answer template and (Person $p) (Born $p $y) as the conditions of the search. The computer returns (Socrates (468 BC)) as the answer. Note that Herbrand and Turing cannot be shown to be persons with the present knowledge base. If we want to take the viewpoint that Born is about persons only (and not other mammals) we can add the assertion:

(I– (Person $p) <– (Born $p $y))

then repeat the query:

(ALL ($p $y) (Person $p) (Born $p $y))
((Socrates (468 BC)) (Herbrand (1908 AD)) (Turing (1912 AD)))

this time obtaining a larger list of answers deduced from the new information.

Logic programming applied to qualitative analysis

When the researcher develops a working hypothesis, he or she wants to explore aspects of it by examining data represented by combinations of knowledge-base information. Using queries which contain formalized expressions of relationships among knowledge-base information, the researcher can identify text segments relevant to the working-hypothesis focus. By developing such queries, the researcher also documents the

conceptual associations between concrete and more abstract representations of the phenomena under study.

A query is a formalized expression of a question about a relationship
involving coding and/or file information (and/or any other information
in the knowledge base). It is the means by which the researcher invokes
the deductive capacities of logic programming; that is, the logic uses the
information in the knowledge base to deduce responses which meet the
conditions established in the query. We suggest that there is a sequence
of thought that results in the set of conditions in any query (see Figure
8.3). Our experience indicates that working hypotheses tend to be
abstractions which can be broken down into several manageable units
of analysis. We call each of these units a focus. As a sub-set of the
working hypothesis, a focus is one particular lens through which the
researcher studies the data to confirm or to refine an aspect of the
working hypothesis. A focus is also defined by the knowledge-base
information used to specify relevant data. To use the deductive capa-
bilities of logic programming, the researcher defines the focus as a set
of characteristics, then formalizes the focus as a set of conditions, that
is, knowledge-base characteristics. Using this set of conditions, the
logic identifies knowledge-base information, which in turn identifies
text segments pertinent to the current focus. These data must then be

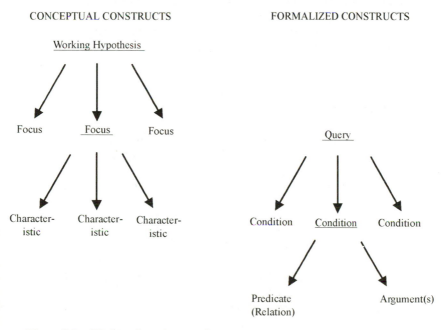

CONCEPTUAL CONSTRUCTS   FORMALIZED CONSTRUCTS

Working Hypothesis

Focus   Focus   Focus   Query

Character-   Character-   Character-   Condition   Condition   Condition
istic   istic   istic

                                                    Predicate   Argument(s)
                                                    (Relation)

Figure 8.3   *Working hypothesis and query trees*

studied for supporting evidence and/or refinement of the working hypothesis.

To illustrate, we will build a small knowledge base of code categories associated with a few well-known methodology writings:

Becker and Geer's *Participant Observation: The Analysis of Qualitative Field Data* (1960)

Bogdan and Biklen's *Qualitative Research for Education: An Introduction to Theory and Methods* (1982)

Glaser and Strauss' *The Discovery of Grounded Theory: Strategies for Qualitative Research* (1967)

Spradley's *The Ethnographic Interview* (1979)

To start, we prepare each writing as a text file, numbering the lines of text, thus creating a database of text files. Next we code these articles for patterns we label 'coding', 'decoding symbols', or 'generating working hypotheses'. Using the logic system, we define a relation Code, expressing the notion that a code category is associated with a text segment in a data file.

```
(l- (Code $file ($begin-line $end-line) $category-label))
```

In this assertion, we have structured Code as a relation involving a data file, $file, a set of lines demarcating a text segment, ($begin-line $end-line), and a code-category label, $category-label. We use the form of this relation to assert the association of code-category labels to text segments:[2]

```
(l- (Code BeckerGeer.1960 (592 657) (coding)))
(l- (Code Spradley.1979 (964 985) (decoding symbols)))
(l- (Code Spradley.1979 (5563 5594) (decoding symbols)))
(l- (Code BogdanBiklen.1982 (6951 6959) (coding)))
(l- (Code BogdanBiklen.1982 (6520 6625) (coding)))
(l- (Code GlaserStrauss.1967 (3980 4092) (coding)))
(l- (Code BeckerGeer.1960 (592 569) (generating working
hypotheses)))
(l- (Code Spradley.1979 (5111 5132) (generating working
hypotheses)))
(l- (Code BogdanBiklen.1982 (6951 6959) (generating working
hypotheses)))
(l- (Code BogdanBiklen.1982 (6582 6625) (generating working
hypotheses)))
(l- (Code GlaserStrauss.1967 (4026 4039) (generating working
hypotheses)))
```

Our sample working hypothesis is as follows: although coding and hypothesis generation may co-occur in all stages of analysis, the systematic approach to the inductive analysis process depends on working hypotheses being generated from properly integrated (that is, defined and illustrated) code categories. We break down this hypothesis into multiple focuses, such as the following:

1. It is characteristic of induction that the process of coding depends on identifying patterns in the data, not on the development of topics of interest to the researcher.
2. Coding and hypothesis generation co-occur in all stages of analysis.

For the purpose of illustration, we will examine the first focus. We start this exploration by asking for all co-occurrences of our two code categories, 'coding' and 'generating working hypotheses', defining 'co-occurrence' as a code pattern corresponding to overlapping text segments. Thus, we formalize the focus as a set of search conditions as we write the query:

```
(ALL ($file ($line-a $line-b) ($line-c $line-d))
     (Code $file ($line-a $line-b) (coding))
     (Code $file ($line-c $line-d) (generating working hypotheses))
     (Overlap ($line-a $line-b) ($line-c $line-d)))
```

which yields the answers:

```
(BeckerGeer.1960 (592 657) (592 569))
(BogdanBiklen.1982 (6951 6959) (6951 6959))
(BogdanBiklen.1982 (6620 6625) (6582 6625))
(GlaserStrauss.1967 (3980 4092) (4026 4039))
```

The ALL query asks for all answers of the form given by the 'answer template' ($file ($line-a $line-b) ($line-c $line-d)) which satisfy the two Code conditions and the Overlap condition. The Overlap condition holds just when the specified intervals have at least one line in common. Note that the labelled text segments must be in the same file. Note too that there is no answer for Spradley.1979, since it contains no text segments labelled 'coding'.

Having identified some text segments that may be relevant to the focus of current interest, we (re-)examine the data:

BeckerGeer.1960 (592 657) (592 569)
A systematic assessment of all data is necessary before we can present the content of a perspective. . . . We have tentatively identified, through sequential analysis during the field work, the major perspectives we want to present and the areas . . . to which these perspectives apply. We now go through the

summarized incidents, marking each incident with a number or numbers that stand for the various areas to which it appears to be relevant. This is essentially a coding operation . . . its object is to make sure that all relevant data can be brought to bear on a point. (Becker and Geer, 1960: 280–281)

BogdanBiklen.1982 (6951 6959) (6951 6959)
Preassigned Coding Systems. . . . researchers are sometimes employed by others to explore particular problems or aspects of a setting or subject. . . . Many evaluation research coding schemes are affected by and (at times) are a direct reflection of the agreement between the researcher's sponsors and the people conducting the research. Then the codes derive from the agreement. (Bogdan and Biklen, 1982: 162)

BogdanBiklen.1982 (6620 6625) (6582 6625)
There are three general points to make before moving on to the next section, 'Analysis after Data Collection.' Like some of the ideas and procedures we described under the heading, 'Analysis in the Field,' these points carry importance for both ongoing and final analyses.

The first point. . . . Do not be afraid to *speculate*. . . . We do not suggest that the facts and the details are not important, for ideas *must* be grounded in the data, but they are a means to clear thinking and to generating ideas, not *the end*.

Finally we suggest that while you review your data during the collection phase of research, mark them up. Jot down ideas in the margins of your field notes. Circle key words and phrases that subjects use. Underline what appear to be particularly important sections. (Bogdan and Biklen, 1982: 154–155)

GlaserStrauss.1967 (3980 4092) (4026 4039)
We wish to suggest a third approach to the analysis of qualitative data – one that combines, by an analytic procedure of constant comparison, the explicit coding procedure of the first approach and the style of theory development of the second. The purpose of the constant comparative method of joint coding and analysis is to generate theory more systematically than allowed by the second approach, by using explicit coding and analytic procedures. (Glaser and Strauss, 1967: 102)

We see that the data do not support the notion that coding must always be divorced from topics of interest to the researcher, so the first focus needs further consideration. Clearly, it would also be a mistake to assume, based merely on co-occurrences of the two code categories, that Becker and Geer describe the relationship between 'coding' and 'generating working hypotheses' in the same way as Bogdan and Biklen do. In addition, it would be a mistake to assume, based on the absence of Spradley from the list of responses, that he does not identify relationships between 'coding' and 'generating working hypotheses'. In the first case, the researcher closes the deductive inference loop by examining the actual text segments identified by the query. In the latter case, the researcher formulates additional queries to identify text segments which allow him/her to examine the hypothesis from a different focus.

It is worth pointing out again that, in the example above, the researcher is working with information about the data (that is, codes, file names, line numbers, relations) which make up the knowledge base. These are all researcher-generated representations of the data by which he or she moves to some description, principle or theory about the phenomena under study. The knowledge-base assertions are, throughout these activities, used to retrieve the actual data identified by answers to queries.

Through this illustration, we wish to emphasize that we make a distinction between using the logic system to analyse information about data and using it to facilitate data analysis. First, we use the logic to develop formally expressed queries about our knowledge base. Thus, it is appropriate to consider these queries as analyses of knowledge-base information. However, our purpose in writing queries and our interpretation of text segments derived from queries are not mechanical tasks; they remain the conceptual tasks of the researcher. Thus, we distinguish these data analysis tasks as those which are facilitated by the logic system.

Conclusion

Symbolic-computation programs offer the researcher a highly flexible computing environment:

1. for representing and storing the products of inductive inference, and
2. for expressing universal propositions about those products, that is, deductive inferences.

These products and processes comprise the qualitative researcher's operational definition of induction:

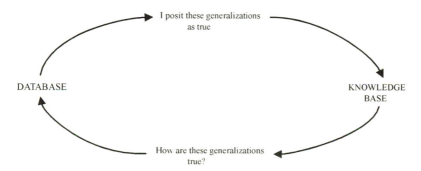

Figure 8.4   *The induction-deduction cycle*

Coupled with the researcher's memos, such documentation provides a chronological account of the researcher's conceptual activities and associated mechanical tasks. Together, these traces of the process comprise a methodological database by which a researcher can analyse his or her or another researcher's analytic journey through the induction process (Hiemstra et al., 1987; Shelly et al., 1986). Through analysis of many such methodological databases, we can begin to describe the tasks of analysis and to examine the characteristics of a methodology which is based on human judgement and inference.

Notes

1. We recognize that data may take many forms. However, to simplify the discussion we will refer to *text* with the understanding that the ideas are applicable to other forms of data as well.

2. We have not in fact constructed a database of the sort described. The line numbers in the example are only approximate.

9

Hypothesis Testing in Computer-aided Qualitative Data Analysis

Sharlene Hesse-Biber and Paul Dupuis

In this chapter a second approach to the implementation of computerized deductive reasoning in the qualitative research process will be presented. The goal of this approach is similar to that proposed in the last chapter: the examination and refinement of hypotheses – either those that the researcher has generated inductively from the data, or those that were derived from a pre-existing set of theoretical ideas about a given data set. But there is an important difference to the strategy discussed by Sibert and Shelly, who recommend the use of queries for the retrieval of text segments relevant to the hypotheses: following their approach the analyst identifies evidence or counter-evidence for his or her hypotheses by the careful examination of the original text. In contrast, we propose a strategy for information retrieval that mainly uses the information contained in the knowledge base and not the original textual data. The purpose of the automatic hypothesis tester, which we will present in this chapter in a step-by-step format using examples from our research practice, is to identify coincidences and associations between certain codes in a given document in order to confirm or disconfirm a specific hypothesis. But this strategy, in which the analyst does not use the raw data, but information about the co-occurrence of codes as supporting evidence, requires that the process of coding be conducted with special care. In particular, attention must be paid to the directionality of codes, since otherwise valid results cannot be obtained.

In the following, we will present examples for such a strategy of hypothesis testing and discuss its theoretical and data analysis implications for qualitative research.

An automatic hypothesis tester for qualitative data analysis

The strategy we propose for hypothesis testing in qualitative research requires the application of an automatic hypothesis tester which is embedded in a software environment for computer-aided qualitative data analysis. The hypothesis tester is composed of, first, a *coding component*, which allows for the coding of text segments and displays index cards for each case and, second, *searching and reporting components*, which enable the researcher to select codes by Boolean searches and output data about the codes in a report.[1]

The application of the proposed hypothesis tester requires, however, that particular attention is paid to the development of the coding scheme and its implementation. As has been pointed out in Chapters 4 and 6, a distinction must be drawn between the factual and the referential function of coding: if the referential function is in the foreground, codes are mainly used to denote a certain text passage. Most qualitative analysts use referential coding at the early stages of the analysis process, and this is often referred to as 'open coding'. At this stage the material will be coded mainly for 'topics' or 'themes' (for example, those mentioned by an interviewee). The factual information contained in such codes is often ambiguous. The code **self-image**, for example, can be used to denote text passages where the interviewee expresses a negative self-image, as well as those segments where he or she displays a very positive self-image, or may even denote those passages where the interviewee talks about other people's self-images. Since such referential codes cannot be seen as representations of facts, the researcher always has to draw on the original textual material if he or she wants to look for evidence or counter-evidence for his or her hypotheses.

If codes have been used that mainly fulfil a factual function another hypothesis testing strategy can be employed. Factual codes are codes that denote a certain fact – given the above example the code **self-image** would fulfil a factual function if it were only used in cases where an interviewee expresses, for instance, a positive self-image. In this case the information contained in the code (together with the information that a certain case is coded with this code) can represent sufficient evidence or counter-evidence for certain hypotheses. If factual coding has been conducted by computer-aided methods it is then possible to use an algorithm (an 'automatic hypothesis tester') that retrieves this information.

To ensure that the codes do indeed fulfil a factual function the first step in utilizing the hypothesis tester would be to consciously code for the presence or absence of a given phenomenon, that is to use *directional codes*, and not, as is common in qualitative analysis, to code for topic alone. The code **self-image**, used in the first example, has no consistent directional meaning, since its presence in a given case gives no hint as to whether a certain person has a positive image of him- or herself or a negative one. However, by consistently coding to include directionality, by using codes such as **positive self-image** and **negative self-image**, a hypothesis about influences on the self-image can be expressed and tested automatically. Thus, the development of directional codes can be regarded as a special form of the 'dimensionalization' of categories (Strauss and Corbin, 1990).

By treating the presence or absence of codes in a source as indicating a true or false value for that code, the program creates a *knowledge base* (made up of all the cases in the study and the individual codes for each case).

A hypothesis based on directional codes is then represented by a set of propositions stated in terms of 'if-then' statements, applicable to the created knowledge base. In the following we will call these 'if-then' statements which describe a particular theory, hypothesis, or proposition that the researcher desires to test, *production rules*. The basic form of such a production rule is that of an implication: IF some set of conditions is true, THEN infer some set of conclusions to be true. The hypothesis tester can then be used to infer new codes from existing codes. A single 'if-then' production rule describes the inference of one or more new codes, which were initially not used for coding the data directly, but inferred from the presence of other codes in the same case. In a sense, a production rule is employed to aggregate or condense the existence of several related codes into one or more new codes.

If applied to a qualitative knowledge base the production rule must take the form IF *Expression* THEN *Actions*. *Expression* is a Boolean combination of codes from the master code list that has been developed while coding the data. *Actions* is a list of instructions to add codes to or remove them from the knowledge base. This formulation of a hypothesis provides a formal mechanism for describing the inference or thought process used to draw conclusions from the data.

The following example of the implementation of a hypothesis tester in the process of qualitative analysis comes from a research project on 'Women, Weight and Body Image' (Hesse-Biber 1991). This research is based on sixty intensive interviews with college-age women concerning their weight and body image issues and the development of eating disorders. A grounded theory approach was initially utilized to generate code categories. During the initial phase of coding for this project, it became clear that a mother's attitude, in particular her criticism of her daughter's body image, was an important factor in a daughter's feelings about her self-image and the extent to which a daughter went on to develop a weight problem. From this a single production rule concerning the influence of a mother's attitudes on her daughter's body image was created.

IF Mother critical of Daughter's body image AND Mother Daughter relationship strained AND Daughter experiencing weight loss, THEN ADD Mother's negative influence on Daughter's self-image

The 'THEN' indicates the 'action'; in this case it is 'ADD'. This single rule is interpreted by the hypothesis tester as follows:

IF the code Mother critical of Daughter's body image exists in this case AND the code Mother Daughter relationship strained exists in this case AND the code Daughter experiencing weight loss exists in this case, THEN add the code Mother's negative influence on Daughter's self-image to this case.

Production rules may be also based upon codes inferred from the code list, that is, added to it by previous rules. In this manner a logical chain of proposed inferences can be developed to support the major statement of a hypothesis. An example of a second production rule based on the above may be:

IF Mother's negative influence on Daughter's self-image AND Daughter dislikes Daughter's appearance, THEN ADD Mother has damaged Daughter's self-image

This rule is also interpreted as:

IF the code Mother's negative influence on Daughter's self-image exists in this case AND the code Daughter dislikes Daughter's appearance exists in this case, THEN add the code Mother has damaged Daughter's self-image to this case.

Therefore, only if the codes Mother critical of Daughter's body image AND Mother Daughter relationship strained AND Daughter experiencing weight loss are found in the case does the hypothesis tester infer Mother's negative influence on Daughter's self-image, and only if that code is inferred and the code Daughter dislikes Daughter's appearance is present does the hypothesis tester add Mother has damaged Daughter's self-image to the case. Using multiple production rules, the researcher can construct a model of his or her theory in terms of relations between codes that is grounded in the research material.

In executing these production rules against the knowledge base, the hypothesis tester reports on the success or failure of a given hypothesis in each case in the study, and if the hypothesis failed, the hypothesis tester will report why it failed. The program will apply the rule set (hypothesis) to each case, comparing the codes used in each *Expression* (the antecedent of each rule) with the actual codes appearing in the case. If a code in the *Expression* actually appears in the case, it will be evaluated as 'true'; if not it will be evaluated as 'false'. If the entire

Expression is evaluated as 'true', then any *Actions* listed will be applied to the case. This process continues for each case until no rules can be found that apply (the antecedent is not evaluated as 'true') or until a special rule is found, which indicates success.

The hypothesis tester reports which rules were evaluated in each pass and which rules were applied, until no rules can be applied or a terminal rule (the conclusion) is applied for each case. A successful arrival at the terminal rule in a majority of cases will indicate that the hypothesis has some degree of validity. If there is a failure to arrive at the terminal rule in a majority of cases, the researcher can use this report to re-examine the original textual data to see whether materials were coded incorrectly, whether codes that should be present do not exist within the data, or whether some theoretical assumptions are erroneous.

If the method of theory building consists of strict coding with the development of theory after all coding has been accomplished, this strategy of hypothesis testing offers the researcher a tool for continuously revising and evaluating his or her theory from a complete list of all codes used in the study. For the researcher whose method focuses on the development of theory first and coding second, a fully developed hypothesis can be represented as a set of production rules expressed in the system and then 'run' to provide a report (output) with a list of the codes required to be present in each case for the hypothesis to be valid. The researcher can then turn his or her attention to validating that these codes are in fact present in the data. For researchers who use a grounded theory approach to qualitative analysis, rules can be added as new relationships among codes are discovered in the data. For a researcher working by analytical induction, hypotheses can be tested and additional coding can be performed afterwards to verify the validity of the hypothesis on more extensive data. Regardless of method, an automatic hypothesis tester can be a powerful tool for theory generation and the validation of theoretical assertions derived from qualitative data.

Implications for the qualitative researcher of using the hypothesis tester

The implementation of an automatic hypothesis tester in the research process raises a number of issues ranging from coding of text segments and researcher accountability to theory construction and generation of theoretical ideas.

The coding process: coding for directionality
As we have tried to indicate in the preceding discussion, the usefulness of the hypothesis tester for the purpose of testing logically constructed hypotheses is highly dependent upon the strategies used by the researcher

during the coding process. Directionality of codes (coding for the positive or negative support of a concept) is critical, since the codes must represent Boolean facts for the hypothesis tester to produce meaningful results. A code that references source material that neither positively nor negatively supports some fact, but serves only to mark a block of related material, is unusable for the hypothesis testing strategy outlined above. In addition, the readability of the rule set as a formal specification of a hypothesis is enhanced or diminished by the choice of wording for codes.

Making the researcher more accountable
The *ex post facto* interpretation of unstructured textual material by the researcher, a method which is at the core of qualitative analysis, has always prompted the warning that this can lead to arbitrary results. Indeed, it is often possible to develop different interpretations for a single segment of text, a fact which makes the process of independent verification very difficult. Being more explicit about the procedures used to analyse data can make secondary analysis or replication of research studies of qualitative data more feasible.

To apply a formal language for describing the reasoning chain from the codes to the researcher's conclusion would be one way to handle this problem. Hence, the strategy of hypothesis testing we have outlined in this chapter requires researchers to be more explicit in the procedures and analytical processes they went through to produce the data and the interpretations. It captures a researcher's thought process or reasoning chain about his or her theory in a step-by-step formal manner, so the researcher can share it with others. The data and coding scheme are in a convenient electronic form and can be transported to various environments. For example, a researcher can go out and do a whole different set of interviews and still work with the same master code list, so that he or she is coding for the same things.

On the problem of validity, a further advantage of the strategy outlined here is that the decision rules are based on codes and coded material and not variables, as in quantitative analysis, so that a researcher can always go back to the text to discern its original meaning, as opposed to, in quantitative research, going back to a variable whose meaning has already been taken out of context. Thus, an automated strategy of hypothesis testing holds out the promise and peril of enabling qualitative researchers to answer the question of how confident they are in their analysis (that is, do they really have the core categories right? Are the categories detailed?).

Assisting the process of theory generation
The use of the hypothesis tester also supports the researcher in theory generation by allowing many propositions to be tested with relatively

low costs in terms of time and money. But this can also have a problematic impact on the research process. The ability of a hypothesis testing program to ascertain quickly the number of cases which support a hypothesis, or set of hypotheses, can easily seduce some researchers into using such a tool for the sake of data dredging.

Furthermore, the application of an automatic hypothesis tester of the kind we have described above may require the establishment of something akin to significance levels for qualitative analysis, something that qualitative researchers have largely avoided dealing with up until now. Nevertheless, as Barton and Lazarsfeld (1974) have already pointed out, many qualitative researchers have been using the terms 'some', 'many' or 'few' to signify when a theme is prevalent or not prevalent in their data (see also Lazarsfeld, 1972). But the use of such a vague 'quasi-statistical terminology' always raises questions like: in how many cases did the hypothesis hold up? Should a qualitative researcher apply significance tests to qualitative data? When, if at all, is this appropriate? On the other hand, we must ask ourselves whether we are falsely applying the logic of quantitative research to qualitative research when we pose such questions. One must keep in mind that some qualitative researchers would argue that even the single occurrence of a given phenomenon can be theoretically important (see Seidel, 1991: 113). These scholars would argue that the fact that this theme is not supported quantitatively by the data is applying the logic of quantitative analysis to qualitative data. It must be emphasized here that the quantification of qualitative data can enhance its validity only if one is careful about how this is conducted. Counting themes or categories in the data always needs to be linked to the respondent's own method of ordering the world (gathered from qualitative analysis). As Silverman notes: 'The aim is not to count for counting's sake, but in order to establish a thoughtful dialogue with qualitatively-derived insights about the setting and actors' version of the situation at hand' (1985: 148).

But if the analyst proceeds properly, quantification will offer the opportunity to assess the representativeness of the data as a whole. Researchers will then be able to tighten their analysis and perhaps specify more clearly the application of their research findings to the data (Silverman, 1985).

Note

1. The authors have developed the software program HyperRESEARCH, which represents a technical application of the automatic hypothesis tester presented in this chapter. Chapter 14 contains more details of the program.

10

Qualitative Hypothesis Examination and Theory Building

Günter L. Huber

This chapter describes how strategies of computer-assisted hypothesis examination and refinement relate to the process of theory building in qualitative research. For practical reasons it is assumed that the first steps of qualitative analysis have already been conducted; that is, the content of specific text passages has been reduced to categories and labelled with appropriate codes. Additionally, it is assumed that the consistency of the decisions that underlie the allocation of the codes has already been checked. However, it should be clear from the preceding chapters that there is no logical restriction on theory building that says it has to be performed during a particular phase of the qualitative analysis. Indeed, when concentrating on theory building the qualitative researcher has already been supplied with a number of notes or 'memos' about specific code patterns that caught the analyst's eye when they were reading and coding the database.

Blueprints for theory building

In all empirical sciences, theory building proceeds from descriptive or categorial analysis of a set of phenomena and the postulation or observation of some kind of regularity, to statements tentatively explaining these relations. Whether the result is a taxonomic order, a correlational matrix or a causal model of the phenomena under study, this process can be conceived of as a further step of reduction leading to higher levels of abstraction. The essentials become visible by 'abstracting away . . . all the accidental elements of the real world' (Galtung, 1990: 98).

There are, of course, fundamentally different approaches to researching the 'real world'. I will refer to the pattern of principles or rules guiding these approaches as a 'blueprint', as a plan of action for achieving insights into the regularities of the phenomenon under scrutiny. These regularities are then used as construction units or 'building blocks', when the researcher tries to build an adequate theory of the phenomenon he or she is interested in. Two types of blueprint can be distinguished: the blueprint for reconstruction and the assembly blueprint.

The blueprint for reconstruction

- A study using a *blueprint for reconstruction* would define its 'construction rules' by focusing on a small number of general assumptions. These rules would then be applied in the search for building blocks (regularities) in the area being studied.
- Reconstruction is realized by deduction, and tentatively explaining or predicting specific properties.
- The end product of a reconstruction study would be a report accentuating how the reconstruction rules were tested and what the results were.

The assembly blueprint

- An approach using an *assembly blueprint* would try to reveal the specific properties of potential building blocks in the field and to find their distinguishing and/or shared characteristics.
- Assembly is realized by induction.
- The assembly study would inform the researcher which parts had been found, how they were identified as parts of what, and how they were finally assembled.

With the results of either an assembly or reconstruction study, the researcher would then construct a theory to explain the observed phenomenon. The differences in the methods that the two approaches use to arrive at a final report, and the consequences of these differences, are best illustrated by the controversy between Glaser (1992) (representing the assembly blueprint approach) and Strauss and Corbin (1990) (representing the reconstruction blueprint approach). In order to establish connections between coding categories, the latter authors introduce 'axial coding' as a 'set of procedures whereby data are put back together in new ways . . . by making connections between categories. This is done by utilizing a coding paradigm involving conditions, context, action/interactional strategies and consequences' (Strauss and Corbin, 1990: 96). Glaser's 'theoretical coding families emerge as connections between categories and their properties. If one category is a condition of a property, then this will emerge as such' (Glaser, 1992: 62).

Whereas researchers using the reconstruction approach decide in advance which coding family to apply, or in other words which kind of relations between codes to reconstruct from the building blocks analysed in the database, users of the assembly method have to remain 'theoretically sensitive' (Glaser, 1978) and constantly compare specific statements and emerging general concepts, asking under which broader class this statement could be subsumed and whether the conditions for applying the more abstract concept are given in this case.

Another difference between the two types of blueprints has to do with idiographic vs. nomothetic orientations. The idiographic perspective focuses on single cases, for example on revealing the tacit personality theory of a person in charge of a company's career decisions. Comparing several single-case analyses may lead to a typology of individually held personality theories. From the nomothetic perspective, theory building is achieved by generalizing over a large number of people, situations or events. Miles and Huberman (1984a) and Huberman and Miles (1985) established the interrelation of both approaches as well as the cyclic interrelation of inductive and deductive operations most lucidly in their description of the inferential component and verification in qualitative data analysis. They underline that qualitative analysis of a single case or a local context not only describes in great detail 'what happens within it, but is particularly well prepared to develop explanations, i.e., to disclose the rules and reasons that determine why things happen the way they do' (Miles and Huberman, 1984a: 132). This 'local causality' is only significant, however, within the boundaries of case-specific conditions. Given the database for across-case analysis, it seems possible to obtain generalizable explanations.

In summary, it may be concluded that the goal of establishing systematic relationships between categorized data segments can be attained by a variety of strategies. However, the strategy chosen is not a matter of personal routines or preferences, but depends on the research question. For example, in an ongoing study we observed how groups of three students handled their learning tasks. If we had been primarily interested in generating hypotheses about learning processes in team situations, we would have tried to identify meaningful segments in our field notes and assign them to an appropriate category. Then we would have looked for recurring sequences of codes, signalling regularities among our categories. Finally we would have tried to assemble these patterns of occurrences by means of more abstract categories, gradually clarifying an emerging hypothesis. On the other hand, we could have started with a theory of group decision-making in mind and tried to apply it to the learning situations observed. During the coding phase we would have looked primarily for segments of the field notes exemplifying the interaction incidents which we deduced from the theory guiding our efforts. This theory would also supply us with the appropriate categories and code labels. During the stage of theory building we would have tried to find supporting evidence in the form of co-occurrences of these codes which had been predicted by our general theory.

However, in both approaches it is always a good idea to keep an eye on the other type of blueprint. When trying to build theories, the researcher will not be able to completely rely on either the data given or on pre-established concepts and constructs. Indeed, without at least tacitly borrowing from everyday and professional constructs of learning, groups, communication, decision-making, etc., a purely data-driven assembly approach would be in danger of either getting lost in a mass of tiny pieces of evidence for something (but what?), or of ending up with some huge, immobile parts representing highly formalistic categories. In order to proceed from a conceptually-driven starting point, the researcher must be able to make sense of concrete data in the light of abstract constructs, that is, to illustrate them by some empirical knowledge. Therefore, software supporting theory building in qualitative analysis should offer tools for both data- and theory-driven orientations and for within-case as well as across-case applications.

Blueprints and software tools

In a chapter about different types of qualitative analysis Tesch (1990) distinguishes between structural and interpretational analysis. The first group of approaches seek to create 'models that mirror the structure of the phenomenon under study, such as events, interactions, language usage, or the organization of cultural knowledge'; the second group is 'characterized as research whose purpose is to discover regularities and as research that is meaning-oriented' (Tesch, 1990: 98). In view of the focus here on theory building, I will concentrate on interpretational analysis without elaborating on the sometimes fuzzy distinctions between orientations toward regularity vs. meaning of data. Instead, the operation of comparing and contrasting, which is the main intellectual tool for both interpretational orientations (Glaser, 1978; Tesch, 1990), is differentiated in two ways:

- *the analysis of linkages* builds upon the identification of critical elements in the database, for which the researcher tries 'to discern a structure . . . either as a pattern or as a network of relationships' (Tesch, 1990: 60);
- *the analysis of configurations* is based on commonalities across the cases while at the same time respecting their uniqueness (see Tesch, 1990).

Although several cases may display a particular theme, this theme will only be related to other commonalities of these cases in specific contexts. In many studies commonalities in terms of cause–effect relations are of special interest. By means of comparing configurations it is possible to formulate causal statements that 'account for the differences among instances of a certain outcome . . . determining the different contexts in which a cause has an impact' (Ragin, 1987: 167).

Software tools that assist in linkage analysis may be used for reconstruction and assembly approaches to theory building, although their functions differ within the underlying cycle of deduction and induction. Configuration analysis and its software tools on the other hand clearly serve analytic ends, however, without destroying the wholeness of individual cases. The tools and tables shown here are taken from the English version of the software package AQUAD IV (Huber, 1994; for more details see Chapter 14) for the analysis of qualitative data.

Theory building by linkage analysis

In the debate about using computer technology for assisting with qualitative analysis, the term 'linkage' generally refers to any connection between the elements of the qualitative database (for more details see the Introduction to Part II). However, in this context it will be exclusively focused on linkages between codes. 'Linkage analysis' as it is proposed here is conducted by searching for regularities, or patterns of codes, for instance in the form of repeatedly co-occurring codes. These regularities are regarded as signals for correlational or even causal links between the information in the text segments referred to by the 'linked' codes. In other words, these co-occurrences of coded text segments in the database indicate linkages between codes.

Context analysis or distance analysis
An analysis of linkages through the search for co-occurring codes starts with a distance analysis. In this all text segments belonging to a particular, critical category (that is, with a particular code) are identified and then a search is made for text segments belonging to other categories that can be found in the vicinity of the critical text segments. As an example I refer to an analysis of biographical interviews, where the focus was on how interviewees cope with critical life events, that is, sudden changes in the course of their lives. Table 10.1 shows a small part of the results of a distance analysis which identified all text segments beginning within a distance of ten lines from the end of text segments belonging to the category critical life event (cle). In the following I will no longer refer in detail to text segments and categories, but only to the codes which were attached to these segments, because all analyses were performed in the software package AQUAD, primarily with these codes.

The example starts with text file bios1. The code cle, which has been chosen as the focal code (the code on which the analysis focuses), appears for the first time between lines 22 and 23. The program gathers together all other coded text segments beginning within a defined distance (ten lines) from line 23.

Table 10.1   *Distance analysis: codes in the vicinity of* cle

Retrieval of codes – particular structures: code distances

CODE FILE bios1

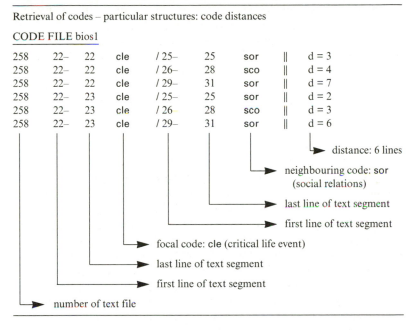

258	22–	22	cle	/ 25–	25	sor	‖	d = 3
258	22–	22	cle	/ 26–	28	sco	‖	d = 4
258	22–	22	cle	/ 29–	31	sor	‖	d = 7
258	22–	23	cle	/ 25–	25	sor	‖	d = 2
258	22–	23	cle	/ 26	28	sco	‖	d = 3
258	22–	23	cle	/ 29–	31	sor	‖	d = 6

distance: 6 lines

neighbouring code: sor
(social relations)

last line of text segment

first line of text segment

focal code: cle (critical life event)

last line of text segment

first line of text segment

number of text file

When the focal code cle appears for the first time in bios1, its context seems to be characterized by **social relations (sor)**, in other words the critical life events are coupled primarily with social relations. As there is no conceptual condition for the selection of neighbouring codes, just the formal criterion of closeness in terms of transcript lines, this result can viewed as a *context of unconditioned categories*. What is gained from this contextual information? Well, the gain matches the conceptual investment – which was rather low. All that was done was to decide on a focus of interest, in this case the code cle. All we get back is a hint that cle is frequently found in close proximity to sor. The meaning of these correlated manifestations of two codes still has to be constructed by interpretation. Thus, context analysis serves as a heuristic tool – it indicates a direction in which the investment of more cognitive effort may be promising. Of course, in this example the possible meaning of the relations with sco (**self-concept**) as well as non-relations with other codes should also be considered.

Matrix analysis or table analysis
Matrix analyses require more conceptual preparation and consequently it is reasonable to expect to discover more information. Miles and Huberman (1984a) recommend the use of a matrix of selected codes as

an important analytical procedure because it helps to reveal underlying structures in the database. This will be demonstrated with a shortened example from Marcelo's (1991; Huber and Marcelo, 1993) study of the influences on newly qualified teachers. It was clear from coding the interviews that further analyses had to consider differences between different types of school. With this distinction in mind a matrix or table of codes was designed using 'profile' and 'conceptual' codes. *Profile codes* refer to the variables saved with each case, such as socio-demographic data about the interviewee and type of school in which the interviewee works. *Conceptual codes* relate to the categories, or topics, identified in the interview transcripts. Profile codes, such as **elementary school** and **secondary school**, define the columns, and conceptual codes, such as **classroom memories**, **actual experiences** and **additional training**, define the rows of the table. The construction of the table and the following retrieval of the contents of its cells, that is the text segments matching the conditions of column and row definitions, were performed with the assistance of the computer program. Table 10.2 shows a summary of selected results, where the numbers in each cell indicate the frequency of similar findings.

Since the retrieval of conceptual codes defining a matrix row is determined by a particular profile code serving as column header, a matrix analysis allows the reconstruction of interrelations within the *context of conditional categories*. Matrix analysis can therefore be conceived of as

Table 10.2   *Matrix analysis: 'influences' by 'school type'*

	Elementary school		Secondary school
		Memory of own teachers	
0		9	'What I really do in the classroom is to follow what my teachers did with me, I treat my students the same way, maybe somewhat milder.'
		Experience	
4	'I believe that a teacher develops, that for me in the school, if they give you some rules . . . but nevertheless you develop by experience . . . for example, I guess, I am much more patient than earlier, I believe, that I am always more patient, the more I understand them.'	8	'One learns something every day.' 'The only valid education is by experience.'
		Additional training	
0		5	'I joined some training courses in order to complete my education.'

a special type of *selective retrieval* (see Chapter 14). Only in those cases where the additional condition of selection is fulfilled does a text segment appear as the content of a matrix cell. According to Miles and Huberman (1984a) these matrices can help to:

1. gain an overview, since data and analysis are expressed in combination;
2. notice very quickly where additional, more differentiated analyses are necessary;
3. compare data as well as interpretations; and
4. communicate results more easily.

From this example there was a strong indication that differences in the teachers' education for different types of schools should be scrutinized. Novice teachers at secondary schools seem not to start with much educational knowledge, but to depend heavily on memories from their own time as grade school students and on additional training.

The results of a matrix analysis provide more direct information for the interpretation of data than mere statements about spatially or temporally neighbouring but otherwise independent codes. However, two constraints have to be kept in mind:

1. The introduction of a second group of (profile) codes serving as a 'condition' for retrieving conceptual codes requires many more assumptions and/or analytic findings than a distance analysis.
2. The intention was to reconstruct or assemble patterns of conceptual codes, but what we got was a table of conceptual codes (or their corresponding text segments) sorted by the profile characteristics of their database. This result supports theory building excellently, but additional, more differentiated procedures will be needed.

Analysis of elementary linkages

In the more advanced stages of qualitative analysis, researchers, depending on their blueprint for theory building, will try to either reconstruct expected code patterns or to assemble meaningful patterns of codes from the database. In both cases codes are tentatively linked in search of meaning and the database is explored for whether and/or to what extent these linkages can be supported by co-occurrences of coded segments in the database. If such a hypothetical code pattern does not include more than three codes and only one type of logical link (for example, only AND links without any NEGATION) I call them 'elementary' linkages. The functions of these logical links correspond to those of Boolean operators that are used to search for co-occurring codes in many software programs for qualitative data analysis (see Chapter 14).

Let us assume that an elaboration of the heuristic information received from the distance analysis described above (see Table 10.1) is desired. For example, a hypothesis could be formulated such that every manifestation of critical life events in the database (of biographical interviews) is closely followed by remarks about social relations, in other words that there are regular co-occurrences of the codes cle and sor. For computer-assisted retrieval the 'closeness' of this link is expressed in terms of spatial distance (line numbers) in the transcript. For instance, if the researcher wanted to find both components of the hypothetical linkage within maximally five text lines from each other, the first of the twelve simple linkage structures built into AQUAD could be used to investigate our assumption.[1] Table 10.3 shows the findings from an analysis using two interviews as a database.

On the right-hand side of Table 10.3 the information that was entered into the program is noted. In the database bios1 the expected co-occurrence (cle and sor) is found three times. The database bios2, however, does not contain the code pattern at all. However, if these results are compared with the findings of the distance analysis (Table 10.1), it becomes apparent that the fourth appearance of sor in bios1 is not retrieved as co-occurring with cle in lines 22–23. Restricting the closeness of the relation to five text lines obviously prevented the software from including this (potential) co-occurrence. Retrieval of text segments coded by sor reveals that it is better to enlarge the distance, because the content of lines 29–31 (statement about being alone) is clearly related to the critical life event (separation from husband) in 22–23.

The details of this example should shed some light on the possible functions of the resulting information. First, it is important to remember that the software neither interprets nor analyses the database, but serves as a tool – in the above example in a phase of theory building. Retrieving some specimen of the expected pattern in some databases may be taken as an indication that the theory being built is on safe

Table 10.3   *Linkage analysis: elementary linkage of two codes*

LINKAGE 1/CODE FILE bios1							Entries in AQUAD during run-time:
22	22	cle	–	25	25	sor	
22	23	cle	–	25	25	sor	Code 1: cle
255	256	cle	–	255	256	sor	Code 2: sor
							Distance: 5

└──▶ Result: 3 linkages found

LINKAGE 1/CODE FILE bios2

└──▶ Result: no linkage found

ground, but it cannot serve as proof. Analogically, if no evidence for the expected code pattern (see database bios2 in Table 10.3) is found, the hypothetical linkage must not be immediately rejected. This database may belong to a specific cluster of cases where the focal code may be linked meaningfully to other codes, or the range of proximity may have been too narrow to find positive evidence. The researcher should not forget to look for negative evidence, that is appearances of the focal code that are coupled with codes other than sor, especially those that contradict the original assumption. In cases where positive evidence has already been found, it may then be concluded that too broad a range of proximity was chosen, since other codes that appeared in the neighbourhood of the focal code were retrieved, but at such a distance as to make them meaningless in terms of the hypothetical linkage.

In many cases, distance in terms of space between the appearance of codes, that is the text passages to which they pertain, plays a critical role for linkage analysis. Of course, linkage analyses looking for the presence of just two or three particular codes in a database can also be conducted. In terms of a retrieval logic, this would mean searching for codes linked by the logical conjunction 'OR'. However, in order to make sure that linkages represent more than just co-occurrences in a text, an additional criterion has to be introduced. Of course, some type of linkage-, macro- or hypercode signalling the relationship of particular codes associated with specific text segments could be invented, but to make the appropriate semantic decisions it would be necessary to re-read all the texts in detail at least once more. In order to profit from the potential of available software tools, although they do not perform true semantic analyses, a retrieval in which particular codes (text passages) are linked by the logical conjunction 'AND' could be conducted, but the range of retrieval is limited by the distance of co-occurring text segments in the database to which the linked codes have been attached.

How does the criterion of distance contribute to a search for meaningful linkages? Let us assume that the researcher suspects that one of the interviewees had dissociated his emotions (emo) from the critical events he experienced in his life (cle). By running a linkage analysis without distance criterion three critical life events and five emotional expressions were retrieved from the interview transcript. Is this clear evidence against the hypothesis? Not necessarily! if the retrieval is now limited to those co-occurrences between cle and emo, where cle precedes emo and the text passages to which the two codes were attached are maximally five text lines apart. Now it may be that this person never really mentioned emotions in connection with critical life events, which were reported early in the interview, but talks a lot about his momentary feelings, which fill the last page of the interview transcript.

Linkage analysis is not a test, but a constructive tool producing stepping-stones for moving in the stream of comparisons and contrasts of meanings. Line numbers and codes in the program output give information on the location of text segments that may be linked in a meaningful way. But to ensure that these links are meaningful the original text should be checked, either manually or by means of routines for text retrieval, and by analysing alternative linkages. The results of a linkage analysis assist tremendously in the task of permanent comparisons.

Analysis of elaborate linkages
When dealing with complex phenomena or when proceeding to higher levels of abstraction the researcher may want to analyse linkages that are more elaborate than a sequence or a hierarchical pattern of two or three codes. Of course, software cannot offer linkage structures for every possible combination of varying numbers of codes. However, software tools can offer an open environment for researchers to enter their own linkage postulates. Without explaining the details here, I will give an example of the analysis of elaborate linkages. The prerequisites for this analysis and the significance of its results are basically the same as in the case of elementary linkages – the only difference is that the demands are more complex.

In Marcelo's (1991) interview texts already quoted above there were many hints that some newly qualified teachers thought a lot about teaching methods, but unfortunately from a very narrow perspective: Teaching methods (MET) were often mentioned together with other aspects of teaching (TEA); however only on rare occasions did these teachers relate personal reflections (personal dimension; PDI) or institutional reflections (institutional dimension; IDI) to this class of statements. In other words a complex linkage could be postulated: 'There were some teachers in the sample whose reflections on teaching methods were connected with considerations about other aspects of teaching, but not with personal or institutional reflection.' The next step in theory building is to reformulate this hypothetical linkage in a manner that allows it to be investigated with computer assistance.

The conditions for this linkage are met if:

• there is an entry MET in a specific teacher's database,
• and there is an entry TDI,
• and there are no entries PDI or IDI,
• and only those entries are relevant that appear within five lines of MET,
• and all solutions or a negative report for every teacher are to be retrieved.

Table 10.4 shows the beginning of the program's output for this linkage formulation.

Table 10.4   *Linkage analysis: elaborate linkage postulation*

LINKAGE 1/CODE FILE ini001					
98	120	MET	—		MET linked to TDI,
	122	130	TDI		not to PDI or IDI
132	134	MET	—		MET linked to TDI,
	137	140	TDI		however also to PDI
	134	136	PDI	negative	

LINKAGE 1/CODE FILE ini002					
278	285	MET	–		MET linked to TDI,
	287	291	TDI		not to PDI or IDI

LINKAGE 1/CODE FILE ini003			
85	94	MET	–
	98	111	TDI
241	246	MET	–
	249	259	TDI
454	456	MET	–
	458	460	TDI

The analysis of interview ini001 produced counter-evidence, while the other findings correspond with the postulated code pattern. Teacher 001 combines personal reflections with her thoughts about classroom methods and teaching in general. In the other two cases reflections on topics other than teaching were not found within five lines of MET. The function of these findings in the process of theory building is the same as in the case of the elementary linkages discussed above.

Theory building by configuration analysis

Glaser and Strauss (1967) defined the core activity of qualitative analysis as the permanent comparison of text segments, categories and codes within one text and across texts. In many studies these comparisons reach such a level of complexity that the mere retrieval of co-occurrences and code-patterns no longer meets the analytical demands.

For instance, in order to look for causal relations one must search the database for hyperlinks of codes or connections between particular codes (see Ragin, 1987: Chapter 3 for the relationship between causality and case-oriented methods). However, one of the most distinctive features of qualitative research is that there is no intention to introduce fixed links as a sort of hypothesis to be tested 'variable by variable', but the researcher wishes to address complex constellations of phenomena in the database, paying attention to the variety of meaningful configurations.

To this end Ragin (1987) suggested the use of the procedure from Boolean algebra called *logical minimization* (of empirical conditions to logical 'implicants') for qualitative comparisons (see Chapter 13 for an explanation of this process). This entails the transformation of codes (maybe according to their frequency in the individual database), or some significant linkages which have been reconstructed or detected, into 'truth values'; that is, they are reduced to binary statements 'condition true' (that is, given) or 'condition false' (that is, not given). Then a table of truth values (see Table 10.5) is constructed, where the conditions chosen for analysis define the columns, and the particular values of these conditions for every case constitute the rows. The conditions for each case are combined with Boolean multiplication (logical AND). The different configurations, that is, the rows in the resulting table, are combined additively (logical OR). With these preparations completed, the minimization procedure will help to uncover patterns of invariance and constant linkages by the thorough comparison of all cases (Ragin, 1987: 51). The Boolean concept of minimization in qualitative approaches corresponds to the variable-oriented experimental design on the level of comparisons of single cases: if the critical effect Y is found in two cases, and in one case the condition X is given but X is absent from the second case, then this condition X can be eliminated from further analyses as irrelevant. This strategy results in a simplified, that is, a minimized, configuration of conditions for Y.

As a heuristic tool, this type of configuration analysis may facilitate the task of generating adequate categories, even if only a few texts have been analysed. During the final steps of category generation, when the researcher wants to summarize or group findings, to differentiate between types of texts or speakers, the process of logical minimization seems to be indispensable.

Analysis of implicants
In efforts to find causal relations beyond the boundaries of case-specific conditions, valid for the above mentioned 'local causality', one category that reoccurs across cases has to be identified as the effect in which the researcher is interested, or as the effect whose possible causes the researcher would like to learn more about. For instance, in the study described above, Marcelo (1991) became more and more interested in finding reasons for some newly qualified teachers' problems with classroom discipline. In the logical formulation 'if . . . then' of empirical causality, the 'then-part' is the effect category or 'critical' effect. Stated concretely in the above example: if some yet unknown

things happen, then newly qualified teachers are confronted with discipline problems. What he then wanted to find was the content of the 'if-part', that is, those groups or configurations of categories that cause the critical effect. Since this if-then linkage is known as the 'logical relationship of implication', it can also be said that the propositions within the if-part imply or implicate the proposition determining the then-part, and these causal propositions can be called the effect's implicants.

For example, Marcelo found that newly qualified teachers talked most frequently about discipline problems in the classroom, although not all of them mentioned this. Looking for critical differences between the teachers, which might also explain their problems, the analysis concentrated on six categories:

A   self,
B   teacher–student relations,
C   teaching methods,
D   discipline problems,
E   student motivation, and
F   classroom climate.

Table 10.5 shows the frequencies of these categories (for the first 12 of 106 teachers). According to the cut-off (high vs. low frequency) that the user has defined for distinguishing between the states of 'true' (condition given) and 'false' (condition not given), a table of truth values is then produced from these frequencies. Capital letters represent the value 'true', lower case 'false' (see the example in Table 10.5).

Table 10.5   *Frequencies of categories*

Data table		INICIA.DTA						
Condition		A	B	C	D	E	F	
case	1	3	2	6	1	2	2	
case	2	1	3	6	2	0	0	
case	3	6	0	7	2	3	1	Example for transformation
case	4	5	4	2	1	2	0	into truth values:
case	5	2	1	2	0	0	1	
case	6	4	3	6	2	1	2 →	A B C D e F
case	7	5	3	3	1	1	1	Teacher 6 talks often
case	8	0	2	1	0	0	0	('true') about topics
case	9	1	1	2	1	1	1	represented by the
case	10	6	4	3	0	0	2	categories A, B, C, D and F,
case	11	2	1	1	1	0	0	but only rarely ('false')
case	12	3	1	1	1	1	1	about category e (therefore
. . .		continued until case 106						entered in lower case)

An analysis of configurations for condition D (discipline problems) as a criterion resulted in three groups of implicants:

D = ABC + ACEF + abcef

From this reduction three groups of newly-qualified teachers who frequently mentioned discipline problems (D) can be distinguished:

- The first group is characterized by the configuration ABC; this means that they reflect about themselves, teacher–student relations, and teaching methods – but not about student motivation and classroom climate.
- The second group, characterized by the configuration ACEF, talks about self, teaching methods, student motivation and social climate – but does not seem to reflect on teacher–student relations.
- The third group, typified by the configuration abcef, mentions discipline problems frequently in their interviews, but none of the other central categories!

This example illustrates how configuration analysis in terms of 'logical minimization to implicants' assists in structuring even a large number of single cases.

Analysis of clusters
The analysis of clusters is simply a variant of the analysis of implicants. For theoretical and methodological reasons, as well as for practical ones, the researcher may wish to switch from the wide-angle view of general findings about different configurations of conditions for a critical category to a close-up view of single cases. In other words, the researcher may be interested in re-reading the interview transcripts of all the teachers who belong to one of the sub-groups experiencing discipline problems (see previous section), but this time concentrating on particular codes. After minimizing the table of truth values to implicants, AQUAD will scan it and create a list of those cases in the database that display a particular configuration of conditions. Thus, the software also supports permanent comparison at this level of analysis, opening the road from the heights of abstraction back to the lowland of case-specific formulations.

The function of configuration analysis in the process of theory building
How should researchers treat the implicants derived from configuration analysis? Do they serve as evidence to prove or reject underlying theories, the blueprints for reconstruction, or theories emerging in the

process of qualitative analysis? The answer is a maybe puzzling 'neither . . . nor'. As this is not the place for elaborate methodological considerations, Ragin's (1987) explanations of the dialogue of evidence and ideas in Boolean configuration analysis can be recommended for further reading: 'The Boolean approach to qualitative comparison . . . is a middle road between two extremes, variable-oriented and case-oriented approaches – it is a middle road between generality and complexity. It allows investigators both to digest many cases and to assess causal complexity' (Ragin, 1987: 168).

Note

1. I speak of linkage 'structures' because the program provides a set of abstract analytical algorithms which become concrete linkage blueprints when specific codes and their distance (in terms of line numbers) are filled in.

PART IV

COMPUTERS AND TRIANGULATION

Introduction: Between Quality and Quantity

*Gerald Prein and Udo Kuckartz in discussion with
Edeltraud Roller, Charles Ragin and Udo Kelle*

During the last two decades there has been a quite intensive debate about the integration of qualitative and quantitative methods, referred to by notions like *triangulation, micro–macro link* or *mixed methods approach* (see Bryman, 1988; Denzin, 1977; Flick, 1992; Fielding and Fielding, 1986; Padilla, 1992).

The starting point for this discussion was the idea that the different research methodologies, interpretive analysis of qualitative data on the one hand and statistical analysis of numerical data on the other, each have specific weaknesses but also specific strengths: the weaknesses should be overcome by combining qualitative and quantitative data sources and methods of analysis in the same research project. As Bryman (1988: 131–156) has pointed out, researchers usually follow one of two different goals when applying such a strategy:

- Either they try to find further evidence to *confirm or disconfirm their previous research results* by using a different research methodology. The underlying assumption is that the validity of research results is enhanced if there is a convergence of findings about the same empirical domain produced by using different methodological approaches (see Campbell and Fiske, 1959; Denzin, 1977; Padilla, 1992).
- Or they want to establish a more complete picture of the investigated phenomena by combining different research strategies. The idea behind this comes much closer to the original meaning of the word 'triangulation', a paronym from land surveying and navigation: quantitative and qualitative methods represent different

perspectives and can therefore be employed to investigate *different aspects* or *levels* of reality (see Flick, 1992; Fielding and Fielding, 1986; Burgess, 1927).

In practice, the implementation of a mixed-method approach or strategies of triangulation quite often means that the research design is split into two distinct and mutually exclusive parts: different data sets are collected, one of them consisting of numerical data, for example collected with survey questionnaires, and the other of unstructured textual material, for example transcripts from open-ended questions in questionnaires, interviews or verbal records from participant observation. These different data can then be analysed in accordance with the widely accepted division of labour between the two methodological paradigms: numerical data by means of statistical procedures, unstructured verbal data using some kind of interpretive or hermeneutic method. The purpose of this strategy is to produce different results that can be related to each other. In comparison, the integration of qualitative and quantitative methods in using the same data poses quite serious methodological problems: until now there have been no statistical methods available for the analysis of small, purposefully (sometimes self-)selected samples whose results could be generalized with a good conscience. On the other hand, from the perspective of research economy, it would not be feasible to apply widely used methods of interpretive analysis, for example fine-grained hermeneutic analysis or discourse analysis, to large random samples similar to those collected in quantitative studies. For example, analysing hundreds of voluminous interview transcripts by means of a careful text interpretation would be a task demanding enormous resources in terms of time and personpower, and would most certainly lead to a superficial analysis. As Ragin (1994c) has pointed out, there is a trade-off between the number of cases and the number of attributes of cases a researcher can study. In short, it is difficult to study social phenomena both extensively and intensively at the same time.

For a long time quantitative content analysis – especially its variants using computer algorithms to classify and count semantically similar units of texts (see Krippendorf, 1980) – represented the only available method for quantitatively analysing large sets of textual data. The strength of this quasi-automated approach – primarily based on the calculation of word frequencies in given texts – certainly lies in the opportunities it offers for the analysis of highly formalized speech events (for example, in certain political discourses or in mass media communication). Nevertheless, the shortcomings of this type of analysis become rapidly evident when it is applied to texts arising from everyday communication, such as interview transcripts or field notes from unstructured observations. Since the meaning of many words used in these settings is either ambiguous or strongly dependent on the context, severe difficulties are created for analyses based on counting their mere occurrences in a given text. In contrast, qualitative approaches have always been concerned with these matters of context-relatedness and indexicality, and have therefore drawn on the researcher's ability to *Verstehen*.

For these reasons it seems a rather promising, albeit challenging, task to combine hermeneutic methods for the understanding of the meaning of texts with techniques for the reduction and 'standardization' of information contained in large amounts of textual data.

Since the introduction of computers to qualitative research the idea has been expressed that, with the help of this tool, the different traditions of qualitative and quantitative methodology could be reconciled. But there have also been warnings that the application of quantitative methods to qualitative research may do harm to the virtues of person-relatedness, richness, relevance and the capturing of idiosyncrasies that are at the core of non-experimental qualitative research. Consequently, the question of how the quantitative analysis of formal structures can be linked to the hermeneutic analysis of semantic content seems to be a methodologically difficult one.

An attempt to find an answer is made by Edeltraud Roller, Rainer Mathes and Thomas Eckert in Chapter 12 where they present their approach towards 'hermeneutic-classificatory content analysis'. Using examples from their research projects, in which semi-structured interviews had been collected from large samples, they describe a procedure for information reduction partly based on fine-grained hermeneutic analysis: after structuring the texts according to topics and speakers through a process of *formal coding*, a *conceptual network of categories* is developed that defines the code categories and (possible) relations between them on different levels of text. Using this network of categories (which remains modifiable) and *hermeneutic techniques* for coding, the relevant information contained in the text segments is then transformed into a quantitative data matrix. This data set can then be statistically analysed in order to generate *frequency distributions* of certain codes or code patterns. On the basis of the statistical analyses, researchers are then able to identify *cases from important modal categories* or *marginal cases* that may contain information relevant to the research question. Using text segments from marginal cases and from cases from modal categories the researcher can then switch back to fine-grained hermeneutic analysis in order to elucidate or modify the results obtained until this point.

Another approach to the generation of quantitative data from textual material is offered by Udo Kuckartz in Chapter 11, drawing on

Max Weber's and Alfred Schütz's theoretical and methodological considerations about *typification*. Kuckartz thereby addresses the problem of how cases can be *classified* and how a typology can be constructed without referring exclusively to predefined categories (for example, the respondents' socio-demographic characteristics). Instead, the relevant dimensions for typification have to be developed from the empirical material, a process that requires a thorough analysis of the whole case using phenomenological and hermeneutic methods. In Kuckartz's approach, code-and-retrieve techniques are employed to help with this process. The next step of analysis is the comparison of cases according to the dimensions found by this process in order to classify them on the basis of *genus proxima* and *differentiae specificae*. But for this purpose 'manual' case-by-case comparisons are not sufficient – while they are often feasible and useful for small samples and a limited number of dimensions, they may easily lead to arbitrary results when applied to a larger number of cases and dimensions. Therefore, Kuckartz draws on formalized methods of comparison, such as cluster analysis and correspondence analysis. For this purpose the dimensions which were initially developed from the data have to be transformed into *case-oriented variables* and *case-specific variable values*. This will provide the researcher with an ordinary matrix (cases × variables) to which formal algorithms for clustering or comparison can be applied in order to establish a data-driven typology. Like Roller and her colleagues, Kuckartz also proposes a final step for the qualitative analysis in order to validate the quantitative results. A careful inspection of the textual 'raw data' should help to identify further *similarities* and *differences* between the mechanically produced clusters or groups.

It should be emphasized here that the mathematical procedures employed by Kuckartz are quite well suited to the analysis of qualitative research data. One has to keep in mind that only in rare cases, like the one described by Roller, can samples be drawn at random and be sufficiently large to permit methods of inferential statistical analysis. Numerical variables derived from textual data can mostly be measured only on a nominal or ordinal scale. In most cases it is also doubtful whether other requirements for the application of standard multivariate statistical techniques, for example the requirement for the normality of residuals or for homoscedasticity, are fulfilled. Consequently, the use of methods of multivariate analysis and inferential statistics for such data seems to be a somewhat dubious endeavour. On the other hand, given the complexity of the investigated phenomena, it is often hardly satisfying to restrict statistical analysis to the use of simple descriptive measures like frequencies or percentages. Hence the application of complex methods of exploratory data analysis like cluster analysis which Kuckartz proposes seems to be a workable solution for the problems outlined above. However, it should be mentioned that these explorative techniques also contain certain methodological assumptions which can have an impact on the process of analysis. For example, it is usually assumed in cluster analysis that all single variables are equally relevant to all cases, an assumption implying causal homogeneity for all cases. This can sometimes become problematic, especially if these techniques are employed in order to establish inferences from qualitative data where multiple different causal paths or configurations are present.

Therefore, many analysts – mainly those who are interested in investigating causal relationships – will still find that these methods do not fulfil their demands. Strategies for causal modelling are now widely applied in statistical analysis. However, their application almost always rests on far-reaching mathematical requirements that can only rarely be fulfilled by qualitative data material. A solution for this problem is offered by Charles Ragin. He proposes a method for formalizing the intuitive process of multiple comparisons, used for example by a historian or political scientist conducting a comparative analysis of macro-phenomena, which is employed in the search for causal explanations of such phenomena. Unlike Kuckartz and Roller et al., Ragin does not describe the process of variable generation in detail, but takes as a starting point the situation that a researcher has already defined certain characteristics of a case as outcomes and others as possible causes. Instead of introducing statistical standard procedures *into* qualitative data analysis, as Roller and her colleagues or Kuckartz do, Ragin presents a case-oriented approach that rests on the application of Boolean algebra. The goal is to identify all possible configurations of causes that lead to a specific outcome. For this purpose, a strategy of redundancy elimination is applied, using logical minimization in order to further simplify the model. By doing so, the causal heterogeneity of cases can be taken into account: different causal configurations that lead to the same outcome can be identified.

Since every single case that contains a specific causal configuration, but not the outcome, would lead to the abandonment of a causal hypothesis, this strategy can be extremely helpful for researchers who have intimate knowledge of their cases and seek to account for every single case. Hence, it has a strongly deterministic emphasis and is therefore less suited for the investigation of processes including elements of 'chance' in the probabilistic sense.

These three approaches represent promising attempts to overcome the weaknesses of interpretive analysis as well as of quantitative methods by combining their strengths: the consideration of the context-relatedness of everyday language on the one hand and the ability to efficiently analyse enormous amounts of numerical information on the other. But to reach this goal, the researcher has to meet high standards of methodological rigour. The use of codes for the purpose of information reduction through quantification always requires that one can be sure that the code scheme is highly reliable and stable, and that the coding is done inclusively and exhaustively (see Chapter 4). But if these demands are fulfilled, the pay-off in terms of rich and valid information about the domain under study can be high.

11

Case-oriented Quantification

Udo Kuckartz

The *case-oriented quantification* approach is based on the method-ological works of Max Weber and Alfred Schütz, and aims for a methodologically controlled *typification*. According to Schütz, the actor's common-sense knowledge, which represents an integral part of their 'natural attitude' towards their life-world, is a system of con-structs of its typicalities. Thus, Schütz indicated that the cognitive process of *typification* is a fundamental anthropological technique, which enables us to understand our everyday world as well as to con-duct scientific inquiries (see Schütz, 1962: 7ff.). Since abstract notions and typifications form the basis of our everyday reasoning, the proce-dures of classification, quantification and typification are always present on a subliminal level, even if no formal classification or act of counting, in the algebraic sense, takes place.

For Max Weber, the construction of understandable types of action, which he considered to be a connecting link between single-case-oriented hermeneutic *Verstehen* on the one hand, and quantitative methods which are meant to discern statistical relationships in order to find law-like regularities on the other, was the central goal of empirical social science (see Weber, 1964; Kuckartz, 1991).

To a certain extent this is the classical position of *unified science*. In opposition to approaches that try to draw a sharp distinction between *idiographic* and *nomothetic methods*, between *Verstehen* in *Geisteswissenschaften* and nomic explanations in natural sciences, my aim is an integration of qualitative and quantitative research methods. This does not mean that epistemological differences between the two methodological perspectives, and especially their different criteria for reliability and validity, are ignored. Methodologically speaking the aim must be to identify patterns in social regularities *and at the same time* to understand them in the sense of controlled *Fremdverstehen* (under-standing the other).

Thus, the endeavour to construct empirical types within the social sciences has a long tradition, going back to one of the most outstand-ing sociological debates of the nineteenth century (see Kuckartz, 1991). Later, mainly during the heyday of positivistic methodology, this discussion about typologies and typification faded from the scene, although specific methods of quantitative analysis were designed on the basis of a typological approach, such as Lazarsfeld's latent class analysis (see McCutcheon, 1987). In the realm of qualitative methods, for a long time detailed, explicit research techniques to support typification were missing. The case-oriented quantification approach, which is presented here and was initially developed within the framework of studies employing semi-structured interviews consisting mainly of open-ended questions, tries to bridge this gap. In the context of this approach typification always relates to individuals, that is, to the interviewees. This does not mean that the types necessarily refer to personal traits; they could also be types drawn from the respondents' reported actions, situations, experiences and attitudes.

The overall purpose of the case-oriented research method is to classify and, if necessary, quantify the qualitative data or parts of it, whereby the 'case', that is, the respondent in question, forms the referential basis of this method. In the following discussions this analysis was performed with the assistance of the software program MAX (see Chapter 14 for more details).

From transcription to analysis of themes

The *case-oriented quantification* model combines qualitative and quantitative operations during the evaluation of qualitative research data. The first steps of the method are hermeneutic; this means that, to a large extent, the method parallels processes used in the fields of phenomenology or ethnography (see Geertz, 1973). Consequently, the first goal is to isolate the subjective meaning of a text. The first steps are shown schematically in Figure 11.1.

It could be asked, why does a method whose objective is the comparison of 'cases' and which works with thematic categories start with the hermeneutic analysis of single cases? The background is provided by the principle of 'interpretive understanding' (*deutendes Verstehen*), based on Weber's concept of social interaction (see Weber, 1964: 3ff.).

Social interaction is a form of human behaviour to which the actors involved attach subjective meaning and which is related to the behaviour of others. The term 'meaning' is related to the subject and is not, according to Weber's definition, 'any kind of objectively correct or metaphysically explored *true* meaning' (Weber, 1964: 4). '*Verstehen*' therefore primarily means 'understanding' the behaviour of those *individuals* who take part in social interaction. Only on this basis can the search for regularities, for 'understandable types of action' (*verständliche Handlungstypen*), be conducted.

This is also the reason why the first steps of the case-oriented method

Step	
1	Transcription of texts
2	Interpretation of each text = single case analysis
3	Interpretive comparison of single cases = comparative single case analysis
4	Development of codes, i.e. a system of thematic categories
5	Allocation of codes to text segments
6	Compilation and interpretation of all text segments with the same code (analysis of themes)
7	Analysis of relationships between codes (comparative analysis of themes)

Figure 11.1   *The first coding process: from the interview transcripts to thematically structured and ordered text segments*

are not a segmentation of the texts and a removal of the text segments from their context, but an analysis of the whole case. The codes that are developed during the following two methodological stages and then allocated to the text segments can, in this form of analysis, be characterized as *topic-oriented categories*. They are used to identify topics in the transcribed interviews. Coding is the preliminary step and the necessary prerequisite for the following evaluation of the data, in which the first step is to compare all text segments belonging to the same category. By means of contrasting comparisons, the aim of this analysis of topics is to identify similarities between individuals, peculiarities of single cases and relationships between categories.

Although these coding and retrieval techniques are relatively simple, they consume a great deal of time and effort on the part of the researcher. The result initially appears to be rather meagre: the data has been clearly structured and ordered. It is similar to the way in which medicines are stored in a pharmacy; everything is neatly tucked away in drawers and on shelves. Labels on the drawers indicate what is to be expected when the drawer is opened.

In an empirical study about the motivations of young men doing voluntary work (Carstens et al., 1990) some of the 'labels on the drawers' are shown in Table 11.1. The text segments from different interviews are stored in these single drawers; the allocation was determined by the coding process conducted earlier. This material lends itself to a simple descriptive evaluation: the contents of the drawers are spread out and rearranged into a new text. If the data is comprehensible, a close

Table 11.1   *An example of thematic categories*

Background to the voluntary activity	Relationship to assistants	Personal reflections
The activity itself	Relationship to clients	Personal philosophy
Training and support offered by organizers	Relationship to professionals	Reaction of the social environment to the voluntary activity

inspection and interpretation reveals typical patterns and it is possible to give 'thick descriptions' (see Geertz, 1973) of the social life-worlds under investigation.

The more extensive the sample, and therefore the data, the harder it is to identify complex patterns. It is common to conduct twenty or more interviews during a qualitative study, but even with this population size (which is small compared to the sample size in mainstream social research) it becomes increasingly difficult to determine whether the apparent or intuitively observed relationships, which are often labelled with quasi-statistical terms (typical, mainly, pattern, orientation pattern, model, leitmotiv), are indeed verified by the data.

The method of case-oriented quantification addresses this problem. By means of careful classification of the data and by the rating of individual statements on scales the aim is, on the one hand, to extract the maximum amount of information from the data and, on the other hand, to identify complex relationships on the basis of these newly constructed variables.

From dimensional analysis to classification and quantitative analysis

If the initial application of coding and retrieval techniques is termed as first-order coding, then the further steps in case-oriented quantification could be regarded as a process of *second-order coding* (for the distinction between first-order and second-order coding see also p. 66 in the Introduction to Part II).

The process of second-order coding, roughly schematized in Table 11.2, has as its starting point the compilation of text segments belonging to the same topic-oriented category, and has as its finishing point the rating of individuals, the respondents, on scales. The simplest possible case would be a process of coding in which only a single variable on a yes/no scale is rated. Interpretation and classification processes, requiring repeated readings of the data, take place between the starting and finishing point of the second-order coding. Two examples help to demonstrate how the second-order coding process works.

Table 11.2   *Starting point and goal of the second coding process*

Starting point	Goal
Pool of all segments belonging to one code	Rating of individuals on scales

Example 1. In the previously mentioned study about voluntary workers the code **reaction of the social environment towards the voluntary work** was used to code all parts of the text in which the respondents talked about how their environment, that is, their parents, partner, friends, acquaintances, relatives, etc., reacted towards their voluntary work. The next step is to investigate the semantic spectrum of the category. A dimensional analysis is conducted whose natural starting point is a re-examination of the material. The process of dimensionalization was described in detail by Anselm Strauss (see Strauss and Corbin, 1990: 69–72; Strauss, 1991: 44ff., 204). The principal aim is to identify *distinctions* in a particular section of the data. The distinctions do not necessarily have to be inductively drawn from the data, but can also be based on existing contextual or theoretical knowledge (see Strauss, 1991: 41). The process of dimensionalization can be conducted in several steps and on several levels, so individual distinctions can be further distinguished to construct subdimensions.

In the example mentioned above the result of the comparative analysis of the text segments is a distinction between the reaction of close members of the respondent's *reference group* (for example, parents, partner) and the reaction of more distant members (for example, acquaintances, colleagues, etc.). Further, a dimension entitled **evaluation** can be observed, which registers the reported reaction of the environment. Two variables can now be constructed:

1. Reaction of partner/parents
2. Reaction of acquaintances/colleagues.

The next step is to define the distinctive features of the **evaluation** dimension for these two variables. In order to do this it is usually necessary to re-examine the material. The simplest form of coding is a dichotomous positive/negative scale. If the level of differentiation in the statements allows it, ordinal scales can be used, for example ranging from 'unconditionally positive/supporting' to 'strongly rejecting, they don't understand why I'm doing this for nothing'. The number of variables defined and the values chosen for them have to be oriented around the information provided by the material within each code. It should also be kept in mind that the aim of the second coding process is to compare the respondents and not to analyse the single cases; in other words there is no point in defining values for the variables which only apply to single cases and display only a negligible frequency.

Example 2. In a study conducted in a school the subjective meaning of computers for girls was investigated (see Schründer-Lenzen, 1994). The methods employed were qualitative interviews, essays written in class and group discussions. A central issue was questions concerning gender-specific self-images. Relevant passages of text from the open interviews were coded with 'gender modalities'. The second process of coding works by dimensionalizing these statements relating to self-image. Among others, the following dimensions were distinguished:

1. Resisting an ideal self-image.
2. Exuberant masculine self-image.
3. The desire for higher cognitive achievements.
4. The desire for higher achievements in maths and science.
5. The desire for higher achievements in general.
6. The desire to be able to cope better with problems.
7. The desire to be a more of a 'fighter'.
8. Orientation towards education.
9. Orientation towards a job.

For the second coding process each dimension is defined as a self-contained variable, producing nine variables for self-image. In the next step (a further re-examination of the material) each respondent, or text segment of her interview that fits the 'gender modalities' code, is classified according to these nine variables. Therefore a decision is made about whether the appropriate dimension is addressed in the statements or not. It is recommended to work with 0/1 coding, so that the 9 dichotomous variables are used to code the question of self-image.

These two examples show that one can employ a variety of different coding procedures within the case-oriented quantification model. In the 'girls and computers' study a simple classification of the content of the text and identification of self-image patterns, which were already known from the research, was involved. In the 'voluntary worker' study a scaled evaluation of interview statements was made. What the two examples have in common is a model of coding presented in Figure 11.2.

An examination of the material is necessary at three points: at steps 1, 4 and 7. If the material is extensive, it is recommended that the analysis of dimensions and the definition of variables and their values are conducted with only a part of the material. For the case-oriented coding an examination of all the material is of course necessary.

The model is not conceived of as an inflexible, sequential, forward progressing schema. At certain points it might be crucial to take a step backwards. It might happen that 'case-oriented coding' reveals that the nominal scale values are not sufficiently differentiated so the coding instructions have to be changed. Another possibility is that the initial ordinal scale exhibits a degree of differentiation which is not

1.	Examination of all text segments belonging to one code
2.	Analysis of dimensions
3.	Definition of variables
4.	Renewed examination of all text segments with this code
5.	Determination of the type of scale and definition of scale values
6.	Formulation of coding instructions with prototypical examples
7.	Case-oriented coding
8.	Entering the values of each case

Figure 11.2   *From the analysis of dimensions to case-oriented coding: model of the second coding process*

appropriate to the quality of the data. In this case steps 5 to 7 have to be repeated.

After a complete examination of the material and the entering of the code values the initial statistical analysis, counting the frequencies, can be conducted. If necessary the values the variables can take should be modified after this analysis. This is the case if the frequency of certain values on the scale is 0 or negligible, and it does not seem meaningful, in terms of the research question, to continue.

If we now ask which univariate and multivariate statistical methods can be used to analyse the newly created variables, we must first of all look at the general criteria for statistical analysis. The main criteria are:

- type of scale;
- distribution of characteristics or variables;
- sample size;
- appropriateness of the statistical model.

For data generated by *second-order coding* the scale is usually not metric, the distribution is not known and the assumption of a normal distribution usually cannot be justified. The size of the samples is rather small, and compared to the size of well-known surveys (ISSP, ALLBUS, EUROBAROMETER, etc.) is in fact tiny. What avenue of statistical analysis remains open in the face of these adverse conditions?

Univariate analyses, by means of frequency counts with the results expressed as percentages, are certainly possible. Robust statistics, such as the median, are more appropriate as measures of central tendency than the arithmetic mean because of the restrictions of this type of scale.

Cross-tabulations, with the figures also expressed as percentages, are the method of *bivariate* analysis best suited for this kind of data. With such tabulations it is easy to recognize cells in the table where the observed frequency differs greatly from the expected frequency. To identify such cells, which can indicate meaningful configurations, the *chi-squared test* can be used and the chi-squared residual of the single cells can be calculated. Cells that show a particularly large deviation between the expected and the observed frequency can then be more closely investigated by means of, for example, retrieval of the corresponding text segments.

Classical multivariate methods based on the General Linear Model, such as variance, regression and factor analysis, as well as the modern methods of linear structural analysis and confirmatory factor analysis, are certainly not suitable for this type of data. However, exploratory multivariate analysis methods, such as correspondence analysis and especially cluster analysis, are well suited (see Aldenderfer and Blashfield, 1987; Anderberg, 1973; Bailey, 1983).

The aim of the case-oriented quantification method is not just the frequency evaluation, or quantification, which the second-order coding process makes possible. Its real advantage lies in its possibilities for analysing relationships and for selective retrieval, in which the values of the variables for different respondents serve as a selection criterion for accessing the text segments. Analysis of relationships, employing proven statistical methods, can now be conducted without any further preparatory work. In the 'girls and computers' study for example descriptive statistics could be used to analyse the relationships between statements about self-image, and multivariate methods enabled us to create profiles of self-images.

Case-oriented methodology

The integration of quantitative operations into the analysis of qualitative data occurs in case-oriented quantification with the objectives of the comparison of investigated cases and the creation of types. There is an important difference concerning second-order coding between the method of case-oriented quantification and those methods of computer-aided qualitative data analysis that are restricted to code-and-retrieve procedures. Of course, when employing the latter, it is also possible to proceed to some sort of second-order coding. Therefore code-and-retrieve procedures can assist researchers who do not wish to restrict themselves to mere description and interpretation, but who want to do some more theoretical work with their coding categories, whereby new codes, integrating codes, etc., are defined. But ordinary code-and-retrieve procedures do not, as the case-oriented approach does, offer possibilities for coding the values of a variable. In the case-oriented approach the unit of analysis is the person, the case, for whom a score on each variable is calculated.

The advantage of classification is immediately applicable; assumptions of and statements about correlation can be verified immediately. This does not have to be oriented towards the *significance* of relationships. The method would have been totally misunderstood if the only concern were the significance of relationships; this would also be a scarcely adequate strategy with samples that, in most cases, are not random. However, the coefficients, as a descriptive measure, could highlight the strength of relationships within the sample. Their value lies, therefore, not so much in hypothesis testing, but they have a heuristic value in terms of constructing a theory. The second-order coding process also highlights a problem which, until now, applied to qualitative data analysis and the coding processes involved, namely the question of reliability and validity. A task for future research will be to develop practicable strategies for controlling the quality of coding (see also Chapter 4 about Coding).

It must be emphasized that the method is currently most appropriate for qualitative research dealing explicitly with individuals (see Kuckartz 1990a). In observational studies, for example an ethnographic study in a school, the problems are different, because the field notes are not related to individuals but, in most cases, several people are referred to in a field report, and the classification of individuals might not even be at issue, but the characteristics of interaction or situations. Further developments are planned to adapt the case-oriented method for these types of questions.[1]

Note

1. This also applies to the software program MAX, which was designed especially to facilitate this type of analysis (see Kuckartz 1990b, 1992 and Chapter 14).

12

Hermeneutic-classificatory Content Analysis: A Technique Combining Principles of Quantitative and Qualitative Research

Edeltraud Roller, Rainer Mathes and Thomas Eckert

Quantitative approaches to content analysis have often been criticized for being too atomistic and oversimplistic in analysing complex statements. On the other hand qualitative approaches have often been criticized for not being systematic, for lacking intersubjectivity, and for not being applicable to large quantities of texts. *Hermeneutic-classificatory content analysis* combines quantitative as well as qualitative approaches to content analysis and takes these objections into consideration. It relies on quantitative classification for the analysis of large quantities of texts and it focuses on a network system of categories in order to record complex statements. The principle underlying this system is that of the separate analysis of a multitude of characteristics whose co-occurrences are recorded. Moreover, the coding and ensuing process of analysis of data is a twofold process, combining both quantitative and hermeneutic-interpretive elements. This chapter describes the operation of this technique using the example of a study into support for the welfare state in Germany as an illustration.

Principles of quantitative and qualitative content analysis

On the most general level content analysis is 'any technique for making inferences by objectively and systematically identifying specified characteristics of messages' (Holsti, 1969: 14). Whereas the criterion of objectivity – now usually replaced by intersubjectivity – refers to the fact that scientific statements can be tested by other scientists, the term 'systematic' means that every research step is based on explicitly formulated rules and that these rules are consistently applied. *Quantitative* approaches to content analysis have to reduce the complexity of whole messages and isolate the single elements in order to count specific characteristics of such messages. These elements are then classified according to theoretically relevant criteria. *Qualitative* approaches, which seek to identify the meaning of a message as a whole, reconstruct the substantive meaning by interpreting the messages. As a result of these different procedures, quantitative approaches to content analysis have been criticized as being too atomistic and oversimplistic (Kracauer, 1952/53: 632), and thus lacking validity. On the other hand qualitative approaches to content analysis could be criticized for not being systematic and for lacking intersubjectivity. Since they have the ambitious goal of describing whole messages, they are too time- and cost-intensive for analysing large numbers of texts.

Hermeneutic-classificatory content analysis

The hermeneutic-classificatory method of content analysis is a technique that was developed in the late 1980s (Mathes, 1992; Mathes and Geis, 1990). It combines principles of quantitative as well as qualitative content analysis. Like qualitative techniques, it aims to record complex statements but, at the same time, is intended to be applicable to large quantities of texts. Hermeneutic-classificatory content analysis attempts to fulfil these criteria by employing the following specific techniques:

1. a quantitative classification for the analysis of large numbers of texts,
2. a new approach, called the network technique, is used to construct the system of categories for recording complex statements,
3. the interpretive aspects are emphasized during coding and data analysis, in order to maintain validity when recording complex statements,
4. a method of hermeneutic interpretation (see Oevermann et al., 1979), based on explicitly formulated rules, is used as an interpretive technique.

In the following we will use the framework of a content-analytical research process (see Table 12.1) to describe hermeneutic-classificatory content analysis. A study about support for the welfare state is used to illustrate this technique. In this study semi-structured interviews were conducted with a representative sample of 231 Germans (Roller and Mathes, 1993).[1]

The preparation of the material
The entire text (for example the tape-recorded semi-structured interviews) is transcribed and divided into individual text segments. Identification numbers are assigned to these segments on the basis of formally defined characteristics such as interview number, question number, speaker (interviewer or respondent) and sentence. The identification numbers are, technically speaking, 'formal' codes. By

Table 12.1 *Steps of the hermeneutic-classificatory content analysis*

Steps	Elements	Data-files
Preparation of material	1. Transcription of the texts 2. Assigning identification numbers to text segments according to formally defined characteristics such as interview number, question number, speaker, sentence etc.	Text data-file
System of categories and recording units	Network system of categories covering different recording units: 1. Specific level of statement unit 2. General level of respondent unit	
Coding	1. Qualitative element: Hermeneutic interpretation of message meaning in group discussions 2. Quantitative element: Classification of meanings and transformation into numeric codes	Numeric data-file
Analysis	1. Quantitative element: Quantitative structure-analysis 2. Qualitative element: Hermeneutic detail-analysis of specific text segments	Numeric data-file Text data-file

numbering individual text segments we have a common reference system for text segments and 'substantive' codes (for example, the code negative **general evaluation of the welfare state**), which refer to theoretical categories and will be assigned to the text segments later in the research process.[2] The identification numbers allow the linking of text segments with their 'substantive' codes at any time during the analysis. The result of this process is a text data-file that contains the text of all interviews and the identification numbers for text segments. This file can be managed with text-analysis programs such as Textpack (Mohler and Züll, 1990 and see Chapter 14).

The system of categories and recording units
After the reference system (that is, the identification numbers) has been constructed the next step is to develop a content-analytical instrument. Such an instrument consists of, first, a system of categories and, second, units of analysis, for example recording units (see Holsti, 1969:

116). The characteristics of the messages that interest the researcher are used to define *categories*. In our research we used categories such as general evaluation of the welfare state that include simple positive or negative statements about the welfare state. A system of categories not only includes all of the developed categories but also specifies the relationships between categories. In other words, it defines when individual characteristics are recorded in isolation or in co-occurrence with other characteristics. Conventional systems of categories only contain one or a small number of categories and have to ignore the co-occurrence of certain events. However, in hermeneutic-classificatory content analysis many characteristics or categories are isolated through analysis and the co-occurrences between them are recorded. This means that complex statements can be reconstructed.

In order to maintain a clear structure within this complex system of categories, subdimensions of categories are combined into networks, so that each category can be represented by one network. These networks are then united in one system of networks (see Figure 12.1, explained in detail below, for an example). Consequently, a multi-dimensional and relational system of categories emerges which we will call a '*network system of categories*'.

In principle, there are two ways of constructing a (conventional or network) system of categories. Either it can be constructed before coding, on the basis of theoretical reasoning (a theory-driven system of categories), or on the basis of the empirical material (a data-driven system of categories). Ideally, the construction method employed is a combination of both approaches. Whereas the *a priori* theoretical construction ensures that the categories are theoretically significant, a later modification and completion of the system of categories on the basis of the empirical material ensures empirical significance, that is, validity.

Whereas the system of categories is defined by the substantive interests of the researcher, the *recording unit* – the second element of a content-analytical instrument – is defined by 'the specific segment of content that is characterized by placing it in a given category' (Holsti, 1969: 116). In other words: categories define *what* is of interest and recording units define *which* part of the text is classified. There can be many different types of recording units (Krippendorf, 1980: 60–63) such as physical units (books, issues of a newspaper, respondents), syntactical units (paragraphs, sentences), referential units (objects, events), propositional units (statements) or thematic units (issues). The network approach allows the simultaneous application of different types of recording units. In addition, different levels of recording units can be used for a multi-level analysis of the text. Interview material can be analysed at the specific level of statements (defined as an object or term and a statement about it) and on a more general level of respondents. With *statement units* each of the respondent's statements that refer to the categories of interest are recorded. With *respondent units* categories of interest are recorded only once per respondent. Categories applied at this level refer to respondents' dominant statements. If the category general evaluation of the welfare state is applied at the statement level, each of the respondent's statements that refer to this category are recorded. At the respondent level the dominant general evaluation of the welfare state is recorded instead.

To illustrate the network technique we will use the system of categories developed for analysing the respondents' support for the welfare state in Germany. The study investigated to what extent, positively or negatively, respondents supported the welfare state as a whole as well as its single elements, and what the bases of this support were. The network system of categories was constructed on the basis of theories about the welfare state and was modified and completed on the basis of the empirical material. Central parts of the network system of categories employing statements as the recording unit are illustrated in Figure 12.1. Single categories are marked as boxes. All categories were divided into many subcategories (due to limitations of space these subcategories are not included in Figure 12.1). The recorded relationships are shown as connecting lines with arrows. Categories that form subdimensions of more general dimensions build networks. Networks are also depicted as boxes but with broken lines.

At the most general level, this system covers three networks referred to as the main networks: the main network of objects, the main network of evaluation and the main network of references.

1. The main network of *objects* covers categories referring to objects at different hierarchical levels. At the general level, the category refers to the global objects of the welfare state/social state.[3] At the more specific level of objects the categories refer to the goals and means defined as the central parts of the welfare state.
2. The main network of *evaluations* includes different types of evaluations given by the respondents. At the general level, the category refers to general evaluations such as good and bad. At a more specific level evaluations via outcomes are recorded. The latter are further differentiated into the intended outcomes category, such as having social security, and unintended outcomes category such as financial problems.
3. The main network of *references* covers categories such as space and time that are used as frames of reference for individual objects and evaluations.

From this example the main characteristic of a network system of categories becomes clear: namely, the recording of relationships or

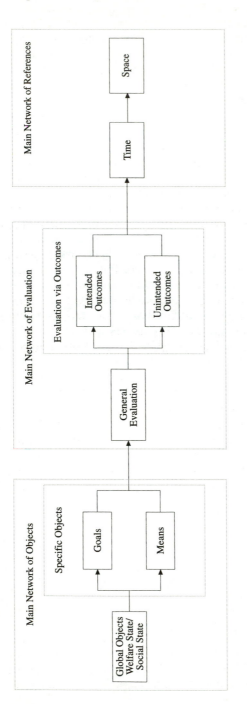

Legend:
□ Categories
   Network
▲ Recorded relationships or co-occurrences

Figure 12.1   *Partial network system of categories for analysing support for the welfare state*

co-occurrences between categories. If people speak about unintended outcomes, such as the financial ruin of the state, and they see social security payments – a subcategory of the means category – as the cause of this financial ruin, then this co-occurrence is recorded. If these aspects were mentioned together with other categories, for example a negative general evaluation of the welfare state, then these further co-occurrences are also recorded. Consequently, the characteristics of messages are not recorded in isolation but in their context, enabling us to reconstruct complex statements.

The network system outlined in the example above includes more categories than those presented in Figure 12.1. Two additional categories are worth mentioning as examples of categories recorded at the general level of respondents. These two categories are general conception of the welfare state/social state and general evaluation of the welfare state/social state. They were introduced to cover additional information about the general level of basic conceptions and general evaluations of the welfare state. The recording of this general information then allowed us to analyse other questions referring to the relationship between general information and the information recorded at the specific level of statements. Such a question could be whether or not different general conceptions of the welfare state/social state are associated with different unintended outcomes at the specific level.

Coding
With hermeneutic-classificatory content analysis the process of coding, that is, assigning codes to text segments, has both a qualitative and a quantitative part. The first step, the hermeneutic interpretation of the meaning of the messages, is *qualitative*. It is carried out by a group of coders who discuss the various options open to them. The ensuing classification of these 'meaning' elements, which are transferred into numeric codes suitable for data processing and then assigned to the text segments, is *quantitative*. This second step results in a numeric data-file which also contains the identification numbers for the relevant text segments. The numeric data-file can then be analysed with statistical programs such as the commonly used SPSS.

Every coding process includes these two parts, but it should be emphasized that the relevance of the first qualitative step increases under certain conditions. Such conditions would be a high level of ambiguity in the message (which is especially the case with spoken messages), a high 'latency' of content and large recording units. In our study of support for the welfare state the hermeneutic interpretation of the 'meaning' of the message during the coders' group discussions was of particular importance when coding the information using respondents as the recording unit. Most of the interviews included a lot of information, which was partially inconsistent, about the general conception and evaluation of the welfare state, dispersed widely over the whole text.

Analysis

With hermeneutic-classificatory content analysis the analysis strategy is also twofold and has both quantitative and qualitative elements. In the first step the *quantitative structure-analysis* is conducted on the basis of the content-analytical coding. This analysis, manageable with statistical programs, gives a quantitative overview of the relevant characteristics of the messages, the co-occurrence of their characteristics and their quantitative importance. In the second step a *hermeneutic detail-analysis* can be conducted based on the texts. Using the results of the quantitative structure-analysis, the researcher is able to selectively retrieve relevant text segments such as frequent, typical cases or infrequent, rare cases. These selective retrievals can be managed with the help of text-analysis programs using the identification numbers as pointers for the search, or, more conveniently, with the help of code-and-retrieve software (for more details see Chapter 14). The researcher can then conduct a more in-depth interpretation of the results on the basis of these retrievals. With the use of different recording units, analysis is possible at both the statement level and the respondent level.

As an example of such an interactive analysis we examined the reasons for supporting single elements of the welfare state. One question was, 'What are the reasons for the described outcomes?' Financial problems were named most frequently by respondents as an **unintended outcome** of the welfare state. One of the central questions is whether or not respondents believe that the causes of the financial problems are to be found in the welfare state itself or whether they can be explained by external causes. The first answer would place blame on the welfare state itself and would therefore be a fundamental criticism of the welfare state.

For the analysis of this question we first conducted a quantitative structure-analysis. We counted how often the **unintended outcome** of financial problems co-occurred with **specific objects** and its subcategories. The empirical analysis indicated that approximately 45 percent of all statements about financial problems co-occurred with **specific objects**. The arguments refer to several subcategories of **specific objects**. The organizational principle underpinning the German pension system, known as the '*generation contract*', was criticized most frequently (26 percent), followed by unemployment (24 percent). Of the remaining subcategories, benefits are mentioned relatively frequently (17 percent). Unfortunately, these subcategories of the category **specific objects** are not detailed enough to answer the question of whether financial problems are caused by external causes or by the welfare state itself.

Therefore, a second analytical step was necessary. We conducted a fine-grained hermeneutic analysis based on the corresponding text segments. Typical examples of arguments referring to the organizational principle of the 'generation contract' are those which cite the declining birth rate as the cause of financial problems:

> well, one should see that the population is declining in Germany and that the financing of pensions for instance is therefore very difficult . . .

In reference to unemployment:

> If nobody works anymore, nobody pays any social insurance and then no pensions can be paid and then the pensioners don't get money anymore because nobody is working . . .

Arguments about the benefits of the welfare state refer to the extent and level of the benefits paid:

> now and then we tend to give the people too much and, on the other hand, we find ourselves indebted because we cannot finance it . . .

These arguments differ from one another. The first two types make up half of all arguments and refer to external causes such as the falling birth rate and increasing unemployment. Arguments about the extent and size of benefits, however, refer to internal features of the welfare state. So the viewpoint that external developments cause financial problems for the welfare state is dominant; in other words fundamental criticism of the welfare state is not the dominant perspective.

This analysis has demonstrated that without a more detailed hermeneutic interpretation of statements the question of whether or not there is fundamental criticism of the welfare state could not have been answered satisfactorily. In addition, without the preceding quantitative structure-analysis no information about the relative frequency of the fundamental criticism of the welfare state would have been available.

Application, advantages and problems of hermeneutic-classificatory content analysis

Although hermeneutic-classificatory content analysis can be applied to virtually all written and spoken documents, the example given above has shown that this technique is especially suited for analysing unstructured or semi-structured interviews in which people describe and explain their views on specific topics in their own words. If a researcher who worked with such material is interested in analysing complex statements, or is interested in the general analysis of the entire text, or wishes to conduct both types of analysis, then hermeneutic-classificatory content analysis offers systematic procedures for achieving these goals. It does this by combining quantitative and qualitative approaches to content analysis.

Compared with quantitative approaches to content analysis this new technique has the advantage that a multitude of characteristics and their co-occurrences can be recorded. Consequently, complex statements can be reconstructed. In other words, characteristics are recorded in the context in which they appear. Compared with qualitative approaches the method works well with large numbers of interviews. Therefore representative samples can be drawn which then allow valid generalizations. By going beyond quantitative and qualitative approaches the technique permits a wide range of possible analyses that did not previously exist given the separate and competing approaches to content analysis. There is now the possibility of combining quantitative structure-analysis with hermeneutic detail-analysis.

The multi-level analysis of the text is another attractive feature resulting from the combination of quantitative and qualitative approaches. A further analytical possibility exists if additional information about the respondents, such as socio-demographic data, is available. This information can be integrated into the numeric data-file and can then be used in all steps of analysis. However, this advanced technique has one drawback: it requires significant resources (in terms of time and money) to train coders to systematically apply the complex system of categories and to do the coding. Nevertheless, these costs are balanced by the increased range of analytical possibilities.

Note

1. With small modifications, hermeneutic-classificatory content analysis was also used in a study of educational research including 264 interviews (Eckert, 1993).

2. It should be noted that this formally defined reference system does not determine the definition of recording units.

3. The objects 'welfare state' and 'social state' must be used because in German there are two competing terms, with slightly different meanings, for the welfare state (see Roller, 1992: 59–60).

13

Using Qualitative Comparative Analysis to Study Configurations

Charles C. Ragin

Qualitative Comparative Analysis (QCA) is a new analytic technique that uses Boolean algebra to implement principles of comparison used by scholars engaged in the qualitative study of social phenomena (Ragin, 1987). Typically, these scholars examine relatively few cases, but their analyses are both *intensive* – addressing many aspects of cases – and *integrative* – examining how the different parts of each case fit together. QCA (Drass and Ragin, 1991) formalizes the configurational logic of cross-case qualitative analysis and brings some of the empirical intensity of qualitative approaches to studies that embrace a moderate or large number of cases.

Researchers are often advised to use variable-oriented, quantitative methods when studying many cases because these methods are powerful data reducers (King et al., 1994). However, quantitative methods embody strong assumptions about social phenomena that are at odds with the interests of qualitatively oriented investigators. For example, most quantitative methods assume that causal factors are additive in their effects on outcomes. Most qualitative approaches, by contrast, assume that causation is fundamentally conjunctural – that is, different causal conditions must combine in specific configurations to produce particular qualitative outcomes. Quantitative approaches also tend to assume that causal forces operate in the same way across all cases in a sample or population. Most qualitative approaches, by contrast, assume that there may be many paths to the same outcome in a given set of cases. As I show in this chapter, QCA provides an alternative to conventional quantitative analysis and avoids many of its troublesome assumptions. The key to this new approach is the strong analytic foundation it provides for studying cases as configurations (Ragin, 1989, 1994a).

This chapter uses the contrast between qualitative, case-oriented research and quantitative, variable-oriented research to introduce QCA and then presents an overview of the technique. Special attention is devoted to practical issues in constructing and analysing truth tables, an important tool for studying configurations.

Case-oriented and variable-oriented research

The case-oriented strategy starts with the simple idea that social phenomena in similar settings may parallel each other sufficiently to allow comparing and contrasting them. This strategy sees cases as meaningful but complex configurations of events and structures, and treats cases as singular entities purposefully selected, not as homogeneous observations drawn at random from a pool of equally plausible selections. While comparative analysis of cases is advocated, the analyst must proceed with caution because much may be lost when cases are decomposed into their component parts.

In variable-oriented work, by contrast, investigators begin research not by postulating the existence of comparable entities, but by positing general dimensions of variation. In this approach, empirical instances are viewed as partial, jumbled or impure representations of underlying theoretical concepts or relationships. Instances vary in the degree to which they express these underlying properties, and researchers view their task as one of uncovering basic patterns of covariation among essential properties. Investigators initiate their research by defining the issue to be explored in a way that allows observation of *many* cases, conceived as substitutable empirical instances. Next, researchers specify relevant causal and outcome variables, matched to theoretical concepts, and then collect information on these variables. From this point on, the language of variables and the relations among them dominate the research process. The resulting understanding of empirical relationships is shaped by examining patterns of covariation, observed and averaged across many cases, not by studying how different features or causes fit together in individual cases (Lieberson, 1991).

The methodological gulf between case-oriented, qualitative research and variable-oriented, quantitative research is wide. Case-oriented work typically examines many causal and outcome conditions in different configurations in a limited number of cases, while variable-oriented work typically examines relatively few variables across a large number of cases. Is there a methodology appropriate for systematically analysing similarities and differences across many cases that preserves the integrity of cases as configurations? The basic problem is to implement methods and strategies that bring the logic of intensive, case-oriented research to investigations with large numbers of cases.

Relevant features of case-oriented research that should be preserved in large-N qualitative studies include:

1. *Attention to cases as configurations.* In case-oriented studies the different parts of a case are defined in relation to each other. For example, one aspect of a hospital's authority structure (for example,

its degree of hierarchy) is understood in the context of other features of the hospital (for example, its ethnic division of labour). This way of approaching cases is not the same as using one aspect to account for another. It is a matter of interpretation: having a high degree of hierarchy conveys and signifies different things about a hospital depending on whether or not there is a substantial ethnic division of labour.

2. *Attention to causal conjunctures.* In case-oriented investigation, explanations of outcomes typically cite combinations of conditions – causal conjunctures and configurations. John Stuart Mill (1967) called this type of causation 'chemical' because the outcome, a qualitative change, emerges from a combination of causal agents.

3. *Attention to causal heterogeneity.* In case-oriented research a typical finding is that different causes combine in different and sometimes contradictory ways to produce roughly similar outcomes. The effect of any particular causal condition depends on the presence and absence of other conditions, and several different conditions may satisfy a general causal requirement – they may be causally equivalent at a more abstract level.

4. *Attention to deviating cases and concern for invariance.* There is no such thing as error in case-oriented studies; investigators account for every case in their attempt to uncover patterned diversity. Cases often deviate from common patterns, but these deviations are identified and addressed on a case-by-case basis. Thus, conclusions typically are rarely stated in probabilistic terms.

5. *Attention to qualitative outcomes.* Qualitative studies typically address specific qualitative changes in specific contexts. In some studies the qualitative changes are dramatic; in others the changes emerge slowly through time. Often the boundaries of an investigation are set by the universe of relevant qualitative changes.

The question that is explored in the remainder of this chapter concerns the nature of the analytic operations that preserve basic features of qualitative research in investigations with large Ns. Many of the basic features of qualitative research can be preserved once it is recognized that the logic of the methods used in cross-case qualitative research can be formalized. The formalization I present uses Boolean algebra, the algebra of logic and sets. Most statistical techniques use linear algebra, a system that is less compatible with the logic of qualitative research.

A brief overview of qualitative comparative analysis

In qualitative comparative analysis (QCA) each case is conceived as a configuration of conditions, not as a collection of scores on variables.

The simplest type of analysis involves dichotomous causal and outcome variables, but more complex variable types can be examined
(Ragin, 1994b). It is important to point out that the treatment of any
feature or characteristic of a case as a cause or as an outcome is entirely
up to the investigator. Based on theory, empirical knowledge, prior
research, in-depth case studies or even vague hunches, investigators
specify some characteristics as causes and others as outcomes.
Causality is inferred based on patterns identified in the data; it may or
may not be observed directly.

As in statistical analysis, an important part of a qualitative comparative investigation involves the selection of outcome variables and the
specification of causal conditions. In qualitative comparative analysis,
however, the causal variables define the different configurations that
are possible within the limits of the analysis. For example, the specification of five dichotomous causal variables provides for 32 (that is, 2^5)
logically possible, qualitatively distinct configurations of conditions.
Causal variables are not examined one at a time or in terms of their
unique contribution to explained variation as in statistical analyses, but
as basic elements that define configurations.

Once causal conditions have been selected, cases conforming to each
combination of causal conditions are examined to see if they agree on
the outcome condition. If there are many causal combinations with
cases that disagree on the outcome variable, the investigator takes this
as a sign that the specification of causal variables is incorrect or incom-
plete. Alternatively, the investigator may use probabilities to construct
the truth table (see Ragin and Bradshaw, 1991; Ragin et al., 1984). The
close examination of cases that have the same values on the causal
variables yet display contrasting outcomes is used as a basis for select-
ing additional causal variables. The investigator moves back and forth
between specification of causal variables (using theory, substantive
knowledge and substantive interests as guides) and examination of
cases to build a combinatorial model with a minimum number of cases
having the same configuration of values on the causal conditions but
contrasting outcomes.

Once a satisfactory set of causal conditions has been identified, data
on cases can be represented as a truth table and then the truth table can
be logically minimized. A truth table lists the different configurations
of causal conditions and the value of the outcome variable for the
cases conforming to each combination. An analysis with three dichotomous causal conditions yields a truth table with eight rows; four causal
conditions produce a truth table with 16 rows; five causal conditions,
32 rows; and so on.

Consider, for example, the simple truth table presented in panel A of
Table 13.1. This truth table lists the different combinations of values for

three dichotomous causal conditions (variables **A**, **B** and **C**) and the outcome value (variable **Y**) associated with each combination. The last column shows the number of cases with each causal combination and is included simply to remind the reader that each row may contain any number of cases (including no cases; see below). As presented, this truth table is ready to be logically reduced because there are no causal combinations that include cases with contrasting outcomes. In the extended example that follows this brief overview, however, I demonstrate techniques for assessing truth tables that include contradictions.

The goal of the logical minimization is to represent in a logically shorthand manner the information in the truth table regarding the different combinations of conditions that produce a specific outcome. In the example in Table 13.1, the goal is to specify the different combinations of **A**, **a**, **B**, **b**, **C** and **c** that produce **Y** (where an upper case letter

Table 13.1   *Simple example of Boolean minimization**

A. Truth table

Causes			Outcome	N of cases
A	B	C	Y	
0	0	0	0	4
0	0	1	0	6
0	1	0	1	8
0	1	1	0	3
1	0	0	0	10
1	0	1	1	9
1	1	0	1	2
1	1	1	1	7

B. Reduced to prime implicants for positive outcomes (Y = 1)

A – C = Y
A B – = Y
– B c = Y

C. Prime implicant chart

		Relevant truth table rows			
		ABC	AbC	ABc	aBc
	A–C	x	x		
Prime implicants	AB–	x		x	
	–Bc			x	x

D. Final equation

Y = AC + Bc

---

* Upper case letters and 1s are used to indicate presence; lower case letters and 0s are used to indicate absence. Dashes indicate that a causal factor has been eliminated.

indicates the presence of a condition and a lower case letter indicates its absence). The first step in the minimization process is to compare rows with each other and simplify them through a bottom-up process of paired comparison. These paired comparisons follow a simple rule which mimics a series of *ex post facto* experimental designs: combine rows that differ on only one causal condition, but produce the same outcome. The last two rows, for example, differ on only the third causal condition, and both produce **Y**. Thus, they can be combined to produce a single, simpler expression, **AB**.

The process of paired comparisons culminates in the production of *prime implicants,* shown in panel B of Table 13.1. Often there are more prime implicants than are needed to cover all the original causal combinations for an outcome. This result obtains in Table 13.1, as is shown in panel C. This panel shows the next phase of logical minimization which involves constructing a *prime implicant chart* mapping the correspondence between the prime implicants (just derived) and the original causal combinations for the outcome of interest drawn from the truth table. It is apparent from simple inspection of this chart (panel C) that only two prime implicants are needed to cover all the causal combinations for the presence of **Y**.

Use of the prime implicant chart is the final phase of logical minimization and culminates in a logical equation for the outcome of interest. The final reduced equation for the presence of **Y** is reported in panel D of Table 13.1. The equation states simply that two combinations of causal conditions result in **Y**: (a) presence of **A** combined with the presence of **B**, and (b) presence of **B** combined with **c** (the absence of **C**).

When the number of causal conditions is greater than four, it is difficult to perform these operations by hand, and computer algorithms are necessary, especially for the simplification of large prime implicant charts. In the 1950s several algorithms were developed by electrical engineers (described in McDermott, 1985; Mendelson, 1970; Roth, 1975) and have been adapted for social science data by Drass and Ragin (1991).

A re-analysis of data from *The Strategy of Social Protest* using QCA

The brief overview just presented uses unrealistically simple data. Most qualitative researchers are interested in more complex configurations. The following demonstration uses data from Gamson (1975). This data set exhibits some of the typical problems associated with social science data: first, there are many combinations of causal conditions in the truth table that lack empirical instances and, second, among the causal combinations with empirical instances, some include cases with contrasting outcomes.

In *The Strategy of Social Protest* William Gamson (1975) presented a systematic examination of fifty-three social movement organizations, drawn from about a hundred years of US history. Gamson's analytic strategy was simple and straightforward. With only fifty-three cases, he was able to establish some familiarity with each case. To complement this familiarity, he used simple descriptive techniques. Armed with a series of hypotheses from the literature on social movements, Gamson computed a series of two-way cross-tabulations and reported them in the form of bar graphs with percentages and chi-square statistics. The small size of the data set limited Gamson to simple statistical methods. As will be clear in the analysis that unfolds below, QCA does not suffer these same limitations.

Specifying outcome variables

Gamson examined two dependent variables: *acceptance* and *new advantages*. The first, *acceptance*, concerns the relationship between the social movement organization and its antagonists and can take several forms. The organization may be accepted as a spokesperson for the collectivity it represents, or it may be consulted by political authorities or by antagonists. Acceptance is coded for the period of the organization's activity. *New advantages* concerns whether or not any gains occurred for the organization's constituency. Unlike acceptance, new advantages can occur after the period of the group's challenge, up to fifteen years later.

However, the correspondence between acceptance and new advantages is strong. Altogether, 42 out of 53 organizations (79 percent) fall into the two cells on the main diagonal in the cross-tabulation of these two variables. In the analysis that follows, acceptance is treated as a causal condition – as a factor that may contribute to new advantages, the main outcome of interest. It is likely that methodological limitations encouraged Gamson's restricted use of acceptance – as only a dependent variable – and constrained his analysis and results. These methodological limitations derive from the modest number of cases in his study and from the logic of the statistical procedures he used (Ragin, 1989).

Specifying causal conditions

The analysis focuses on five different causal conditions relevant to the success of social movement organizations:

1. presence/absence of bureaucracy,
2. class origins of the organization's constituency,

3. presence/absence of displacement as a primary goal (explained below),
4. presence/absence of help from outsiders and
5. presence/absence of acceptance of the organization, as defined above.

The first three characteristics concern basic features of the organizations; the fourth and fifth concern events that occurred or failed to occur while it was active.

Presence/absence of bureaucracy distinguishes between organizations with full, formal bureaucracies and those lacking full formal bureaucracies. *Class origins of the group's constituency* is coded to pinpoint organizations with exclusively lower strata constituencies. Gamson identified six class-origin categories: (a) middle class and professional; (b) blue-collar workers, manual workers and craftsmen; (c) farmers; (d) mixtures of working class and middle class or of workers and farmers; (e) students; and (f) disadvantaged ethnic groups, including blacks. In the present analysis, categories (b) and (f) are lumped together to indicate organizations with exclusively lower strata constituencies. *Displacement as a primary goal* appears in Gamson's work as a dichotomy used to distinguish organizations that were trying to destroy or replace their antagonists from organizations that were not. Organizations with displacement as their primary goal, on the whole, had very low success rates. *Help from outsiders* concerns whether or not an organization received more than verbal support from an established interest group, political party or government agency that was not a target of the group, but could, by its actions, help the group.

Constructing truth tables

The next step is to construct truth tables, which show the different combinations of the five causal conditions (coded 1 for yes or present and 0 for no or absent) and the outcomes associated with each combination. Table 13.2 presents data on the fifty-three organizations studied by Gamson (1975) in truth table form. The different logically possible combinations of values of the five causal conditions are listed along with their codes on the outcome variables. For each combination of causal conditions that exists in the data (the first five columns), the number of organizations is listed along with the breakdown of these groups on the main outcome variable, *new advantages* versus *no new advantages*. The last three columns show the outcome codes assigned to organizations in each row based on the distribution of cases with and without new advantages.

The codings of the three outcome variables (right-hand side of Table 13.2) reflect the distribution of outcomes for organizations in a given row. The first outcome column is labelled U for uniform new

Table 13.2   *Truth table for causes of new advantages**

BUR	LOW	DIS	HLP	ACP	Number of cases	New advantages	No new advantages	U	L	P
0	0	0	0	0	4	2	2	0	0	1
0	0	0	0	1	2	2	0	1	1	1
0	0	0	1	0	2	2	0	1	1	1
0	0	0	1	1	2	2	0	1	1	1
0	0	1	0	0	4	0	4	0	0	0
0	0	1	0	1	1	1	0	–	–	1
0	0	1	1	0	2	0	2	0	0	0
0	0	1	1	1	1	0	1	0	0	0
0	1	0	0	0	2	0	2	0	0	0
0	1	0	0	1	0	remainder	term	?	?	?
0	1	0	1	0	0	remainder	term	?	?	?
0	1	0	1	1	2	2	0	1	1	1
0	1	1	0	0	5	0	5	0	0	0
0	1	1	0	1	0	remainder	term	?	?	?
0	1	1	1	0	2	0	2	0	0	0
0	1	1	1	1	0	remainder	term	?	?	?
1	0	0	0	0	3	0	3	0	0	0
1	0	0	0	1	4	1	3	0	0	1
1	0	0	1	0	1	1	0	–	–	1
1	0	0	1	1	1	1	0	–	–	1
1	0	1	0	0	1	0	1	0	0	0
1	0	1	0	1	0	remainder	term	?	?	?
1	0	1	1	0	0	remainder	term	?	?	?
1	0	1	1	1	0	remainder	term	?	?	?
1	1	0	0	0	2	1	1	0	0	1
1	1	0	0	1	7	6	1	0	1	1
1	1	0	1	0	0	remainder	term	?	?	?
1	1	0	1	1	5	5	0	1	1	1
1	1	1	0	0	0	remainder	term	?	?	?
1	1	1	0	1	0	remainder	term	?	?	?
1	1	1	1	0	0	remainder	term	?	?	?
1	1	1	1	1	0	remainder	term	?	?	?

* Column headings: BUR = bureaucratic organization; LOW = lower strata constituency; DIS = displacement as primary goal; HLP = help from outsiders; ACP = acceptance of the organization. 1 indicates presence; 0 indicates absence. The output is coded as follows: U = uniform new advantages; L = new advantages likely; P = new advantages possible. The don't care output coding is indicated with a dash.

advantages and indicates whether or not the cases in the row uniformly display an outcome of new advantages. Note that to receive a code of yes (or 1) in this column, a row had to contain at least two cases. Rows with only one case of new advantages and 0 cases of no new advantages were coded don't care (dash) on outcome U. (The don't care outcome is explained below.) The second outcome column is labelled L for new advantages likely and indicates rows where at least a substantial majority of the cases had new advantages. Again, rows with only one case with new advantages and 0 cases with no new advantages were coded don't care (dash). The third column is labelled P for new advantages possible and indicates those rows in which at least one case had new advantages, regardless of the number of cases with no new advantages.

In effect, these three outcomes are nested: uniform is a subset of likely, and likely is a subset of possible. The nesting of coded outcomes offers a clear alternative to the statistical analysis of outcomes, which focuses only on relative probabilities. The second outcome (L) is the closest to a statistical treatment of these same data because it distinguishes between likely and unlikely. The first and third outcomes (uniform and possible), however, have no counterpart in statistical analysis. The analysis of outcome P (possible), for example, offers the researcher a Boolean analysis of possibilities. In the framework elaborated in this chapter, probabilistic outcomes are intermediate between uniform and possible outcomes.

With five dichotomous variables, there are 2^5 (32) logically possible combinations of causal conditions. Only 20 of these 32 logically possible combinations actually exist (see Table 13.2). An important decision in qualitative comparative analysis concerns the treatment of logically possible combinations of causal conditions that lack empirical instances (Ragin, 1987: 104–113). There are several ways to treat these *remainder terms* as they are known (Drass and Ragin, 1991). Two are plausible in the present context.

One is to assume that if organizations with these characteristics existed, they would not be among those with new advantages (that is, they would be coded 0 on all three outcome variables: U, L and P). This coding of the remainder terms is based on the simple idea that organizations constantly seek new advantages and are likely to try whatever works. Thus, according to this reasoning, if a causal combination does not exist, its absence may indicate simply that it involves a combination of conditions that would not lead to new advantages.

An alternative approach to the remainder terms is to assign them the same don't care value (the dash) assigned to the rows with only one case of new advantages and no cases of no new advantages. A coding of don't care allows algorithms internal to computer programs capable of such analyses[1] to determine the appropriate value for the row: if coding the row yes (1) on an outcome results in a logically simpler solution of the truth table, then the algorithm assigns that output value to the row; otherwise, it assigns the row an output value of no (0) (see McDermott, 1985; Mendelson, 1970; Ragin, 1987; Roth, 1975.) Both treatments of the remainder terms are presented below.

Results of qualitative comparative analysis

With three outcome variables and two analytic strategies (one with non-existent combinations assigned 0s and the other with non-existent combinations assigned don't care outcomes), there are six different analyses. Each of these six analyses is based upon a different truth table. Remember that the goal of each analysis is to represent the information in a truth table in a logically minimal manner. The simplification of these six truth tables follows the procedures sketched in Table 13.1. Of course, not all the rules for simplifying truth tables are represented in Table 13.1. Interested readers should consult McDermott (1985), Mendelson (1970), Roth (1975) or a comparable introduction to switching circuit theory.

Applying appropriate minimization procedures to the six truth tables that can be generated from Table 13.2 yields the six logical equations presented in Table 13.3. In the first column of Table 13.3 are the solutions that result when remainders are set to false (0). The second column shows the equations that result when the remainder terms are set to don't care.

Each equation is interpreted as a specification of functionally equivalent causal configurations for a particular outcome. Variable names in lower case letters indicate absence; variable names in upper case letters indicate presence. For example, the first equation (column 1, row 1) states that uniform new advantages accrue to organizations that display

Table 13.3   *QCA results: minimization of truth tables for new advantages**

Remainder terms = false (0)	Remainder terms = don't care (–)

UNIFORM = dis*HLP*ACP
        + low*dis*HLP
        + bur*low*dis*ACP
	UNIFORM = dis*HLP
	        + bur*dis*ACP

LIKELY = dis*HLP*ACP
        + low*dis*HLP
        + bur*low*dis*ACP
        + BUR*LOW*dis*ACP
	LIKELY = dis*HLP
	        + bur*dis*ACP
	        + LOW*ACP

POSSIBLE = dis*HLP*ACP
        + low*dis*HLP
        + bur*low*dis
        + BUR*dis*ACP
        + BUR*LOW*dis*hlp
        + bur*low*hlp*ACP
	POSSIBLE = dis*HLP
	        + bur*low*dis
	        + BUR*LOW
	        + hlp*ACP

* Variable names are explained in notes to Table 13.2. Variable names in upper case letters indicate presence; variable names in lower case letters indicate absence; addition indicates logical OR; multiplication (*) indicates logical AND.

any of three configurations of causes: (a) non-displacement goals combined with help from outsiders and acceptance as a representative of its constituency, (b) representation of middle strata combined with non-displacement goals and help from outsiders and (c) representation of middle strata combined with a low level of bureaucracy, non-displacement goals and acceptance as a representative of its constituency.

Notice that when the remainder terms are given the don't care coding on this outcome, a simpler result obtains (row 1, column 2). This simplification reflects the addition of a sub-set of the remainder terms to the equation that appears in column 1. Thus, the equation for uniform new advantages in the second column specifies two configurations of conditions: (a) non-displacement goals combined with help from outsiders and (b) a low level of bureaucracy combined with non-displacement goals and acceptance as a representative of its constituency. Equations in the first column are sub-sets of equations in the second column because those in the second column reflect the addition of selected remainder terms.

Because of the structure of the outcome variables, each equation is a sub-set of the equation below it. Looking down the first column, for example, organizations that uniformly won new advantages constitute a sub-set of the organizations likely to win new advantages. Not surprisingly, moving down a column reveals more complex equations because a greater diversity of organizations is covered.

It is important to evaluate any remainder terms that are used to generate simplified equations. With a list of the remainder terms used to simplify an equation, it is possible to check their plausibility. Consider, for example, the solution for likely new advantages, using remainder terms (row 2, column 2 of Table 13.3). This equation uses the following remainder terms:

LOW*DIS*ACP,
bur*LOW*hlp*ACP,
LOW*dis*HLP*acp,
BUR*low*dis*HLP and
BUR*dis*HLP*acp.

Is it plausible to assume that organizations with these characteristics, if they existed, would win new advantages for their constituents? The first remainder term in the list (LOW*DIS*ACP) states that an organization representing lower strata, with displacement goals and acceptance as a representative of its constituency, would be likely, if it existed, to win new advantages. In fact, this assumption is not plausible. Gamson (1975) has shown that organizations with displacement goals generally fail, and I have shown elsewhere (Ragin, 1989) that organizations representing lower strata must mobilize more resources than organizations representing middle strata in order to win new advantages. If some remainder terms seem implausible, they can be omitted, and a new equation generated. In this way, the investigator can formulate more plausible equations intermediate between those in the first column and those in the second column.

Those who seek simple answers might scan Table 13.3 and ask: which equation is correct? The answer to this question depends on the purposes of the investigation and the assumptions that the investigator is willing to make. Essentially, all equations are correct, for they all provide different representations based on different goals and different assumptions. QCA clarifies the consequences of decisions that are central to the research process.

Conclusion: recreating intensive investigation

Systematic analysis of cases as configurations of causes and outcomes is the essence of case-oriented comparative work. When the number of cases and configurations is great, it is a cognitively demanding task, especially in the absence of computer algorithms to aid the researcher.[2] The formalization of qualitative comparative methods sketched here (and explained in detail in Ragin, 1987) allows the preservation of essential features of case-oriented work in the analysis of many cases and provides an important methodological bridge between case-oriented and variable-oriented work. The re-analysis of Gamson's data demonstrates that basic features of intensive investigation can be maintained in studies with many cases. The qualitative comparative analysis of these organizations shows that it is possible (a) to approach cases as configurations, (b) to apply a configurational approach to causal conjunctures, (c) to allow for multiple causal conjunctures, (d) to find general patterns without resorting to error vectors and probabilistic statements and (e) to examine qualitative outcomes.

By formalizing cross-case qualitative analysis, its distinct strengths and virtues are highlighted. These strengths distinguish it from techniques that rely on probability theory and additive causal models. QCA is uniquely well suited for examining configurations of similarities and differences across many cases.

Notes

1. For example, the program QCA developed by Kriss Drass and Charles Ragin for analysing truth tables.

2. Although the programs QCA and AQUAD are capable of such analyses (see Chapter 14).

14

An Overview of Software

Gerald Prein, Udo Kelle and Katherine Bird

The purpose of the preceding chapters was to discuss recently developed strategies for using computers in qualitative research and to introduce current methodological debates related to these developments. This chapter focuses on the computer software specifically designed for practically implementing such strategies.

During the 1980s, due to the fact that standard software (such as ordinary database management systems) could not easily be used to employ most of the methods discussed in this book, many qualitative researchers began to develop their own computer programs. Initially, these were not particularly user-friendly; in most cases such programs consisted of routines for limited purposes based on batch processing without providing any menus or dialogue boxes. With such programs the user had to execute commands directly from the operating system, sometimes having to specify numerous parameters. However, some of these routines formed the foundation for powerful and user-friendly software packages for qualitative data analysis. Many of these programs are now widely available to the scientific community, and the developers regularly issue new and enhanced versions, and some also provide extensive support for users.

Although the general principles of textual database management supported by the programs tend to be similar, there is enormous variation between the programs with respect to additional features, which sometimes have far-reaching methodological implications. Consequently, it is important for the analyst of qualitative data to acquire an overview of what the different programs offer before choosing one. In this chapter such an overview of the programs developed especially for qualitative research is presented, so that the reader who wishes to apply the methods discussed in the previous chapters can gain an impression of which software is most suitable for his or her purposes.

The program descriptions are based on questionnaires sent to the developers or distributors and on our own knowledge of the programs. The descriptions focus mainly on issues relevant to the methodological discussions in this book and, additionally, provide the most important technical specifications.[1] We decided not to include an evaluation of the user interfaces (which vary enormously – ranging from simple command shells to sophisticated graphically oriented user interfaces), since subjective preferences vary significantly here. We will, however, give some general information, for example whether there is a graphical interface or whether a mouse can be used. It is worth noting here that graphical user interfaces may help novices, but they can also disturb users if a confusing multiplicity of icons appears on the screen. Users with a fairly advanced knowledge of, for example, database structures may sometimes be more comfortable with one of those programs (for example, MAX or AQUAD) that currently have a simpler, menu-based user interface, but nevertheless offer an 'open environment', allowing the user to develop his or her own subroutines that interface with the program.

Due to the rapid evolution of software for the analysis of qualitative data, and variations in personal preferences, we would recommend that anyone intending to purchase one of these programs also asks the developer for further information or a demonstration version, which sometimes also contains a tutorial (for example, NUD.IST or QUALPRO), or refers to a recently published source (for example, Weitzman and Miles, 1995) that gives a highly detailed account of such programs.

All of the programs described here can be used for the management of unstructured textual data. Their common basic feature is that they offer facilities for the 'coding' and 'retrieval' of text segments, either by allowing the researcher to copy text segments onto 'cards', or by attaching pointers to codes that contain the address of text segments. Hence, all programs allow for 'ordinary retrieval', that is, the retrieval of all text segments to which a certain code has been attached. Most of the programs also allow for other kinds of retrieval, based on the *search for co-occurrences* of codes in a document. Co-occurrences can be defined in various ways: indicated by overlapping or nested text segments to which the codes under investigation are attached, or the sequential ordering of text segments, or by a certain maximum distance (proximity) between text segments. The simplest form of *overlapping* text segments would be where, for example, lines 1–10 of a document are coded with code A and lines 8–15 are coded with code B. In this case, lines 8, 9 and 10 (the overlap) are coded with both code A and code B, and codes A and B are said to overlap at this point (see Figure 14.1).

The text segments would be *nested* if code B were attached to lines 1–10, but code A were attached to lines 4–7. In this case, the text segment coded with code A is contained (nested) within the text segment coded with code B (see Figure 14.2).

Figure 14.1   *Text segments with code **A** overlapping with text
segments with code **B***

Sequential ordering is where code **A** is regularly followed by code **B**
(see Figure 14.3). The *proximity* of the codes could be set at, say, eight
lines. Then the researcher would be looking for all instances where a
text segment coded with code **B** starts within up to eight lines of the
start or the end of a text segment coded with code **A**. With this criterion
it is also possible to locate overlapping and nested text segments (see
Figure 14.4).

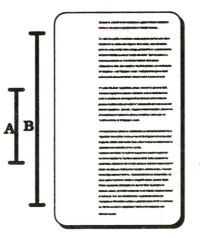

Figure 14.2   *Text segments with code **A** nested into text segments
with code **B***

Figure 14.3   *Sequential order of text segments: code B following*
code A

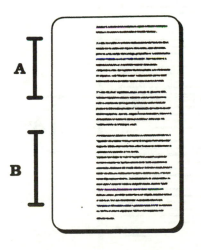

Figure 14.4   *Proximity: text segments with code B following text*
segments with code A at a maximum distance of 8 lines

Searches for co-occurring codes can be realized through quite different algorithms which are useful for different research strategies. Many programs offer facilities for employing the Boolean operators 'AND', 'OR' and 'NOT'. For example using the operator 'AND' to link two codes (for example, search for code A AND code B) will retrieve all text segments to which both codes are attached (that is, which overlap or are nested). Hence this feature permits the identification of nested or overlapping text segments and retrieves this 'nest' or overlap (see Figure 14.5).

If two codes are linked in a query through the operator 'OR', all text segments coded with at least one of these codes will be retrieved (see Figure 14.6). The operator 'NOT' will retrieve all segments to which a certain code is not attached (see Figure 14.7). These definitions, however, do not apply to all of the programs described: for example, when the Boolean operator 'AND' is used in ATLAS/ti, the program will only retrieve co-occurring codes that have been attached to exactly the same part of the document.

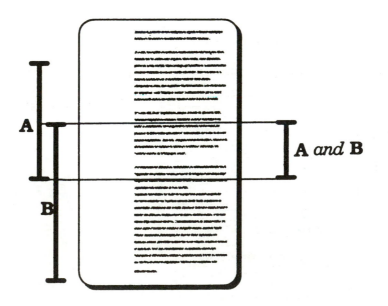

Figure 14.5   *Retrieval using the Boolean operator 'AND'*

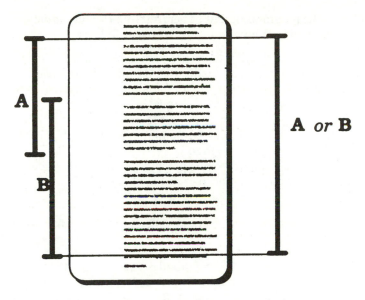

Figure 14.6   *Retrieval using the Boolean operator* 'OR'

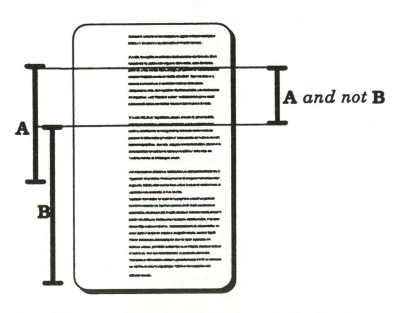

Figure 14.7   *Retrieval using the Boolean operators* 'AND' *and* 'NOT'

In addition, the programs described here also offer a wide variety of other functions; their presentation is structured as follows:

1. Initially, a brief introduction to the program is given highlighting its special or unique features and indicating the analysis strategies for which the program is particularly useful, along with references to the methodological discussions contained in this book.
2. The second paragraph lists the system requirements, that is, operating system environment, and the minimum RAM and disk space required for installing the program.
3. The third paragraph addresses the preparation of text documents, concrete details of coding-and-retrieval facilities, and features for recording memos.

The next three paragraphs relate to the different topics addressed in Parts II to IV.

4. The fourth paragraph of the program descriptions lists those features that can be employed in the strategies for *linking elements of the qualitative database and network building for theory construction* discussed in Part II. The different programs offer a wide range of options for defining linkages between different objects, for example linkages between codes and memos, between memos and text segments, or *hyperlinks* (direct linkages between text segments). Some of the programs facilitate the construction of whole networks from these linkages, and, according to the methodological background and interests of the developers, different types of networks for different purposes can be constructed. An example is the utilization of networks for the construction of hierarchical trees of code categories made possible by programs like NUD.IST, WINMAX or Kwalitan.
5. The fifth paragraph lists features that facilitate different methods of computer-aided *qualitative hypothesis examination*, such as those discussed in detail in Part III of the book. The retrieval techniques employed here are based upon the search for *co-occurrences* of codes in a document. However, it should be pointed out that search functions for co-occurring codes can also be employed in the context of an inductive strategy far removed from deductive hypothesis examination.

   Different conceptions of hypothesis examination are evident in the various programs, which translate into different answers to the question of which parts of the hypothesis examination process should be computerized. Features to assist qualitative hypothesis examination range from automatic hypothesis testers to heuristic devices; the latter are designed so that the identification of evidence or counter-evidence in the original text remains an interpretive task for the researcher. Given the somewhat confusing variety of tools for qualitative hypothesis examination the researcher who wants to employ such methods is well advised to carefully consider the current methodological debate on this issue (outlined, for example, in Part III of this volume).

6. The sixth paragraph refers to features that are helpful if the researcher wants to *combine qualitative and quantitative methods* of text analysis, such as those described in Part IV. The methodological approaches presented in Chapters 11 and 12 require that the information contained in the unstructured texts is reduced and then transformed into a numerical data matrix. This can be achieved in two ways. One way would be to use codes to reduce the textual information. In this case either the code frequencies in a given document or text segment would be a possible product of the transformation. Or the presence or absence of codes in a given document could be represented in a data matrix, thus allowing the calculation of co-occurrences of codes (see Chapter 12). Alternatively, case variables (such as age, gender, occupation) are defined: an ensuing data matrix could contain the values for these variables for each case (see Chapter 11). Two kinds of functions are available to support such transformations: first, features for the calculation of code frequencies and the cross-tabulation of codes or case related variables and, second (since none of the programs presented here contain sophisticated statistical functions), functions for the export of numerical data to statistical software packages like SPSS or SAS.

   If the researcher wishes to concentrate on this type of analysis he or she may also draw on software packages designed particularly for quantitative content analysis such as Textpack (Mohler and Züll, 1990) or Intext/PC, although the coding-and-retrieval facilities are extremely limited in these programs. If the researcher is looking for an alternative to traditional statistical methods, then he or she could experiment with the methodology of 'qualitative comparative analysis' presented by Charles Ragin in Chapter 13. For implementing this methodology the programs AQUAD and QCA can be used. (However, the latter of these two programs does not support the management of unstructured textual data.)

7. The last paragraph presents a list of additional features, for example, functions for counting word frequencies useful in the context of computer-aided quantitative content analysis.

All restrictions that the programs impose (for example, concerning the maximum number of documents that can be handled) and that the developers referred to in the questionnaires or manuals are mentioned. If the reader wishes to compare several programs in order to choose the best software for his or her purposes, then he or she should keep in mind that only the presence of limitations and features is indicated, not their absence.

As mentioned above, this chapter concentrates on programs that have been developed by researchers who wanted to create tools to assist with the qualitative analysis of unstructured textual data. Many commercial software packages are also available that are useful for other purposes in qualitative research, for example:

- *Text retrievers*, which search for words or phrases, can be useful for the investigation of highly standardized texts (for example, instruction manuals or small ads). Examples are Metamorph, Sonar, The Text Collector, Word Cruncher, ZyINDEX or Oracle TextRetrieval.
- *Database programs* that require a fixed, predefined structure for storing text segments can in the context of qualitative research be particularly helpful for the management of short texts (for example, short field notes, memos). Examples are askSam, Folio VIEWS or Tabletop.
- *Network builders* that can be used to represent theories through the visualization of networks, but without any connection to the raw data, such as Inspiration, MECA, MetaDesign and SemNet.

For the reader interested in using such software we would recommend referring to *Computer Programs for Qualitative Data Analysis* (Weitzman and Miles, 1995) which provides a comprehensive and step-by-step introduction to how to use these and other programs.

PROGRAM DETAILS

AQUAD Version 4.03
1994 by Günter L. Huber

Verlag Ingeborg Huber, Postfach 46, 87643 Schwangau, Germany

1. This program is particularly suited for those analysis strategies, described in Part III, that employ logic programming for hypothesis examination. It also contains functions for the logical minimization of truth tables described in detail in Chapter 13.
2. *System requirements*: DOS 2.0 or higher, hard disk with 1.4MB free.
3. *Text documents* must be formatted in ASCII with fixed line ends; the program can analyse a maximum of 1,000 documents at a time.

Code names must have a fixed length; up to 500 codes or variables can be defined per document. The smallest coding unit is the text line. Up to ten codes can start in the same text line. Simple *retrievals* of text segments are possible; selective retrievals of text segments can be made using a 'matrix function' (see Chapter 10). Complex search functions do not retrieve the text segments themselves, but 'references' to the text segments, that is, the relevant document and line numbers. *Memos* can have up to five text lines and can contain references to whole documents, line numbers within a document, codes and user-defined keywords.

4. Several codes can be combined in one 'meta-code'. Using standard DOS commands, these 'meta-codes' can be employed in all types of retrievals. Memos can be linked to codes, texts, text segments and user-defined keywords.

5. *Co-occurrences:* the location, that is, document and line number, of code sequences, code distances, overlapping or nested codes can be retrieved. All Boolean operators can be applied. A wide range of utilities for hypothesis examination based upon these search functions is available. The features for hypothesis examination that the program offers can be extended by a user competent in the PROLOG programming language.

6. Case-variables, such as respondent's gender and occupation, have to be defined as codes. Furthermore, a special type of code is available to which differing numerical values can be assigned, for example, respondent's age. This *numerical information* can then be used in matrices and hypothesis examinations. Code frequencies can be represented in matrix form. The code files containing numerical data are stored in ASCII format; after manual modifications these data can be imported by statistical software.

7. *Additional functions* are available for *matrix building,* for the logical minimization of *truth tables* and for the retrieval of word frequencies.

ATLAS/ti Version 1.1E
1993/94 by Thomas Muhr

Thomas Muhr, Trautenaustr. 12, 10717 Berlin, Germany

1. ATLAS/ti could be the preferred program if an analyst wishes to construct linkages between any elements of the qualitative database – for example text segments, codes and memos. This very flexible tool for constructing any kind of network (for example, containing cycles, hierarchical and non-hierarchical relations) is particularly suited for the approaches to theory building discussed in Part II.

The design of the user interface is such that most of the analysis is conducted on-screen, rather than on paper as with many of the other programs. Consequently, a wide variety of functions to support this style of working is offered. The program is especially useful for research groups whose members want to do coding, memoing and theory building independently, but want to share their results.

2. *System requirements*: DOS 3.1 or later, 4MB RAM, hard disk with 3MB free. The program cannot run under OS/2.

3. The program has a *graphical user interface*; a *mouse* can be used. *Text documents* must be formatted in ASCII with fixed line ends. The smallest coding unit is 1 character. Selective retrievals can be conducted after documents, codes or memos have been assigned to 'families'. *Memos* and *annotations* (brief notes) can be written. Codes can be linked to 'hypercodes' or automatically be replaced by a new code.

4. *Linkages* between all elements (for example codes, entire documents, text segments, memos) can be defined. The nature of the linkages can be defined or 'qualified'; for example the linkage between codes can be defined as a causal link. 'Directional' or 'non-directional' links are possible which come into play when text segments are retrieved. For example, with a causal link between two codes the retrieval of the 'effect' would automatically be accompanied by the retrieval of the 'cause' or chains of causes. After several linkages have been made a network starts to emerge. Networks and parts of networks can be graphically displayed. When the user is in the graphical display mode, elements of the database, for example memos or text segments in their context, can be immediately displayed by clicking on the corresponding nodes. Networks can be edited and linkages between codes used for text retrieval. Non-cyclic networks can automatically be transformed into tree-structured networks. Networks of codes can be stored separately to facilitate 'theory re-use' in follow-up projects.

5. There is a limited number of functions available for *co-occurring code* searches: co-occurring codes that have been attached to precisely the same text segment can be identified by using the Boolean operator 'AND'. With the help of the Boolean operator 'OR', any text segment to which at least one of the specified codes has been assigned will be identified. A 'code matrix' output can be computed as the result of a combination of 'AND' and 'OR': for example (code A OR code B OR code C) AND (code D OR code E OR code F).

6. *Numerical* values can be given to codes. All codes and any numerical information they contain can be exported to SPSS/PC. *Code frequencies* can be calculated.

7. Automatic coding according to user-defined keywords is possible.

HyperQual2 Version 1.0 (stack version)
1993 by Raymond V. Padilla

HyperQual, 3327 N. Dakota, Chandler, AZ 85224, USA

1. A program for the Macintosh based on the Hypercard technology. Copies of text passages are stored separately on 'cards' which can be collected into stacks. The numerous possibilities for sorting, indexing and filtering cards make this a very flexible program. Although the text segments are decontextualized during the coding process, the original context can be rapidly accessed if desired. Furthermore, the program offers various possibilities to 'hyperlink' different elements of the database, for example, text segments or memos and codes.
2. *System requirements*: Apple Macintosh System 6.0.4 or later, 4MB RAM (recommended), Hypercard Version 2.0 or higher.
3. The program has a *graphical user interface; a mouse* can be used. *Text documents* can be formatted in ASCII; other formats can be imported via the clipboard. The program uses the Macintosh Hypercard system. Coding is done by copying a text segment onto a card which includes a reference that allows the user to return automatically to the source of the text segment. Up to 30,000 characters can be placed on a card, but cards can be stacked. The smallest coding unit is one character, the maximum is 30,000 characters. Up to 30,000 characters of codes can be saved with one document. About 500 codes can be saved per case. The program supports selective retrievals of text segments. *Memos* containing up to 30,000 characters can be entered.
4. Several codes can be combined into a new code that can be used in retrievals. *Linkages* between different text segments, memos and codes, memos and documents, memos and coders, and memos and text segments can be defined. These linkages can be used to spring between these objects.
5. *Code frequencies* can be calculated by determining the size of card stacks containing the text segments with a particular code.
6. *Additional functions* are available for the automatic coding of user-defined keywords.

HyperRESEARCH Version 1.5x
1994 by Sharlene Hesse-Biber, T. Scott Kinder, Paul R. Dupuis

ResearchWare, Inc., PO Box 1258, Randolph, MA 02368-1258, USA

1. As well as permitting ordinary coding and retrieval, this program is particularly designed for the approach towards 'qualitative hypothesis testing' discussed in Chapter 9. The researcher formulates a

hypothesis in terms of a series of 'if-then' statements about the co-occurrence of certain codes within a document. Since for this strategy the overlapping, nesting, proximity or sequence of codes is not important, functions that use this information are not implemented.

2.   *System requirements*: Windows 3.1 or later, 4MB RAM, hard disk with 2MB free; or Apple Macintosh System 6.0.7 or later (System 7 recommended), 2MB RAM, hard disk with 1MB free.

3.   The program has a *graphical user interface*; a *mouse* can be used. *Text documents* must be formatted in ASCII. The program can handle 16,000 characters of data at a time; so source texts may have to be divided into 'pages' by using 'break points'. These break points should not be placed within a text passage that the user wants to code as a whole chunk. The smallest coding unit is two characters. Roughly 300 codes can be saved per case. Texts requiring more than 300 codes may be coded to multiple cases. The program supports selective retrieval of text segments, and several codes can be combined into a new code that can be used in retrievals.

5.   *Co-occurrences* of codes within one document can be searched for, regardless of whether the coded segments overlap, are nested, follow each other sequentially or are a certain distance apart. By using all Boolean operators the user can formulate hypothetical if-then statements about the common presence or absence of codes in each document. If the hypothetical statement is confirmed then the program can temporarily add a new code to the document.

6.   *Code frequencies* can be calculated.

7.   The program can automatically code each occurrence of a user-defined keyword.

Hypersoft Version 2.2 (beta)
1994/95 by Ian Dey

Ian Dey, Dept. of Social Policy,
The University of Edinburgh, Adam Ferguson Building,
George Square, Edinburgh EH8 9LL, UK

1.   Hypersoft is a program for Macintosh that is especially suited for the kind of theory building strategy outlined in Chapter 5. The main rationale for developing this package was to overcome the fragmentation inherent in the analysis of isolated text chunks. This is achieved by offering a choice of many different types of direct links between text segments. The program is well suited to develop network-like structures by allowing for the definition of all possible kinds of linkages between different elements of the qualitative database.

2. *System requirements*: Macintosh System 7.0 or later, 2MB RAM

3. The program has a *graphical user interface*; a *mouse* can be used. *Text documents* must be formatted in ASCII. The smallest coding unit is one character. Selective retrievals of text segments are supported. *Memos* can be written.

4. *Linkages* between codes can be defined and represented in different forms, such as relational networks or hierarchical trees. Several codes can be combined to form 'hypercodes'. Memos can be linked to codes, whole documents, users and text segments, and can be retrieved during search procedures. Memos attached to text segments can be displayed and edited at any point during analysis. Text segments can be directly linked with hyperlinks using link words. These link words can indicate the type of relationship between the segments, for example causality. There are functions to support the identification of different forms of linkages between text segments, for example sequential (A B C D), loop (A B C A) or radial (AB AC AD) linkages. Linkages themselves can be coded, and can be 'interlinked' and mapped, that is, graphically displayed. Features for 'matrix displays' are also available.

5. The program is based on hyperlinking and thus has a different approach to coding and retrieval than the other programs featured here. It does offer some search functions for co-occurring codes. It also offers a variety of different display forms for retrieved data with which comparable operations can be performed. For more details please contact the developer.

6. *Numerical* information can be exported via ASCII files. *Code frequencies* can be calculated.

Kwalitan Version 4.0
1994 by V. A. M. Peters

Vincent Peters, Postbus 9108, 6500 HK Nijmegen, The Netherlands

1. Kwalitan is not a classical coding-and-retrieval program, but more like a database management program, since it requires the researcher to divide the textual data into separate segments before importing them into the program. But, unlike a standard database manager, the program has extensive features for changing the boundaries of segments. The hierarchical structuring of codes (see Chapter 6) is also supported.

   Researchers who wish to combine interpretive analysis with classical content analysis (see Chapter 12 for an example and discussion of such a strategy) will be comfortable with the range of functions for content analysis and exporting numerical information that the program offers.

2. *System requirements*: DOS 3.2 or later, 480KB RAM, hard disk with 600KB free.
3. *Text documents* must be formatted in ASCII and have to be divided into meaningful chunks of text, which form the coding units. These segments can be split, matched and expanded during analysis. Up to twenty-five codes can be attached to one segment. Selective retrievals are supported. *Memos* can be classified according to four different categories, such as 'method' or 'theory' memos. Each memo can contain up to 400 lines (or more depending on RAM).
4. The hierarchical structuring of codes is supported. It is possible to retrieve all the text segments attached to a code and to all of its sub-codes. Memos can be linked to codes, to single words in the text and to entire documents.
5. *Co-occurrences* of codes can be searched for using Boolean operators.
6. *Code frequencies* can be calculated. The program can construct several types of data matrices which can easily be exported to SPSS. These matrices can include the frequency or occurrence/non-occurrence of codes in a document, or the frequency of codes within text segments.
7. *Additional functions* are available for quantitative content analysis (such as calculating word frequencies, searches according to word-lists or keywords in context) and automatic coding.

Martin Version 2.0

Simonds Center for Instruction and Research in Nursing,
School of Nursing, University of Wisconsin – Madison,
600 Highland Ave, Madison, WI 53792-2455, USA

1. The program is a card-based 'cut-and-paste' program for Windows, comparable to HyperQual2. Sections of the original text can be copied onto cards which can then be collected together in 'folders'. The folders themselves can also be grouped, for example in a hierarchy.

   The program aids an inductive research strategy that starts with the raw textual data and collects similar text segments together at an ever-increasing level of abstraction.
2. *System requirements*: Windows 3.0 or later, 2MB RAM, hard disk with 5MB free.
3. The program has a *graphical user interface*; a *mouse* can be used. *Text documents* have to be formatted in ASCII with fixed line ends. The manual suggests that text files should not contain more than 50KB. The smallest coding unit is one character. The user can place chosen segments on cards which can be coded and put together in

stacks. These stacks can be ordered or selected using codes, and can be transferred or copied into folders. Folders can be ordered by creating 'groups'. *Memos* of up to 16KB can be recorded.

4. Memos can be *linked* to codes, to groups of text segments, to text segments, to whole documents, to particular marks in the text (similar to footnotes). Memos can also be displayed, edited or printed together with the elements they refer to.

MAX Version 3.5
1993 by Udo Kuckartz, Andreas Maurer

Büro für Softwareentwicklung und Sozialforschung, Schützallee 52, 14169 Berlin, Germany

1. This program was originally developed to support the analysis of open-ended questions in survey questionnaires, whereby the method of case-oriented quantification outlined in Chapter 11 is employed.

   Since then, additional features have been added, for example for the retrieval of co-occurring text segments. All files used and created by the program that contain code or case information are stored in standard dBase format. This offers the competent user extensive possibilities for using other software tools in order to modify these files or to subject them to a different type of analysis than that offered by the program.

2. *System requirements*: DOS 3.3 or later, hard disk with 800K free.

3. *Text documents* must be formatted in ASCII with lines no longer than 60 characters; a maximum of 999 documents can be analysed simultaneously. Texts longer than 999 lines have to be divided into paragraphs of 999 lines or less. One document can contain a maximum of 99 paragraphs. If no paragraph structure is defined by the user, then the program will automatically establish a formal paragraph structure. The smallest coding unit is the text line. The program supports selective retrievals.

4. Two codes can be combined to form one new code.

5. Searches for *co-occurrences* of codes using the Boolean operators 'AND' and 'OR' can be conducted, whereby nested and/or overlapping text segments are retrieved .

6. All files (texts, codes, numerical and other case-oriented data) are saved in dBase format and can therefore easily be exported to statistical programs such as SPSS and SAS and re-imported to MAX after modification. SPSS files can also be directly created for exporting numerical data. Documents can be divided into *paragraphs,* permitting a structuring of texts such as open-ended questions. *Code* and *word frequencies* can be calculated.

206 *Computer-aided qualitative data analysis*

winmax Version 1
1994 by Udo Kuckartz

Büro für Softwareentwicklung und Sozialforschung,
Schützallee 52, 14169 Berlin, Germany

1. WINMAX is a further development of MAX. It contains several additional features, mainly for the construction of hierarchical relations between codes, which can be graphically displayed on the screen and also employed for text retrievals.
2. *System requirements*: DOS 3.3 or later, Windows 3.1 or later, 4MB RAM, hard disk with 820KB free.
3. The program has a *graphical user interface*; a *mouse* can be used. *Text documents* must be formatted in ASCII with fixed line ends. The smallest coding unit is a word. The maximum length of a coded segment is 64KB. The program supports selective retrievals.
4. Hierarchical *linkages* between codes ('trees') can be defined and graphically displayed. It is possible to retrieve all the text segments attached to a code and to all of its subcodes.
5. Searches for *co-occurrences* of codes can be conducted, whereby nested and/or overlapping text segments can be retrieved. In each search the researcher has to decide which Boolean operator (either 'AND' or 'OR') to use.
6. *Numerical data* can be saved in dBase format and therefore easily exported to statistical programs such as SPSS and SAS. *Code frequencies* can be calculated.

qsr nud.ist Version 3.0
1993/94 by Lyn Richards and Tom Richards

Qualitative Solutions & Research Pty. Ltd., Box 171,
La Trobe University Post Office, Victoria 3083, Australia

Distributed by Sage Publications Ltd., 6 Bonhill Street,
London EC2A 4PU, UK

1. NUD.IST is a program for facilitating theory building by identifying the code patterns and relationships in the original data. These are made visible by their coding and retrieval. It is particularly useful for the development of hierarchical networks of categories, a methodology discussed in Chapter 6.

    The strategies of hypothesis examination described in Part III, based on the retrieval of co-occurrences of coded segments, can be integrated into the process of constructing hierarchical categories.
2. *System requirements*: (a) Macintosh with hard disk and 4MB free RAM, System 6.0.4+ or 7.x. A 32-bit clean release is expected early in 1995. (b) IBM-PC compatibles with Windows 3.1 in 386 mode or

NT, 4MB free RAM and 10MB swap file, hard disk and mouse, VGA monitor or better.

3. The program has a *graphical user interface*; a *mouse* can be used. *Text documents* must be formatted in ASCII. The smallest coding unit is 1 character. The program supports selective retrievals and the recording of *memos*.

4. The user is invited (but not forced) to develop a hierarchical code structure that can be represented graphically and can be used for multiple types of retrievals. Among the most powerful retrieval functions are COLLECT, which allows for retrieving all segments or memos attached to a code and all of its subcodes, and INHERIT, which permits the retrieval of all memos or segments attached to a code and its 'ancestors' (that is, the codes in a direct line above the code in question). *Memos* can be linked to codes, case-variables and whole documents.

5. A great variety of retrievals can be conducted to identify the *co-occurrence* of codes, which is defined as the overlapping, nesting, proximity and sequential order of text segment to which the codes under investigation are attached. All Boolean operators can be employed. The program attaches a new code to the retrieved text segments, which may then be incorporated into an existing hierarchical code structure.

6. *Code frequencies* can be calculated.

7. *Additional functions* are available for the building of matrices, and for automatic coding according to user-defined keywords.

QUALPRO Version 4.0
1994 by Bernard Blackman

Impulse Development Company, 3491-11 Thomasville Road, Suite 202, Tallahassee, FL 32308, USA

1. QUALPRO was originally a collection of routines for ordinary coding and retrieval that could be executed via DOS and by using a simple command shell. This collection has now been extended by the addition of functions for co-occurring code searches and matrix displays. Algorithms for the calculation of intercoder reliability and for computing matrices displaying agreement and disagreement between coders are unique features of this program. This information can be used to improve the code definitions and procedures, and hence the precision of coding. The program is particularly useful for research groups concerned with the robustness of the coding scheme (see Chapters 1 and 4).

2. *System requirements*: DOS 2.0 or higher, 128KB RAM

3. *Text* can be entered into the program directly or imported as an ASCII file with line lengths set at 69 characters. The smallest coding unit is the

text line. Up to 1,000 codes can be attached to one document. Selective retrievals of text segments are supported and *memos* can be recorded.

4. Memos can be *linked* to whole documents and text segments.
5. In every ordinary retrieval, the program can retrieve, together with the text, the line numbers of overlapping or nested segments coded with another code. All Boolean operators can be applied in a search for text segments so that nested and overlapping text segments can be retrieved, and also text segments to which a certain combination of codes does or does not apply.
6. *Code frequencies* can be calculated. Matrices displaying code occurrences or code frequencies for each case can be created and exported to statistical packages as ASCII files.
7. *Additional functions* are available for searching uncoded segments. Different coders can be distinguished and the *intercoder reliability* can be determined either by computing *Scott's π measure of reliability* or by generating matrices showing agreements or disagreements.

Textbase Alpha
1994 by Bo Sommerlund

Institute of Psychology, University of Aarhus,
Asylveg 4, 8240 Risskov, Denmark

1. A straightforward code-and-retrieve program particularly suited for researchers who, for methodological reasons, choose to stay with 'cut-and-paste' strategies. It is also a good introduction to computer-assisted qualitative analysis for novices. Additional features for counting word frequencies are of special interest for researchers who wish to integrate content analytic methods (see Chapter 12) into their project.
2. *System requirements*: DOS 2.0 or later, hard disk with 125KB free.
3. *Text documents* must be formatted in ASCII with fixed line ends. The program can analyse up to 200 documents at a time. A maximum of 1,000 *codes* can be defined per document. The smallest coding unit is one character. The program supports selective retrievals of text segments.
6. Textbase Alpha can store up to fifteen *numerical* case variables which – together with information concerning coded text segments – can be exported to standard ASCII files or to SPSS. Code and word frequencies can be calculated.
7. *Additional functions:* to prohibit unauthorized access, text can be scrambled and then descrambled after giving in a password. If keywords (for example, 'Interviewer' or 'Respondent') have been attached in advance to the text, they can be converted into codes.

The ETHNOGRAPH Version 4.0
1994 by John Seidel, Susanne Friese, D. Christopher Leonard

Qualis Research Associates, P.O. Box 2070, Amherst,
MA 01004, USA

1. One of the earliest and most widely distributed programs in the field. The strength of the program is its functions to assist researchers working in the tradition of ethnography and interpretive sociology who are more concerned with the interpretive analysis of texts than with theory building and hypothesis examination.

   Nevertheless, some functions which can be employed for theory building and hypothesis examination, for example searches for co-occurring codes, are also available.

2. *System requirements*: DOS 2.0 or later, 2MB RAM (XT Version: 460KB), hard disk with 2MB free.

3. *Text documents* must be formatted in ASCII with fixed line ends. One document can contain up to 9999 lines of up to forty characters. The smallest coding unit is the text line. Up to twelve codes can be attached to any one text segment. A maximum of seven contiguous nests or overlaps is possible. The program supports selective retrievals. *Memos* can contain up to 2,000 characters and can refer to line numbers and to a maximum of three user-defined keywords. Memos can be retrieved together with the text segments they refer to, or printed individually.

4. *Linkages* can be established between one text segment and up to twenty-six memos. Several codes can be subsumed under one 'Parent Code' for structuring the coding scheme.

5. The 'Multiple Code Search' function helps to find co-occurring codes, whereby co-occurrence can be defined as the overlapping, nesting, sequential ordering or proximity of text segments. These segments can be retrieved by the employment of all Boolean operators.

6. *Code frequencies* can be calculated.

7. *Additional functions* are available for identifying different speakers in transcripts and for entering contextual comments within the texts.

Notes

1. Nevertheless, given the limited space these descriptions cannot be exhaustive. Although we have tried to ensure that all the information is accurate, we cannot guarantee this.

210 *Computer-aided qualitative data analysis*

Contact addresses of developers of other programs mentioned in the book:

Intext   Harald Klein
Universität Jena
Institut für Soziologie
Carl-Zeiss-Str.
07743 Jena
Germany

QCA   Kriss A. Drass
School of Criminal Justice
University of Nevada
Las Vegas, Nevada 89154
USA

Textpack   Peter Ph. Mohler, Cornelia Züll
Zentrum für Umfragen, Methoden und Analysen
Postfach 122155
68072 Mannheim
Germany

References

Agar, Michael (1980): *The Professional Stranger: An Informal Introduction to Ethnography*. New York: Academic Press.

Agar, Michael (1991): The Right Brain Strikes Back. In: Fielding, Nigel G.; Lee, Raymond M. (eds): *Using Computers in Qualitative Research*. Newbury Park: CA.: Sage. pp. 181–194.

Aldenderfer, M.S.; Blashfield, R.K. (1987): *Cluster Analysis*. Beverly Hills/London/New Delhi: Sage.

Allen, Woody (1978): If the Impressionists had been Dentists. In: *Without Feathers*. London: Sphere.

Altheide, David L.; Johnson, John M. (1994): Criteria for Assessing Interpretive Validity in Qualitative Research. In: Denzin, Norman K.; Lincoln, Yvonna G. (eds): *Handbook of Qualitative Research*. Thousand Oaks: Sage. pp. 485–499.

Anderberg, M. (1973): *Cluster Analysis for Applications*. New York: Academic Press.

Araujo, Luis (1992): Comments for the Final Panel Discussion. Paper presented at the conference 'The Qualitative Research Process and Computing', 7–9 October, Bremen.

Bailey, K.D. (1983): Sociological Classification and Cluster Analysis. *Quality & Quantity*, 17. pp. 251–268.

Bain, R. (1929): The Validity of Life Histories and Diaries. *Journal of Educational Sociology*, 3. pp. 150–164.

Barton, Allen H.; Lazarsfeld, Paul F. (1974): Some Functions of Qualitative Analysis in Social Research. In: Adorno, T.W.; Dirks, W. (eds): *Sociologica I*. Aufsätze Max Horkheimer zum sechzigsten Geburtstag gewidmet. Frankfurt am Main, Köln: Europäische Verlagsanstalt (1st edn, 1955 entitled Frankfurter Beiträge zur Soziologie I).

Baszanger, Isabelle (1992): Introduction. Les chantiers d'un interactionniste américain. In: *La trame de la négociation. Sociologie qualitative et interactionnisme*. Paris: Edition l'Harmattan.

Becker, H.; Geer, B. (1960): Participant Observation: The Analysis of Qualitative Field Data. In: Adams, R.N.; Preiss, J.J. (eds): *Human Organization Research: Field Relations and Techniques*. Homewood, IL: The Dorsey Press. pp. 267–289.

Berelson, Bernard (1952): *Content Analysis in Communication Research*. New York: Hafner Press.

Bertaux, Daniel (1988): Qualitative Analysis for Social Scientists. Book Review, *European Sociological Review*, 4 (3, December). pp. 276–277.

Bogdan, R.C.; Biklen, S.K. (1982): *Qualitative Research for Education: An Introduction to Theory and Methods*. Boston: Allyn and Bacon, Inc.

Brownstein, Henry (1990): Surviving as a Qualitative Sociologist: Recollections from the Diary of a State Worker. *Qualitative Sociology*, 13 (2). pp. 149–167.

Bryman, Alan (1988): *Quantity and Quality in Social Research*. London and New York: Routledge.

Burgess, Ernest W. (1927): Statistics and Case Studies as Methods of Sociological Research. *Sociology and Social Research*, 12. pp. 120 ff.

212   *Computer-aided qualitative data analysis*

Campbell, Donald T.; Fiske, Donald W. (1959): Convergent and Discriminant Validation by the Multitrait-Multimethod Matrix. *Psychological Bulletin,* 56 (2, March). pp. 81–105.

Carstens, W.; Gruehn, S.; Harbeke, W.; Kuckartz, U.; Kwon, S.; Zocher, U. (1990): *Hilfsbereite Männer. Eine qualitative Studie über die Motive von jungen Männern in der ehrenamtlichen sozialen Arbeit.* Berlin: Freie Universität.

Cicourel, Aaron (1964): *Method and Measurement in Sociology.* Glencoe: The Free Press.

Clark, K.L.; Tarnlund, S.-A. (eds) (1982): *Logic Programming.* New York: Academic Press.

Colmerauer, A.; Kanoui, H.; Pasero, R.; Roussel, P. (1973): *Un système de communication homme–machine en française.* Research Report. Aix-Marseille: Groupe Intelligence Artificielle, Université Aix-Marseille II.

Conrad, P.; Reinarz, S. (1984): Qualitative Computing: Approaches and Issues. *Qualitative Sociology,* 7. pp. 34–60.

Cook, Thomas D.; Campbell, Donald T. (1979): *Quasi-Experimentation. Design and Analysis Issues for Field Settings.* Boston: Houghton Mifflin Company.

Corsaro, William (1992): Basics of Grounded Theory. Book Review, *Journal of Contemporary Ethnography,* 21 (3). pp. 380–382.

Cressey, Donald R. (1950): The Criminal Violation of Financial Trust. *American Sociological Review,* 15. pp. 738–743.

Cressey, Donald R. (1971): *Other People's Money. A Study in the Social Psychology of Embezzlement.* Belmont: Wadsworth (1st edn, 1953).

Denzin, Norman K. (1977): *The Research Act. A Theoretical Introduction to Sociological Methods.* New York: McGraw-Hill Book Company.

Denzin, Norman K. (1988): Qualitative Analysis for Social Scientists. Book Review, *Contemporary Sociology,* 17 (3). pp. 430–432.

Denzin, Norman K. (1989): *Interpretive Interactionism* (Applied Social Research Methods Series, Vol. 16). Newbury Park/London/New Delhi: Sage.

Denzin, Norman K.; Lincoln, Yvonna G. (eds) (1994): *Handbook of Qualitative Research.* Thousand Oaks: Sage.

Dey, Ian (1992): *Hypersoft: Software for Analysing Qualitative Data.* University of Edinburgh.

Dey, Ian (1993): *Qualitative Data Analysis: A User-friendly Guide for Social Scientists.* London and New York: Routledge.

Drass, Kriss; Ragin, Charles (1991): *QCA: Qualitative Comparative Analysis.* Evanston, IL: Center for Urban Affairs and Policy Research, Northwestern University.

Dreyfus, Hubert L. (1972): *What Computers Can't Do – A Critique of Artificial Reason.* New York: Harper and Row.

Dreyfus, Stuart E.; Dreyfus, Hubert L. (1986): *Mind over Machine – The Power of Human Intuition and Expertise in the Era of the Computer.* Oxford: Blackwell.

Eckert, Thomas (1993): *Erziehungsleitende Vorstellungen und Schulverständnis von Lehrern.* Frankfurt am Main: Lang.

Eisenhart, Margeret A.; Howe, Kenneth R. (1992): Validity in Educational Research. In: LeCompte, Margaret; Millroy, Wendy L.; Preissle, Judith (eds): *The Handbook of Qualitative Research in Education.* San Diego: Academic Press.

Ekerwald, Hedvig; Johansson, Stina (1989): Vetenskap som byråkrati eller som konst? *Sociologisk Forskning,* 2. pp. 15–33. (In Swedish).

Ellis, Carolyn (1992): Basics of Grounded Theory. Book Review, *Contemporary Sociology,* 21 (1). pp. 138–139.

Fielding, Nigel G.; Fielding, Jane L. (1986): *Linking Data* (Qualitative Research Methods, Volume 4). Beverly Hills: Sage

Flick, Uwe (1992): Triangulation Revisited: Strategy of Validation or Alternative? *Journal for the Theory of Social Behaviour*, 22 (2, June). pp. 175–197

Foote, Shelby (1992): Men at War, An Interview with Shelby Foote. In: Ward, Geoffrey C.; with Burns, Ric; Burns, Ken: *The Civil War: An Illustrated History of the War Between the States.* London: Pimlico.

Freidson, Eliot (1975): *Doctoring Together: A Study of Professional Social Control.* Chicago: University of Chicago Press.

Galtung, Johan (1990): Theory Formation in Social Research: A Plea for Pluralism. In: Øyen, Else (ed.): *Comparative Methodology: Theory and Practice in International Social Research.* London: Sage. pp. 96–112.

Gamson, William (1975): *The Strategy of Social Protest.* Homewood, IL: Dorsey.

Geertz, Clifford (1973): *The Interpretation of Cultures.* London: Hutchinson.

Geertz, Clifford (1983): *Local Knowledge. Further Essays in Interpretive Anthropology.* New York: Basic Books.

Giddens, A. (1976): *New Rules of Sociological Method: A Positive Critique of Interpretive Sociologies.* London: Hutchinson.

Glaser, Barney G. (1978): *Theoretical Sensitivity: Advances in the Methodology of Grounded Theory.* Mill Valley, CA: Sociology Press.

Glaser, Barney G. (1992): *Emergence vs. Forcing: Basics of Grounded Theory Analysis.* Mill Valley, CA: Sociology Press.

Glaser, Barney G.; Strauss, Anselm L. (1967): *The Discovery of Grounded Theory: Strategies for Qualitative Research.* Chicago: Aldine.

Green, C.C. (1969): Theorem Proving by Resolution as a Basis for Question-answering Systems. In: Michie, D.; Meltzer, B. (eds): *Machine Intelligence 4.* Edinburgh: Edinburgh University Press. pp. 183–205.

Gusfield, Joseph (1990): Two Genres of Sociology. A Literary Analysis of the American Occupational Structure and Tally's Corner. In: Hunter, Albert (ed.): *The Rhetoric of Social Research.* New Brunswick and London: Rutgers University Press. pp. 62–96.

Hammersley, Martyn (1992): Some Reflections about Ethnography and Validity. *Qualitative Studies in Education*, 5. pp. 195–203.

Harper, Douglas (1988): Qualitative Analysis for Social Scientists. Book Review, *American Journal of Sociology*, 94 (2). pp. 417–419.

Herbrand, J. (1971): Investigations in Proof Theory. In: Goldfarb, W.D. (ed.): *Logical Writings.* Cambridge, MA: Harvard University Press. pp. 44–202. (Original work, 1930 dissertation).

Hesse-Biber, Sharlene (1991): Women, Weight and Eating Disorders: A Socio-cultural and Political-economic Analysis. *Women's Studies International Forum,* 14 (3). pp. 173–191.

Hesse-Biber, Sharlene; Dupuis, Paul; Kinder, Scott (1990): HyperRESEARCH: A Computer Program for the Analysis of Qualitative Data using the Macintosh. *Qualitative Studies in Education,* 3 (2). pp. 189–193.

Hesse-Biber, Sharlene; Dupuis, Paul; Kinder, Scott (1991): HyperRESEARCH: A Computer Program for the Analysis of Qualitative Data with an Emphasis on Hypothesis Testing and Multimedia Analysis. *Qualitative Sociology,* 14 (4). pp. 289–306.

Hiemstra, R.; Essman, E; Henry, N.; Palumbo, D. (1987): Computer-assisted Analysis of Qualitative Research. *Educational Gerontology*, 13. pp. 417–426.

Hillerman, Tony (1990): *Skinwalkers.* New York: HarperCollins.

Holsti, Ole R. (1969): *Content Analysis for the Social Sciences and Humanities.* Reading, MA: Addison-Wesley.

Hopf, Christel (1988): Qualitative Analysis for Social Scientists. Book Review, *Kölner Zeitschrift für Soziologie und Sozialpsychologie,* 40 (4). pp. 781–783.

Huber, Günter L. (1994): *Analyse qualitativer Daten mit AQUAD Vier.* Schwangau: Ingeborg Huber Verlag. (English manual in preparation; Desert Hot Springs: Qualitative Research Management).

Huber, Günter L.; Marcelo García, Carlos (1991): Computer Assistance for Testing Hypotheses About Qualitative Data: The Software Package AQUAD 3.0. *Qualitative Sociology*, 14 (4).

Huber, Günter L.; Marcelo García, Carlos (1993): Voices of Beginning Teachers: Computer-assisted Listening to their Common Experiences. In: Schratz, Michael (ed.): *Qualitative Voices in Educational Research.* London: The Falmer Press. pp. 139–156.

Huberman, A. Michael; Miles, Matthew B. (1985): Assessing Local Causality in Qualitative Research. In: Berg, David N.; Smith, Kenwyn K. (eds): *The Self in Social Inquiry Researching Methods.* Newbury Park, CA: Sage. pp. 351–381.

Janesick, Valerie J. (1994): The Dance of Qualitative Research Design: Metaphor, Methodolatry and Meaning. In: Denzin, Norman K.; Lincoln, Yvonna S. (eds): *Handbook of Qualitative Research.* Thousand Oaks: Sage. pp. 209–219.

Jorgenson, Danny L. (1989): *Participant Observation. A Methodology for Human Studies.* Newbury Park, CA: Sage.

Kaplan, A. (1964): *The Conduct of Inquiry: Methodology for Behavioral Science.* Scranton, PA: Chandel Publishing Co.

Kelle, Udo (1994): *Empirisch begründete Theoriebildung. Ein Beitrag zur Logik und Methodologie interpretativer Sozialforschung.* Weinheim: Deutscher Studienverlag.

Kelle, Udo (1995): Theories as Heuristic Tools in Qualitative Research. In: Maso, I.; Atkinson, P.A.; Vertroeven, J.C. (eds): *Openness in Research: The Tension between Self and Other.* Assen: Van Gorcum.

Kerlinger, Fred N. (1979): *Behavioral Research.* New York: Holt, Rinehart and Winston.

King, Gary; Keohane, Robert O.; Verba, Sidney (1994): *Designing Social Inquiry: Scientific Inference in Qualitative Research.* Princeton, NJ: Princeton University Press.

Kowalski, R.A. (1974): Predicate Logic as Programming Language. In: *Proceedings IFIP 74.* Amsterdam: North Holland Publishing Co. pp. 569–574.

Kowalski, R.A. (1979): *Logic for Problem Solving.* Amsterdam: North Holland Publishing Co.

Kowalski, R.A. (1982): Logic as a Computer Language. In: K.L. Clark; S.-A. Tarnlund (eds): *Logic Programming.* New York: Academic Press. pp. 3–16.

Kracauer, Siegfried (1952/53): The Challenge of Qualitative Content Analysis. In: *Public Opinion Quarterly*, 16. pp. 631–642.

Krippendorf, Klaus (1980): *Content Analysis. An Introduction to Its Methodology.* Beverly Hills/London: Sage.

Kuckartz, Udo (1990a): Computerunterstützte Suche nach Typologien in qualitativen Interviews. In: Faulbaum, F.; Haux, R.; Jöckel, K.-H. (eds): *SOFTSTAT '89. Fortschritte der Statistik-Software 2.* Stuttgart/New York: Gustav Fischer. pp. 495–502.

Kuckartz, Udo (1990b): New Developments in Qualitative Computing: MAX – a new Program for Linking Quality and Quantity. *Bulletin de Méthodologie Sociologique,* published by the International Association of Sociological Methodology, No. 29.

Kuckartz, Udo (1991): Ideal Types or Empirical Types: The Case of Max Weber's Empirical Research. *Bulletin de Méthodologie Sociologique* published by the International Association of Sociological Methodology, No. 32.

Kuckartz, U. (1992): *Textanalysesysteme für die Sozialwissenschaften, Einführung in MAX und TEXTBASE ALPHA.* Stuttgart/New York/Jena: Gustav Fischer.

Kvale, Steinar (ed.) (1989): *Issues of Validity in Qualitative Research.* Lund: Studentlitteratur.

Lakoff, G. (1987): *Women, Fire and Dangerous Things: What Categories Teach About the Human Mind.* Chicago: Chicago University Press.

Laurie, Heather (1992): Multiple Methods in the Study of Household Resource Allocation. In: Brannen, J. (ed.): *Mixing Methods: Qualitative and Quantitative Research.* Avebury: Aldershot.

Lazarsfeld, Paul F. (1972): *Qualitative Analysis. Historical and Critical Essays.* Boston: Allyn and Bacon.

LeCompte, Margaret D.; Preissle, Judith (1993): *Ethnography and Qualitative Design in Educational Research.* San Diego: Academic Press.

Lee, Raymond M.; Fielding, Nigel G. (1991) Computing for Qualitative Research: Options, Problems and Potential. In: Fielding, Nigel G.; Lee, Raymond M. (eds): *Using Computers in Qualitative Research.* London: Sage. pp. 1–13.

Lidz, Charles; Ricci, Edmund (1990): Funding Large-scale Qualitative Sociology. *Qualitative Sociology,* 13 (2). pp. 113–126.

Lieberson, Stanley (1991): Small *N*'s and Big Conclusions: An Examination of the Reasoning in Comparative Studies Based on a Small Number of Cases. *Social Forces,* 70. pp. 307–320.

Lincoln, Yvonna S.; Guba, Egon (1985): *Naturalistic Inquiry.* Beverly Hills: Sage.

Lindesmith, Alfred R. (1968): *Addiction and Opiates.* Chicago: Aldine (1st edn, 1947).

Lofland, John; Lofland, Lyn H. (1984): *Analyzing Social Settings: A Guide to Qualitative Observation and Analysis.* Belmont, CA: Wadsworth Publishing Company.

Lundberg, G.A. (1942): *Social Research: A Study in Methods of Gathering Data.* New York: Longmans, Green (1st edn, 1929).

Mangabeira, Wilma (1992): Contribution to the Closing Session. Paper presented at the conference 'The Qualitative Research Process and Computing', 7–9 October, Bremen.

Marcelo García, Carlos (ed.) (1991): *El primer año de enseñanza.* Sevilla: Grupo de Investigacíon Didáctica de la Universidad de Sevilla.

Mathes, Rainer (1992): Hermeneutisch-klassifikatorische Inhaltsanalyse von Leitfadengesprächen. In: Hoffmeyer-Zlotnik, Jürgen H.P. (ed.): *Analyse verbaler Daten.* Opladen: Westdeutscher Verlag. pp. 402–424.

Mathes, Rainer; Geis, Alphons (1990): The Classificatory-hermeneutic Content Analysis of Guided Interviews with TEXTPACK. In: Faulbaum, F.; Haux, R.; Jöckel, K.-H. (eds): *SOFTSTAT '89. Fortschritte der Statistik-Software 2.* Stuttgart/New York: Gustav Fischer. pp. 503–511.

Mayring, Philipp (1990) *Qualitative Inhaltsanalyse: Grundlagen und Techniken.* Weinheim: Deutscher Studien Verlag.

McCarthy, J.; Abrahams, P.W.; Edwards, D.J.; Hart, T.P.; Levin, M.I. (1965): *LISP 1.5 Programmer's Manual,* 2nd edn. Cambridge, MA: MIT Press.

McCauley, R.N. (1987): The Role of Theories in a Theory of Concepts. In: Neisser, Ulric (ed.): *Concepts and Conceptual Development: Ecological and Intellectual Factors in Categorisation.* Cambridge: Cambridge University Press.

McCutcheon, A. L. (1987): *Latent Class Analysis.* Beverly Hills: Sage.

McDermott, Robert (1985): *Computer-aided Logic Design.* Indianapolis, IN: Howard A. Sams.

McGill, Lawrence (1990): Doing Science by the Numbers. The Role of Tables and Other Representational Conventions in Scientific Journal Articles. In: Hunter, Albert (ed.):

The Rhetoric of Social Research. New Brunswick and London: Rutgers University Press.

Meehan, J.R. (1979): *The New UCI LISP Manual*. Hillsdale, NJ: Lawrence Erlbaum Associates.

Mendelson, Elliot (1970): *Boolean Algebra and Switching Circuits*. New York: McGraw-Hill.

Miles, Matthew B.; Huberman, A. Michael (1984a): *Qualitative Data Analysis. A Sourcebook of New Methods*. Newbury Park, CA: Sage.

Miles, Matthew B.; Huberman, A. Michael (1984b): Drawing Valid Meaning from Qualitative Data: Toward a Shared Craft. *Educational Researcher*, 13 (5). pp. 20–30.

Miles, Matthew B.; Huberman, A. Michael (1994): *Qualitative Data Analysis. An Expanded Sourcebook*, 2nd edn. Newbury Park, CA: Sage (1st edn, 1984).

Mill, John Stuart (1967): *A System of Logic: Ratiocinative and Inductive*. Toronto: University of Toronto Press.

Mohler, Peter P.; Züll, Cornelia (1990): *Textpack PC, Release 4.0*. Mannheim: Zentrum für Umfragen, Methoden und Analysen (ZUMA).

Muhr, Thomas (1991): ATLAS/ti: A Prototype for the Support of Text Interpretation. *Qualitative Sociology*, 14 (4/2, Winter). pp. 349–371.

Muhr, Thomas (1992): Catching Bugs and Butterflies in Networks. Paper presented at the conference 'The Qualitative Research Process and Computing', 7–9 October, Bremen.

Muhr, Thomas (1993): ATLAS/ti. Computer-aided Text Interpretation and Theory Building. User's Manual, Release 1.1.E. Berlin.

Oevermann, Ulrich; Allert, Tilman; Kronau, Elisabeth; Krambeck, Jürgen (1979): Die Methodologie einer 'objektiven Hermeneutik' und ihre allgemeine forschungslogische Bedeutung in den Sozialwissenschaften. In: Soeffner, Hans-Georg (ed.): *Interpretative Verfahren in den Sozial- und Textwissenschaften*. Stuttgart: Metzler. pp. 352–434.

Padilla, Raymond V. (1992): Qualitative and Quantitative Models of Social Situations: The Case for Triangulation of Paradigms. Paper presented at the conference 'The Qualitative Research Process and Computing', 7–9 October, Bremen.

Patton, Michael Q. (1990): *Qualitative Evaluation and Research Methods*. Newbury Park: Sage.

Peters, Vincent; Wester, Fred (1990): Qualitative Analysis in Practice Including a User's Guide to KWALITAN Version 2. Department of Research Methodology, University of Nijmegen, The Netherlands.

Ragin, Charles C. (1987): *The Comparative Method. Moving Beyond Qualitative and Quantitative Strategies*. Berkeley/Los Angeles: University of California Press.

Ragin, Charles C. (1989): The Logic of the Comparative Method and the Algebra of Logic. *Journal of Quantitative Anthropology*, 1. pp. 373–398.

Ragin, Charles C. (1994a): Introduction to Qualitative Comparative Analysis. In Janoski, Thomas; Hicks, Alexander (eds): *The Comparative Political Economy of the Welfare State*. New York: Cambridge University Press. pp. 299–319.

Ragin, Charles C. (1994b): A Qualitative Comparative Analysis of Pensions Systems. In Janoski, Thomas; Hicks, Alexander (eds): *The Comparative Political Economy of the Welfare State*. New York: Cambridge University Press. pp. 320–345.

Ragin, Charles C. (1994c): *Constructing Social Research: The Unity and Diversity of Method*. Thousand Oaks/Lindon: Pine Forge Press.

Ragin, Charles C.; Bradshaw, York (1991): Statistical Analysis of Employment Discrimination: A Review and Critique. *Research in Social Stratification and Mobility*, 10. pp. 199–228.

Ragin, Charles C.; Mayer, Susan E.; Drass, Kriss A. (1984) Assessing Discrimination: A Boolean Approach. *American Sociological Review*, 49. pp. 221–234.

Richards, T.J.; Richards, Lyn (1990): *Manual for Mainframe NUD.IST Software version 2.1.* Melbourne: Replee P/L.

Richards, Lyn; Richards, T.J. (1991a): Analysing Unstructured Information: Can Computers Help? Technical Report No. 17/1991. Department of Computer Science and Computer Engineering. La Trobe University, Melbourne.

Richards, T.J.; Richards, Lyn (1991b): Database Organisation for Qualitative Analysis: the NUD.IST System. Technical Report No. 18/1991. La Trobe University, Melbourne.

Richards, T.J.; Richards, Lyn (1991c): The NUD.IST Qualitative Data Analysis System. *Qualitative Sociology*, 14 (4/2, Winter).

Richards, Lyn; Richards, T.J. (1991d): The Transformation of Qualitative Method: Computational Paradigms and Research Processes. In: Fielding, Nigel G.; Lee, Raymond M. (eds): *Using Computers in Qualitative Research.* London: Sage. pp. 38–53.

Richards, Thomas J.; Richards, Lyn (1994): Using Computers in Qualitative Research. In: Denzin, Norman K.; Lincoln, Yvonna S. (eds): *Handbook of Qualitative Research.* Thousand Oaks: Sage. pp. 445–462

Richards, T.J.; Richards, Lyn (1994): Creativity in Social Sciences: The Computer Enhancement of Qualitative Data Analysis. In: Dartnall, T. (ed.): *Artificial Intelligence and Creativity.* Dordrecht: Kluwer

Robinson, J.A. (1965): A Machine-oriented Logic Based on the Resolution Principle. *Journal of the Association for Computing Machinery*, 12. pp. 23–41.

Robinson, J.A.; Sibert, E.E. (1984): The LOGLISP Programming System. LPRC Technical Report. Syracuse, New York: Syracuse University, Logic Programming Research Center.

Roller, Edeltraud (1992): *Einstellung der Bürger zum Wohlfahrtsstaat der Bundesrepublik Deutschland.* Opladen: Westdeutscher Verlag.

Roller, Edeltraud; Mathes, Rainer (1993): Hermeneutisch-klassifikatorische Inhaltsanalyse. Analysemöglichkeiten am Beispiel von Leitfadengesprächen zum Wohlfahrtsstaat. *Kölner Zeitschrift für Soziologie und Sozialpsychologie*, 45 (1). pp. 56–75.

Roth, Charles (1975): *Fundamentals of Logic Design.* St Paul: West.

Sayer, Andrew (1992): *Method in Social Science: A Realist Approach.* London: Routledge.

Schatzman, L; Strauss, Anselm L. (1973): *Field Research: Strategies for a Natural Sociology.* New Jersey: Prentice-Hall.

Schründer-Lenzen, A. (1994): Weibliches Selbstkonzept und Computerkultur. Eine empirische Untersuchung zur Typisierung der subjektiven Bedeutung des Computers für Mädchen. Research Report. Berlin.

Schütz, Alfred (1962): *Collected Papers I. The Problem of Social Reality.* The Hague: Martinus Nijhoff.

Seidel, John (1991) Method and Madness in the Application of Computer Technology to Qualitative Data Analysis. In: Fielding, Nigel G.; Lee, Raymond M. (eds): *Using Computers in Qualitative Research.* London: Sage. pp. 107–116.

Shelly, A.L. (1984): Inducing Secondary Teachers' Conceptions of Reading: A Qualitative Analysis using Logic Programming. Unpublished doctoral dissertation, Syracuse University, Syracuse, NY.

Shelly, A.L.; Archambault, R.A.; Sutton, C.; Tinto, P. (1986): The Stages of Qualitative Research: Researcher Thinking Facilitated by Logic Programming. CASE Technical Report #8607. Syracuse, NY: Syracuse University, Center for Computer Applications and Software Engineering.

Silverman, David (1985): *Qualitative Methodology and Sociology.* Aldershot: Gower.

Skolem, T. (1928): Ueber die mathematische logik. *Norsk Matematisk Tideskrift*, 10. pp. 125–142.

Smith, J.K. (1984): The Problem of Criteria for Judging Interpretive Research. *Educational Evaluation and Policy Analysis*, 6. pp. 379–391.

Soeffner, Hans Georg (1991): 'Trajectory' – das geplante Fragment. Die Kritik der empirischen Vernunft bei Anselm Strauss. *BIOS – Zeitschrift für Biographieforschung und oral history,* 1. pp. 1–13.

Spradley, J.P. (1979): *The Ethnographic Interview.* New York: Holt, Rinehart and Winston.

Stone, Phillip J.; Dunphy, Dexter C.; Smith, Marshal S.; Ogilvie, Daniel M. (1966): *The GENERAL INQUIRER: A Computer Approach to Content Analysis.* Cambridge, MA: MIT Press

Strauss, Anselm L. (1987): *Qualitative Analysis for Social Scientists.* New York: Cambridge University Press.

Strauss, Anselm L. (1991): *Grundlagen qualitativer Sozialforschung. Datenanalyse und Theoriebildung in der empirischen soziologischen Forschung.* München: Wilhelm Fink Verlag.

Strauss, Anselm L; Corbin, Juliet (1990): *Basics of Qualitative Research: Grounded Theory Procedures and Techniques.* Newbury Park, CA: Sage.

Taylor, Steven J.; Bogdan, Robert (1984): *Introduction to Qualitative Research Methods: The Search for Meanings.* New York: Wiley and Sons.

Tesch, Renate (1990): *Qualitative Analysis: Analysis Types and Software Tools.* London and Philadelphia: Falmer Press.

Tesch, Renate (1991) (Guest Editor): *Qualitative Sociology.* Computers and Qualitative Data II. Special Issue, Parts 1–2. 14 (Fall: 3 and Winter: 4).

Thomas, W.I.; Znaniecki, F. (1958): *The Polish Peasant in Europe and America.* New York: Dower (1st edn, 1918).

Tschudi, Finn (1989): Do Qualitative and Quantitative Methods Require Different Approaches to Validity? In: Kvale, Steinar (ed.) (1989): *Issues of Validity in Qualitative Research.* Lund: Studentlitteratur. pp 109–134.

Weber, Max (1964): *Wirtschaft und Gesellschaft. Grundriß der verstehenden Soziologie.* Studienausgabe, edited by J. Winckelmann. Köln/Berlin: Kiepenheuer and Witsch.

Weitzman, Eben A.; Miles, Matthew B. (1995): *Computer Programs for Qualitative Data Analysis.* Thousand Oaks: Sage.

Wilson, T.P. (1970): Conceptions of Interaction and Forms of Sociological Explanation. *American Sociological Review*, 35. pp. 697–710.

Winograd, Terry; Flores, Fernando (1986): *Understanding Computers and Cognition.* Chicago: Ablex Publishing Corp.

Wiseman, Jaqueline P. (1979): *Stations of the Lost: The Treatment of Skid Row Alcoholics.* Chicago: The University of Chicago Press.

Znaniecki, Florian (1934): *The Method of Sociology.* New York: Rinehart and Company.

Name Index

Agar, M. 9, 12, 60
Aldenderfer, M.165
Altheide, D. 20
Anderberg, M. 165
Araujo, L. 9, 13, 68

Bailey, K. 165
Bain, R. 22
Barton, A. 135
Baszanger, I. 50(N)
Becker, H. 4, 56
Berelson, B. 53
Bertaux, D. 50(N)
Biklen, S.K. 5, 57, 61
Blackman, B. 28(N)
Blashfield, R. K. 165
Bogdan, R. 5, 57, 61
Bradshaw, Y. 180
Brownstein, H. 51(N)
Bryman, A. 152
Burgess, E. 153

Campbell, D. 22, 152
Carstens, W. 160
Cicourel, A. 60
Clark, K. 118
Colmerauer, A. 119
Conrad, P. 6, 9, 19, 20
Cook, T. 22,
Corbin, J. 25, 42, 43, 44, 45, 62, 63, 64,
    67, 78, 80, 105, 106, 137, 131, 162
Corsaro, W. 50(N)
Cressey, D. 106, 107, 110

Denzin, N. 22, 28(N), 44, 46, 49, 50(N),
    55, 106, 152
Dey, I. 12, 62, 66, 78, 79(N), 95, 98, 100,
    102, 103
Drass, K. 177, 182, 186, 189(N)
Dreyfus, H. 2
Dreyfus, S. 2
Dupuis, P. 14, 110, 111

Eckert, T. 15, 154, 176
Eisenhart, M. 20,
Ekerwald, H. 50(N)
Ellis, C. 50(N)

Fielding, J. 152, 153
Fielding, N. 10, 20, 29, 152, 153
Fiske, D. 152
Flick, U. 152, 153
Flores, F. 2
Foote, S. 69
Freidson, E. 57, 58, 61

Galtung, J. 136
Gamson, W. 182, 183, 184, 188, 189
Geer, B. 4, 56
Geertz, C. 55, 159, 161
Geis, A. 168
Giddens, A. 2, 55, 97
Glaser, B. 4, 9, 23, 35, 39, 42, 46,
    50(N), 51(N), 63, 116, 137, 139,
    147
Green, C. 119
Guba, E. 23
Gusfield, J. 51(N)

Hammersley, M. 20, 21 26
Harper, D. 50(N)
Herbrand, J. 108, 119
Hesse-Biber, S. 14, 46, 110, 111, 131
Hiemstra, R. 128
Holsti, O. 167, 169, 170
Hopf, C. 50(N)
Howe, K. 20
Huber, G. 14, 48, 50(N), 111, 142
Huberman, M. 3, 5, 48, 62, 63, 64, 93,
    105, 106, 113, 138, 141-143

Janesick, V. 80
Johansson, S. 50(N)
Johnson, J. 20
Jorgenson, D. 57

Subject Index